A MANUAL OF POLITICAL ECONOMY.

BY

E. PESHINE SMITH.

NEW YORK:
G. P. PUTNAM & SON, 661 BROADWAY.
1868.

STEREOTYPED B. J. [illegible]AN, PHILADELPHIA.

PREFACE.

IN the following pages the writer has made the attempt to construct a skeleton of Political Economy upon the basis of purely physical laws, and thus to obtain for its conclusions that absolute certainty which belongs to the positive sciences. The casual association of its teaching with moral philosophy, is the circumstance to which is to be attributed that metaphysical bias, manifested by almost all Economical writers, in their method of investigation, and which has conducted them to such vague, hypothetical, and unsatisfactory results. It has, indeed, been made matter of set purpose to confine its examination of the laws of the production of the objects which constitute wealth, to "such of them as are laws of the human mind;" as may be seen by consulting the Essay of Mr. J. S. Mill "On the Definition of Political Economy, and the method of Investigation proper to it." The issue, nevertheless, has been, that grossly material estimation of man, which disregards all that is truly human in his nature, and has brought upon Political Economy, thus worked out, the name of the Dismal Science.

Mr. Henry C. Carey led the way, in the better method, by his conclusive refutation of the theory of Ricardo in regard to the occupation of land, which, for more than forty years, has been dominant with the English Economists. This fiction was an inference as to a *physical* fact, from "laws of the human mind," and was for that long period accepted as a fact, without a single Economist, before Mr. Carey, thinking it worth while to test its accuracy by direct observation. Mr. Carey, by showing that the fact is directly the reverse of the hypothesis of Ricardo, and by establishing the consequences which flow from it, restored harmony to what was before a mass of discordances, and rendered it possible, for the first time, to construct a science out of what was, at best, but a mere collection of empirical rules. In addition to the special acknowledgments made to that gentleman in the following pages, it is proper to say, that the author is so thoroughly sensible that he owes whatever his own study of the subject may have effected, to his having been put upon the path and furnished with the clue, in the writings of Mr. Carey, as to be quite indisposed to make pretensions on the score of originality, which, as against others, he might maintain. Upon this point, however, he is reasonably indifferent. The object of preparing this Manual was, to present to his countrymen in a compact form, the principles of what he thinks may justly be called the American System of Political Economy, not less on the ground of its origin, than its signal agreement with our social and political organization. It was desirable to exhibit what might be distinctive, in connection with the general doctrines in which Economists on both sides of the Atlantic agree, in such a manner as to give an outline of the science, adapted to popular reading or to elementary instruction. This imposed upon the writer all the brevity that is consistent with a clear demonstration of the leading principles. He trusts, however, that they have been sufficiently elucidated to afford important aid in the solution of many of the problems, the direct discussion of which he was compelled to forego, with much else that might have given interest to the work; and, that, while a teacher would find room for abundant illustration, any individual of mature years, who may read it without such aid, will meet with no more severe demand upon his reflective powers, than is incident to the treatment of so extensive a subject within such a compass, as to permit the hope of popular circulation.

April, 1853.

CONTENTS.

INTRODUCTION.

CHAPTER I.

THE LAW OF ENDLESS CIRCULATION IN MATTER AND FORCE.

CHAPTER II.

THE FORMATION OF SOILS, AND THEIR ADAPTATION TO OCCUPATION AND CULTURE.

CHAPTER III.

THE GRATUITOUS CO-OPERATION OF THE NATURAL AGENTS WITH HUMAN LABOUR.

CHAPTER IV.

RENT.

CHAPTER V.

WAGES.

CHAPTER VI.

PROFITS.

CHAPTER VII.

EXCHANGE.

CHAPTER VIII.

MONEY AND PRICE.

CHAPTER IX.

GOVERNMENT.

INTRODUCTION.

> "We ought to conceive the study of Nature as destined to furnish the true rational basis of the action of man upon Nature; because the knowledge of the laws of phenomena, of which the invariable result is foresight, and that alone, can conduct us in active life to modify the one by the other to our advantage. In short, SCIENCE WHENCE FORESIGHT, FORESIGHT WHENCE ACTION, such is the simple formula which expresses the general relation of Science and Art."
>
> COMTE.

STARTING from the central highlands of Asia—the loftiest habitable region of the globe, where the great rivers take their rise that flow into the Frozen Ocean, and the Bay of Bengal, the Mediterranean, and the Chinese Sea—the human race has descended in an ever-widening flood, to spread over the earth and to subdue it. Sacred history and Hindoo tradition point to the same region as the cradle of mankind. They are confirmed by the reflection, that it must have been the first to emerge from the primal waste of waters; and the belief, that here it is that wheat and barley are of indigenous growth,* and that the animals run wild who have been tamed by man, and have followed him in his migrations through every clime—the horse, the ass, the goat, the sheep, the hog, the cat, that clings

* "The limit of perpetual snow is wonderfully raised on the northern slope of the Himalaya, perhaps to 2600 toises, or 16,625 English feet, above the level of the sea. Fields of barley (*hordeum hexastichon*) are seen in Kunawur up to 2300 toises, or 14,707 English feet; and another variety of barley even much higher. Wheat succeeds extremely well in the Thibetian highlands up to 1880 toises, or 12,022 English feet."—*Humboldt's Aspects of Nature.*

to his hearth-stone, and the dog, whose fidelity to his person seems like the emanation from a higher nature. As the different offshoots of the race descended to the lower tracts that the receding waters gave up to culture, and as each little tribe waxed in numbers, it has taken on a higher social organization, with a vast increase in the command of the individual members over the elements of physical comfort, a vast accession to their realized property, and to their power to elaborate yet more from the materials and the forces which nature gives without stint to those who know how to ask her. With diminished toil for the satisfaction of the pressing material wants, and diminished fear of inability to meet them in the future, man has acquired leisure for the cultivation of his intellect, and increased freedom to indulge the social affections, which lift him out of the domain of selfishness, soften and refine his nature, and make it capable of all moral improvement. Physical, intellectual, and moral progress, inseparably interdependent, is the historical fact characteristic of our species, and union in societies, its observed condition.

To investigate the laws which explain man's attainment, through association, of enlarged power over matter in all its forms, and the development of his intellectual and moral faculties, in virtue of that power, is the object of Political Economy.

Those things and events are said to be the subjects of law, between which there is a regular and uniform mode of succession, the nature of which may be expressed in one or more general propositions; so that when we observe the things or events which stand in the relation of antecedent, we are enabled to predict those which will be consequent. The collection and methodical arrangement of those laws, make the science of the subject to which they relate.

In the infancy of the race, as of the individual, every appearance and succession of appearances is regarded as accidental, or is attributed to the direct interposition of mythological powers, whose qualities are so vaguely conceived, as to make the idea of an event's depending upon their action scarcely one remove from that of its being absolutely fortuitous, and irreducible to order or rule. Every accession to knowledge diminishes the catalogue of things thus regarded as outside the pale, within which certain effects are confidently anticipated to result from given causes, and arranges them in relations with each other, no longer imagined as fluctuating, but distinctly seen to be constant and invariable. Knowledge gives power, because when a law is once perceived and understood man can conform to it, for the purpose of producing an effect he desires, by arranging the ascertained causes in that method of grouping which the law dictates, instead of wasting his energies and missing his object, in blind endeavours to obtain it in a way other than that which the Lord of Nature has appointed. What a world of barren experiments was saved, for example, when the law of definite proportions was added to chemistry, and men became aware that as oxygen combines with other elements in quantities measured by 8, and its multiples, 16, 24, &c., every attempt to effect a combination in other proportions must end in failure. "Man," says a great philosopher, "commands Nature only by obeying her laws;" laws which undergo no revision, and contain no saving clauses for the benefit of ignorance, or the exemption of favourites.

Is it possible to construct a science of Political Economy? In other words, are there laws grounded in the constitution of things and of man, fixed and invariable successions of effects determined by the causes which precede them,—regulating the progress of men in association with each other, in extending their dominion over matter and their concurrent improvement in intellect and morals?—and are these laws discoverable? What and how many of them have been discovered, is a different question. What is unquestionable, is, that there are professors of what is styled a science of Political Economy, teaching in the schools and through the press a body of precepts, tending more or less to the object we have assigned as that of its investigations. On the other hand, it is denied that there is yet such a science, by some even who concede there will be one at some future time. A writer,* who has brought the acumen of the legal profession, as well as great general ability and sound feeling, to the exposure of fallacies in the existing system of the English Economists, while confidently trusting that "a science of Political Economy will yet dawn that shall perform as well as promise — a

* Mr. Serjeant Byles: Sophisms of Free Trade, page 3, eighth edition.

science that will rain the riches of Nature in the laps of the starving poor—" speaks of its present state in his own country as follows:

"The need of a Political Economy very different from the inert and barren system now in fashion, is but too apparent to any one who looks around him. Modern society presents to the serious observer, as the consequence of past and present systems of Political Economy, practical results by no means flattering. The immense progress of physical science has multiplied a thousand-fold the means of producing wealth. There is in the overflowing and exhaustless bounty of Nature, not only enough, but a superfluity for every one of the children of men. Yet, some mysterious and invisible, but impassable barrier, impedes its distribution, and shuts out the masses from the promised land. Portentous and gigantic social evils, present and approaching, mock the wisdom of the wise.

"Political Economists, look at England's boundless wealth and hopeless poverty! At Ireland's starving myriads! At her dearest children escaping for their lives, like Lot from the cities of the plain! At the periodical alternations of manufacturing prosperity and manufacturing depression and starvation! At the expanse of untilled lands spread abroad amidst a starving, idle, and congested population! At your own differences and disagreements about rent, population, currency, wages, profits! At the theories opposed to yours not only in fashion and in power, in France, Germany, Russia, and America, but supported by the most original thinkers and greatest writers. Some of these writers have been unjust to you. They affirm that instead of a science, solid and practical, you are but the authors of a literature, obscure, presumptuous, and which would be dangerous, were it not eminently tedious."

The gist of the preceding criticism is the insufficiency and falseness of the system of the English Economists, considered rather as an art, giving directions for the practical conduct of men and States, than as a science. It is true, that what inculcates error in practice cannot be deemed sound in theory. But that is not error which is necessary and unavoidable. It is the office of science to instruct us what is the operation of the laws by which things, in the department of which it treats, are governed; it is to discover, not to invent. An American disciple of the modern English Economists says:—"It is natural, and if natural, proper — though we may not see the reason — that poverty and want, and disease and misery should be the next-door neighbours of wealth and unbounded prosperity." This is unanswerable, if true. If such a state of things be natural, that is to say, the result of immutable laws of Nature, then the Economists who have established the fact stand justified, and may claim that their system, however incomplete, is a science, so far as it goes. No man could deny the scientific character of a system of Mechanics based upon the law of gravitation, though that law should cause every one who ascended a ladder to tumble and break his neck. Every fresh instance would serve to confirm the law. So of the system which Mr. Byles rejects from the list of sciences, if it accounts for the facts he deplores, and connects them in a chain of causation with unquestionable truths in the moral nature of man, and the physical nature of his body and the world about him, it has proved its title to the appellation he refuses to it. It would not, perhaps, be Political Economy such as we have described it. It would be, as it has been called, "the Dismal Science," instead of a science of Progress and Hope — but a science, nevertheless.

Mr. Byles unquestionably believes that the gross inequality in the distribution of property, of which England presents the most glaring examples, is not the result of natural laws, but that their tendency is to redress such inequalities, if suffered to act without impediment. The system of which he speaks is obnoxious to his strictures, because it presents as laws of Nature, which it claims to have discovered, certain hypotheses which conduct necessarily to the existing state of things. It substitutes for the actual laws, fictions, more or less plausible, of its own devising. Concurring with him in this belief, we should be obliged to concede that the failure of the many eminent writers who have devoted themselves to this subject, to construct a *science* of Political Economy, creates a presumption that the time is not yet ripe for it, were it not that their principal errors are fancied corrections of what they deem erroneous in the principles taught by Adam Smith.

This great writer, whom the modern Economists, notwithstanding their aberrations from doctrines which he deemed fundamental and firmly established, still claim as the leader, to whom they profess a general adherence, though less scientific, perhaps, in form, was more correct in substance than his European successors. If not always as acute in analysis, or solicitous to devise a general formula for the expression of a number of truths dependent upon a single principle, he was clear in the perception of facts, and not so fettered by any spirit of system, as to prevent his being candid in their statement. This is not the place for criticism, nor yet for a statement of results, but it will appear frequently in the sequel, that the laws at which we arrive, and in respect to which we differ with the modern

Economists of England and the continental writers who have followed them, agree with the conclusions of Adam Smith, and, though deduced through a different process, conduct to the same end.

It is doubtless true, that greater difficulty may be anticipated in forming a science of Political Economy, than in subjects of a less complex character. It involves the relations between man, endowed with reason and will — combined in associations where the reason and will of one conflict with those of another — and the world of physical nature, wherein what of instinct and will exist are subordinate to human dominion. The objects whose relations we have to examine are heterogeneous, and in one of them there is the apparent source of perplexity, that *will*, by its very nature, rejects law which is founded on the notion of a necessary succession of events. The objects — man and the natural world — have each its own distinct system of laws, both operating at one and the same time, co-operating in full force; neither superseding the other, for this would be opposed to the distinctive idea of a law, but producing results by their combined action. This consideration may suggest the method of inquiry most calculated to be successful. It is well understood, as a rule of physical science, that in order to determine the joint action of two forces, we must first discover what would be the independent action of each, considered separately. It is obviously politic to begin with that which is most simple, and in respect to which the greatest amount of accurate knowledge has been attained, because the successions of change in its condition have been ascertained to have an absolute uniformity of relation to the preceding conditions; in other words, to be subject to invariable laws. This would lead us to study first the general laws of the material world, in those aspects which concern man's power of acquisition. Such are the laws of animal and vegetable growth and decay, of the formation of soils and their adaptation to human abode and culture. Here, at least, we tread on firm ground, and can pursue our way with the aid of certain and clear light. If we find the laws of matter are such as to create no necessary obstacle to the free operation of all the faculties with which human nature is endowed, one great stumbling-block to future progress will have been removed.

The strongest instinct of man is that which leads to the increase of population. The European Economists, since Adam Smith, have very generally believed, that the laws of matter were such as to make the repression of this instinct essential to the prosperity of communities. Their system presents a controlling law of humanity as conflicting with the immutable laws of brute matter. It is impossible for them, upon this basis, to construct a science which contemplates the human faculties as acting freely in accordance with their own laws;* and to contemplate them as acting under partial and uncertain restraints, is to clog the problem with an insurmountable difficulty. If the difficulty is purely supposititious we can proceed with good hope, regarding man as he *is*, and trusting that we may safely infer the uniformities of the future from the uniformities of the past. Man, as God made him, we may study and understand; while from the compound, part man and part monk, in indefinite proportions, we should shrink in despair.

We are to regard man then as the lord, not the slave of Nature, but no arbitrary lord—as acting in accordance with fixed laws of his own being, all of which exercise their due force, and none of which are suspended, any more than the law of gravitation,—as securing freedom for that harmonious exercise of all his faculties, in which happiness consists, by means of the intelligence which enables him to apprehend the inevitable necessity that the physical laws *must* operate, and teaches him how to avoid opposing the irresistible, and how to make it work for him.

> "He is the freeman whom the truth makes free,
> And all are slaves beside."

If we undertook to deduce the laws of human nature from their manifestations in the action of a single individual, it would end in failure, because no two individuals, to say nothing of original diversities of constitution, are surrounded by the same circumstances. What concerns us, however, in Political Economy, is the conduct of men associated in communities — a conduct springing not from

* "In reading certain Economists, one might be led to think that the products of industry were not made for man, but that man was made for the products."—*Droz.*

individual will or peculiarities, but from those which characterize the greater part of their members. It has been found by experience that irregularities, taken in sufficient masses, tend to become regular, and susceptible of strict ascertainment and calculation. Nothing is more uncertain, for example, than the period which an individual of a given age will live. Few things, however, are more certain than that, of one hundred thousand new-born infants indiscriminately taken in England and Wales, about fifteen thousand die in the first year, about five thousand more in the second; that something more than a quarter of the whole number will have perished before the expiration of the fifth year, and about one-half only will survive their fortieth year. Upon data obtained from the registration of births and deaths upon a large scale, mathematicians are enabled to construct tables of mortality, which give the probable number of years that any considerable number of persons of a given age will live, in the aggregate, with such precision as to afford a safe basis for the operations of Life Insurance Companies. Nor is this regularity confined to phenomena, which, like death, are so far independent of the human will as to be certain to happen at some time. Quetelet, the eminent statistician of Belgium, affirms that in that country, as he has ascertained from the examination of its registered statistics for twenty years, there is less variation in phenomena directly dependent upon the human will, which we are apt to regard as the most capricious of disturbing elements, than in those of mortality. The Belgian people, he observes, pays its annual tribute to marriage with more regularity than it does to death; though it consults its inclinations in the one case more, and in the other less than in almost any other. Not only does the total number of marriages, as well in towns as in the country, follow a constant mathematical law, but the same regularity is observed in the numbers which indicate the marriages between bachelors and maids, bachelors and widows, widowers and maids, and widowers with widows.* So, in respect to the ages at which marriage is contracted, there is an astonishing uniformity in the annual returns. In regard to suicides, the statistics of France for a period of twelve years

* Du Systeme Social, page 67.

exhibit a similar uniformity. Their number varies very little from year to year, but they are regularly less in December than in any other month; the number increases regularly in every month (except February, which has three days less than the others,) up to June, when it attains its maximum, and then diminishes regularly till it reaches the minimum in December. It is observed that the number of suicides corresponds in its rise and fall precisely with the lengthening and shortening of the day, and that very few suicides are committed in the night.* There is also a sad regularity in the statistics of crime, in ordinary years, when no special cause can be detected as influencing its frequency, together with a regular increase attending any unusual difficulty in procuring subsistence—as from a rise in the price of provisions, caused by a deficiency in the harvest—and a steady improvement with the general march of prosperity.

By observing such facts we may be led to conclude, that such indeterminate causes as arbitrary individual volition produce next to no effect in modifying social phenomena—they occasion individual oscillations, on one side and the other, of a common mid-point, which neutralize each other, and leave the combined action of society what it would be if no such partial perturbations existed. The progress of intelligence, subordinating passion to reason, obviously tends to substitute certainty for doubt in regard to the conduct of communities, to make the private will and the social will correspond, and to reconcile the highest degree of individual freedom with the highest degree of mutual aid and mutual dependence—aid from each other and from Nature, won by conscious and cheerful obedience to the laws of human nature and physical nature.

The considerations we have presented may suffice to indicate the reasons why we have treated Political Economy as having a wider object than that usually assigned to it. "Political Economy," says Mr. Mill,† "concerns itself only with such of the phenomena of the social state, as take place in consequence of the pursuit of wealth

* Annuaire de l'Economie Politique, 1851, page 200.

† Mill's Logic, p. 566, Harpers' edition, quoting from an article written by him in the London and Westminster Review, October, 1836.

It makes entire abstraction of every other human passion and motive, except those which may be regarded as perpetually antagonizing principles to the desire of wealth: namely, aversion to labour and desire of the present enjoyment of costly indulgences. * * * Political Economy considers mankind as occupied solely in acquiring and consuming wealth, and aims at showing what is the course of action into which mankind, living in a state of society, would be impelled, if that motive, except in the degree in which it is checked by the two counter-motives above adverted to, were absolute ruler of all their actions." Mr. Mill concedes that in this mode of pursuing inquiry we arrive only at an approximation, which must be "corrected by making proper allowance for the effects of any impulses of a different description, which can be shown to interfere with the result in any particular case;" and he adverts to the principle of population, as an important correction, "interpolated into the expositions of Political Economy itself; the strictness of purely scientific arrangement being thereby somewhat departed from, for the sake of practical utility."

The idea to which Mr. Mill has given distinct expression in the preceding passage, is that which has silently controlled nearly all the Economical authors since Adam Smith. Our countryman, Mr. Carey, was the first systematic writer on the subject to protest against it,* and to vindicate a wider range for the science. A prominent objection to the method indicated by Mr. Mill, is, that it proceeds upon an hypothesis admitted to be false—it ignores known qualities of man, and, therefore, if it deduces laws from human experience, it is the experience of a different kind of being from that which it conceives as its subject. If, on the contrary, it infers the laws of action governing its ideal man from *à priori* reasoning, *every* conclusion is vitiated with more or less of error, and a new science is necessary to suggest the requisite corrections.

The practical tendency, however, of investigations conducted in this spirit, is to make men lose sight of the necessity of correction, or to apply it, not in conforming hypothetical conclusions to the actual nature of man, but in endeavours to persuade man to conform

* Carey's Principles of Political Economy, vol. 1, Introduction.

his nature to the standard of the Economists. Such is the result in respect to the principle of population, the healthy and natural operation of which, within the limits of morality, is set down as the cause of the great social evils, and men counselled to seek their remedy in abstaining from matrimony and discouraging it in others. Other examples of the same kind will suggest themselves in the sequel.

The definition proposed by Mr. McCulloch, "the Science of Values," and that offered by Archbishop Wheatley, "Catallactics, or the Science of Exchange," are equally narrow. The first, moreover, is liable to the objection, that the material prosperity of nations is dependent, not upon value, but upon the *quantity* of commodities which are produced and distributed among their people. Adam Smith, in entitling his great work "An Inquiry into the Nature and Causes of the Wealth of Nations," and in the manner in which he treated the subject, exhibited a much more just conception of the scope of the science, of which he was laying the foundation. If we attribute to the word "wealth" the signification it once bore, of "*weal*, well-being," this title will differ little from our statement of the object of Political Economy. If the outline of its leading principles we are about to sketch be correct, it will appear that the greatest wealth of nations, in its common acceptation, is only consistent with such a distribution of it, as enables their people, of all classes, to cultivate the higher powers and affections of humanity; that such a distribution is effected by the regular operation of natural laws, and only prevented by attempts to control them, dictated by ignorance and injustice.

MANUAL

OF

POLITICAL ECONOMY.

CHAPTER I.

THE LAW OF ENDLESS CIRCULATION IN MATTER AND FORCE.

THE first and most imperious of human wants is Food.

The functions of our nature are susceptible of a threefold classification, as Vegetative, Animal, and Spiritual; or, as it has been expressed, man includes Plant, Beast, and Angel. The vital or organic functions, which are common to vegetable and animal life, are continuous. They know no intermission. The plant is always assimilating the inorganic elements of the soil and the air, which contribute to its growth, and repair its constant waste. In man, too, the process of nutrition and decay is unceasing: once suspended it is never resumed, for its suspension is DEATH, and man becomes *inorganic*, resolving himself into the dust whereof he was made. The animal functions, on the contrary, experience periodical interruptions; their activity is suspended in regular intervals of sleep.

Another distinction between the vegetative, or organic, and the animal functions, consists in the independence of the first, and the dependence of the other upon the will. The animal sensibility is accompanied by a perception in the mind, as in seeing, hearing, tasting; animal contractility is excited by its volition, communicated to the voluntary muscles by the nerves; while organic sensibility is attended by no perception, and is followed by contraction totally independent of the will. The chyle stimulates the lacteals without our knowledge, and is propelled by them without our aid. The heart beats, the blood circulates, the lungs inhale air, without waiting for a command; all the simply vital processes go on in man as in the mushroom, by their own impelling laws.

Functions which are thus ever-active, which have no natural intermission, and are neither originated nor controlled by the will, must obviously be supplied with the material for their action, before man can devote productive labour to the satisfaction of any want of less intensity. The more they require, the less can be given elsewhere. The less time, either the individual or society finds it necessary to devote to this object, the more will remain available for the gratification of other wants. The latter can employ the time or labour—however much—that remains unemployed for the primary necessity: for it is the characteristic of man, in his higher nature, that his desires are illimitable, always propagated in widening circles, of larger extent—as the ring made by a stone cast in the water creates another beyond it. The animal nature has no such quality, because its functions are carried on in a mechanical way, by the promptings of instinct, which is neither progressive nor improveable. It can find out no new pleasure; for all pleasure resulting from the activity of functions, where these are actuated by an unvarying force, their activity has a fixed limit, and the capacity for pleasure is equally constant. The round of its wants is small and unchanging; once satisfied, the stimulus to action is gone, and the animal nature reposes contented. Its constitution is adapted to a stationary condition, which it never seeks to improve. The foxes that Nimrod hunted had the same fleetness and cunning, and no less greed for poultry, or other vulpine luxuries, than those trapped by David Crockett. Crockett, on the other hand, desired a thousand things, to the wish for which, Ulysses, after all his wanderings and sight-seeing, was a perfect stranger; and the men of the year 1900 will have as many new motives for exertion, as they will have comforts and conveniences of which we have no conception.

The laws which govern the production of Food are therefore at the basis of Political Economy, and upon these it must be built. To trace them in that large generality which the progress of physical science, especially in organic chemistry, within the last quarter of a century, has enabled us to do, a few preliminary considerations are necessary.

The phenomena of the visible universe are resolvable into Matter and Motion. These in conjunction make Force; and Matter itself has been regarded, in a metaphysical analysis, as the result and the evidence of an equilibrium of forces. They are in perpetual flux and circulation. Man can neither create nor destroy a particle of matter, nor can he affect the quantity of force in the world. His power is limited to altering the mode of its manifestation, its direction and distribution. It is latent in matter, and he can set it free by destroying the equilibrium of other forces that hold it bound in quiescence. He may do this by giving the appropriate direction to some independent force existing in the storehouse of Nature, which, after accomplishing its mission, enters into a new equilibrium with one or more of the liberated forces, to remain at rest until again evoked for fresh labour. Every development of force, however, involves a consumption of matter—not its destruction, but its change of form. To generate in the battery a given amount of light or heat, to produce a certain amount of electro-magnetic motion, for the purpose of transmitting a message upon the telegraph wires from New York to Buffalo, a certain quantity of zinc must be burned by an acid and converted into an oxide. To propel a steamboat a hundred miles, a given quantity of coal must be decomposed into gas and cinders, and a given quantity of water turned into steam. To effect a muscular action of the human body, the brain — the galvanic battery of man's frame — must send its message along the animal telegraph wires, the nerves, and in doing so part with a portion of its own substance; and the muscle, in obeying the command, undergoes a change by which a portion of its substance loses its vital properties and separates from the living part, uniting with oxygen and being transformed into unorganized matter, to be thrown out of the system. The gymnoti, or electrical eels of South America, by being stimulated to give repeated shocks, become exhausted, so that they may be safely handled. Long repose and abundant food are required to replace the galvanic force which they have exhausted. It is no otherwise, except in degree, with man.

The Electro-Magnetic Telegraph has made the action of its battery familiar to most of our readers. A number of plates of zinc and copper are arranged alternately in a vessel containing an acid. When the extremities of the apparatus are joined by means of a wire, however long, a chemical action begins upon the surface of the zinc, and a force is propagated along the wire, by which we can raise weights, set wheels in motion, and decompose compounds, the elements of which have the strongest affinity for each other. The moment the continuity of the wire is interrupted and the circuit broken, the force disappears, and the action between the acid and the zinc immediately stops. When the communication is restored the action of the acid upon the zinc is renewed, and the force which had vanished reappears with all its original energy. The substance of the wire, however, is merely the conductor of force, and does not contribute the slightest share to its manifestations. Something analogous to this is the office of man in regard to matter and the forces of Nature. He serves merely to give them circulation, without adding to or detracting from their quantity. His person is but a scene in the theatre of their action, in which they have their exits and their entrances, and each one in his time plays many parts, sustaining transmutations of force, and causing them; but they are immortal in their essence, and run in an endless vicissitude through a round of various utilities, for the maintenance of life and the means of life.

Our concern is with such matter and forces as are employed in human nutrition.

Man feeds upon both vegetables and animals. The animals he consumes are themselves nourished by vegetable aliment. The vegetables, in their turn, digest the inorganic elements supplied by the soil and the air. Modern chemistry has proved that the ultimate constituents of all, are Carbon, Oxygen, Nitrogen, and Hydrogen, the four principal elements of the organic creation, and sulphur, phosphorus, chlorine, lime, potassium, sodium, iron, and a few other inorganic substances.* These must be introduced into the

* "Of the human frame, bones included, only about three-fourths is solid matter—chiefly carbon and nitrogen—the rest is water. If a man weighing

vegetable or animal body, in order that it may live and grow. From these few elements, combined in different numbers and proportions, are formed air and water, the rocks and the earths, which are the result of their decomposition.

That the elements incorporated into the frame of vegetables and animals, are derived from air, water, earth, and rock, has been demonstrated by repeated experiments, exhibiting the fact that the precise quantities of the identical elements gained by the former had disappeared from the latter, under circumstances artificially arranged so as to exclude the possibility of their being drawn from other contributories than those whose loss was to be examined. For detailed accounts of the experiments and reasoning by which these conclusions are demonstrated, we refer the student to the works of Liebig, and other writers on Organic Chemistry, who have pursued the path of inquiry which he opened and so successfully wrought.

The fundamental property of vitality, common to all organized bodies, consists in their constant material renovation; an attribute which distinguishes them from the inert or unorganized bodies, whose composition is always fixed. The latter may be artificially constructed by putting together their constituent parts; while no chemical skill is adequate to the production of wood, sugar, starch, fat, gelatine, flesh, &c., whose elements, though equally simple and equally well known, refuse to combine in organized compounds, otherwise than under the operations of that mysterious power which we call vital force. The growth of a crystal—the highest inorganic process we are acquainted with, involving but one action, that of accretion—may be conducted artificially by the chemist; while the growth of a simple cell, such as compose the yeast fungus, and the

---

160 pounds were squeezed flat under a hydraulic press, 120 pounds of water would run out, and only 40 of dry residuum remain. *A man is, therefore, chemically speaking, a little less than fifty pounds of carbon and nitrogen, diffused through six pailsful of water.* Berzelius, indeed, in recording the fact, justly remarks that 'the living organism is to be regarded as a mass diffused in water;' and Dalton, by a series of experiments tried on his own person, ascertained, that of the food with which we daily repair this water-built fabric, five-sixths is also water." —*London Quarterly Review.*

minute *algæ* which colour the waters of stagnant pools, though the lowest organic process, involves the double action of accretion and disintegration, and defies the power of science to produce. The meanest and least complex form of life it is beyond man's reach to fashion.*

While the ultimate elements of vitality are profusely furnished in the natural world, vegetables alone have sufficient assimilative power to compose their tissues directly from inorganic matter, the liquid and gassy materials, and the earthy particles, which are but minerals decomposed.† Not only so, but no part of an organized being can serve as food to vegetables, until, by the process of putrefaction and decay, it has assumed the form of inorganic matter. It is this capacity which renders vegetable organization the essential base of all other. In the absence of vegetation all animals must be carnivorous, and subsist by mutual destruction, which would soon exterminate their species. For this reason it must necessarily precede animal life. That such has been the fact is abundantly proved by geological research, which, reading the history of buried ages in the rocks, shows us that a period of long duration intervened, after the growth of lichens and ferns in the primitive world, before the lowest order of animals made its appearance upon the earth.

Animal organism, on the contrary, requires for its support and

* I am aware that the English philosopher, Mr. Crosse, supposes himself to have produced insect life, by galvanism, from a soluble glass made of pure black flints and caustic soda, dissolved in distilled water. There is no doubt of the good faith and intelligence of Mr. Crosse. Though not disposed to alter the text, I deem it proper to add this note.

† There is a race of Indians, in Utah and Oregon, who are earth-eaters. They are described in Stansbury's account of the Expedition to the Great Salt Lake, as the very lowest order of human beings. Humboldt mentions that the Otomaas, living on the banks of the Orinoco, who subsist mainly on fish, and are averse to any kind of tillage, are addicted to eating a soft, unctuous clay, which they knead into balls and roast by a weak fire. The balls are moistened again, to prepare them for being eaten. A writer in the Journal of the Royal Agricultural Society of England, (quoted in the Patent Office Report for 1851, page 503,) suggests that dirt is eaten for the purpose of supplying a deficiency of lime in the ordinary food of the tribes, in whom this practice has been observed.

development highly organized atoms. The food of animals, in all circumstances, consists of parts of organisms. While some of them feed directly upon vegetation, others, requiring that matter should have taken on a higher order of life before it can support their own, prey upon other and inferior animals. Having a lower assimilative capacity, it is necessary that their food should have been brought by intermediate agents, into combinations agreeing more nearly with those of their own tissues than even vegetable organization. Without some arrangement and gradation of this character, the higher natures must either perish for lack of food, or consume all their activity in chemical transformations, without reserving any for locomotion or other muscular effort. We may remark here, that with this necessity of overcoming and capturing prey, arises a degree of mental power, enabling the carnivorous animals to devise plans, and to compass by association with their fellows, ends beyond their unassisted power. The spider spins an artful web to catch flies, and wolves hunt their game in packs. The superior functions are everywhere united with less energy in the inferior. Those beings in whom the latter prevail are self-sufficing and independent, but have little reach and power beyond the satisfaction of the low primary wants. As we rise in the scale up to man, the crown and roof of things, we find him, of all, the most dependent, the most prone to association, for which, by the faculty of speech, he is most adapted; and by means of association, though *alone* the least self-sufficing of all beings, he wins the dominion over Nature and her forces, whether animate or inanimate.

Another distinction between animal and vegetable life is this. The growth and development of vegetables depends upon the *elimination* of oxygen from the other component parts of their nourishment. They are perpetually exhaling this gas from the surfaces of their leaves into the air. The life of animals exhibits itself in the continual *absorption* of the oxygen of the air, and its combination with certain component parts of the body. Its office is to generate animal heat by burning the combustible substances of the frame. It combines with the carbon of the food, and in so doing precisely the same quantity of heat is disengaged as if it had been directly burned in the air. The result is carbonic acid gas, which is thrown out of the lungs and the skin; this is absorbed by the leaves of plants, the carbon separated and incorporated into their substance, and the oxygen again exhaled into the atmosphere, to resume its round of circulation.

To trace the cycle a little farther—the carbon uniting with water in the plant, forms, among other things, starch, which the sap conveys to the part requiring it. It is found largely in the seeds. Starch exists in wheat to the extent of one half the weight of the grain, and it consists of carbon and water only. Man eats the wheat, but we find no starch in the human body. When it enters our frames it undergoes a chemical change, a slow burning, in fact, in which the carbon of the starch combines with oxygen, forming carbonic acid gas, which, together with the liberated water in the shape of vapour, is thrown out of the human system into the atmosphere, to be again converted in the laboratory of the plant into the starch from which they were derived. Having served our purpose in keeping up the internal warmth upon which animal life depends, the disengaged elements are recomposed by the plants into part of their substance, which when completed again serve as fuel in the animal economy.

The instances we have given, will, so far as relates to their *organic* constituents, suffice to exemplify the law that animals and vegetables are mutually convertible one into the other, and depend on each other for existence. The interchange of their elements is accomplished through the medium of the atmosphere from which plants derive far the greatest portion of their nutriment.* It is

* "Two hundred pounds of earth were dried in an oven, and afterwards put into a large earthen vessel; the earth was then moistened with rain-water, and a willow tree weighing five pounds was planted therein. During the space of five years, the earth was carefully watered with rain-water. The willow grew and flourished; and, to prevent the earth being mixed with fresh earth, blown upon it by the winds, it was covered with a metal plate full of very minute holes, which would exclude everything but air from getting access to the earth below it. After growing in the earth for five years, the tree was removed, and on being weighed, was found to have gained one hundred and sixty-four pounds. And this estimate did not include the weight of the leaves or dead branches which in five years fell from the tree.

found by burning any form of vegetable matter, in a dry state, that the organic part, which is combustible and disappears in the air, is by far the largest. It ordinarily constitutes from ninety to ninety-seven pounds in every hundred. This part of the plant can only have been formed from air at first, if not directly, yet from compounds whose elements were themselves derived from air, existing in the soil, and taken up by the roots. In the language of Professor Draper, in his Chemistry of Plants, "Atmospheric air is the grand receptacle from which all things spring and to which they all return. It is the cradle of vegetable, and the coffin of animal life."

About one pound in ten, upon an average, of the dry weight of cultivated plants, including their roots, stems, leaves and seeds, is formed of matter which existed as a part of the solid substance of the soil in which the plant grew. Every organ in the stalk, stems, and leaves of a plant has a reticulated framework of inorganic matter, the base of which is either silex or lime. Silex, familiar to us in the various shapes of white sand, flint, and crystal of quartz, constitutes more than sixty per cent. in quantity of the soil, sometimes forming as much as ninety-five per cent. It gives porosity to the soil, in order that water and air may be admitted into its texture. Alumina, the base of clay, on the contrary, renders it compact and retentive. The office of silex in plants is to give strength—to the straw of wheat, for example; it serves as the *bone* of all the grass family. From ninety-three to one hundred and fifty pounds of soluble flint are required to form an acre of wheat.

"Now came the application of the test. Was all this obtained from the earth? It had not sensibly diminished; but, in order to make the experiment conclusive, it was again dried in an oven and put in the balance. Astonishing was the result—the earth weighed only *two ounces* less than it did when the willow was first planted in it! yet the tree had gained *one hundred and sixty-four pounds*. Manifestly, then, the wood thus gained in the above-mentioned space of time was *not* obtained from the earth; we are therefore compelled to repeat our question, "where does the wood come from?"

The writer who narrates this experiment concludes that the wood did not come from the water, and therefore must have come from the air. As both air and water are inexhaustible in quantity, it is of no consequence, for the purposes of our reasoning, whether it came from one or both.

It is unnecessary to remark upon the several inorganic constituents, which, combining in different proportions in the various species of vegetation, exist in the soil, and must be replaced if extracted; inasmuch as the absence of any one which enters into the composition of a particular plant, is as fatal to its further growth, as the absence of all. An able chemist has familiarized the notion of the deterioration, when the crop is carried away so as to return nothing to the soil, by informing us that "for every fourteen tons of fodder taken from the soil, there are carried away two casks of potash, two casks of lime, one cask of soda, a carboy of oil of vitriol, a large demijohn of phosphoric acid, and other essential ingredients."

The soil is composed, like the plants, partly of organic and partly of inorganic constituents. The latter, or mineral portion, called the subsoil, is formed by the crumbling and decomposition of the underlying rock, or of other rocks, which have been drifted over it by the action of water, in the early convulsions of Nature, or brought down by the streams in time of freshets from the formations of their upper waters, are deposited in alluvium upon the plains of the low countries. Above the subsoil lies a deposit of mould, resulting from the decay of vegetation and of animal remains. The roots of plants, penetrating through the mould to the subsoil, extract from each the species of nutriment, organic or inorganic, of which it is composed. The object of tillage is to facilitate this process. In the order of Nature, however, and independent of tillage, it is obvious that the plant, in the decay of the leaves and branches which fall from it, and finally of its entire substance, must return to the soil all the solid matter which it had abstracted during its period of growth. If the plant was itself made the food of an animal, the same result followed at one additional remove. During the life of the animal, the soluble material of its food is returned to the earth in its urine, the insoluble in its solid excrements, and, when its life is ended, its carcass goes to repay to the earth all that remains unpaid of its borrowings. If the animal serves as food for another, or for a human being, there is but one step more in the journey to the same destination; for man, too, returns to the soil the exact equivalent of the food which he consumes, in a state fit for immediate absorption by the roots of plants.

The underlying rocks, from which the subsoil is formed, are themselves but combinations of oxygen, with a few metallic bases. The rocks which make the crust of the earth are in the aggregate about half oxygen. It is sufficiently plain that, if by any means the constituents of the rocks are brought to the surface, and dissipate in air, or enter into the structure of plants and animals, they must return again to the earth and the atmosphere. In the Economy of Nature it is provided that the leaves of trees, which annually fall to the earth, contain from seven to fifteen times more of the earthy minerals than the trunks do. When man has exhausted the surface mould, as has been done in some of our Southern States, by sending its products to foreign lands, and abandons the fields he has impoverished, their fertility is slowly restored by means of that provision. The seeds of the pine are carried by the birds, and scattered by the winds. They sprout in the deserted soil, and, sending down a long tap-root, bring up mineral sustenance from a distance much below the reach of the plants that had sucked the upper surface dry of its nutriment. This is accumulated in the leaves, which falling and rotting upon the earth, gradually form a soil capable of bearing fruit to feed man.

If vegetation be suffered, as in the state of Nature, merely to grow and rot upon the ground, it is apparent that everything is returned to the soil that is abstracted from it. It is, however, material to observe, that if the plant passes through the digestive organs of an animal, it is ground down into minute fragments, and thus prepared to unite more readily with other elements, and to fertilize the soil with more rapidity than if applied in its crude condition. It is combined, moreover, with organic elements which the animal derives from the atmosphere; and what the animal rejects is richer in nitrogen than the food in its original state. For this reason animals are kept stall-fed, in idleness, as *food-producing* machines.*

* "Our Norfolk farmers sometimes feed out a ton of oil-cake a day to their cattle; not to make money by the sale of the cattle, but indirectly, through the richness of the manure obtained by it. In Lancashire there was a large tract of very poor lands, which, thirty years ago, was a com-

Professor Norton, at the conclusion of his "Elements of Scientific Agriculture," thus sums up the matter. "We may follow any particular substance in its course from the inanimate soil to the living plant, from the plant to the living and conscious animal, and finally see it return to the soil once more. In all its changes it remains the same in its nature, but is constantly presented to us in new forms. * * * There is an endless chain of circulation from the earth up through the plant to the animal, and then again back to the parent earth. By watching this chain, and the various transformations of matter during its course, we may hope to grow constantly wiser in every department of agriculture. We discover that *nothing is lost:* if we burn a piece of wood it disappears, but has merely been converted into carbonic acid and water, both of which are at once ready to enter into new combinations. The animal or the plant dies, and also after a time disappears, but in its decay every particle furnishes food for a new series of living things."

It is now more than half a century since Mr. Malthus published his "Essay on Population," in which he proved — what had been shown before without creating any considerable sensation—that the human race is endowed with such a generative power as to enable it to double its numbers in twenty-five years, and that, although this rate of increase has been seldom attained, if ever, for any long period, yet the natural tendency is to increase in a geometrical ratio. He maintained, on the other hand, that, "considering the present average state of the earth, the means of subsistence, under circumstances the most favourable to human industry, could not possibly be made to increase faster than in an arithmetical ratio." He exemplifies the disparate tendencies by saying: "The human species

---

plete moor, in the middle of which was erected a high tower, so that the traveller might know where he was. This great moor is now reclaimed and cultivated, and pays 20 shillings (sterling) rent annually. But it is kept in this state of cultivation by this high farming. They keep cattle, feed them with oil-cake, and, though the cattle may not be worth half the oil-cake used in feeding, yet they obtain in this way a manure, which enables them to raise barley and wheat crops, sustain their families, pay their rent, and lay by something." — *Prof. Johnston's Eighth Lecture before the N. Y. State Agricultural Society: Transactions of* 1849, *page* 249.

would increase as the numbers 1, 2, 4, 8, 16, 32, 64, 128, 256; and subsistence as 1, 2, 3, 4, 5, 6, 7, 8, 9."

The elder Mill, (Elements of Political Economy, page 56,) using the term capital as including the means of subsistence, and everything else capable of being exchanged for them, states the doctrine which he held in common with Malthus, in these terms:

"It thus sufficiently appears that there is a tendency in population to increase faster than capital. If this be established, it is of no consequence to the present purpose to inquire about the rapidity of the increase. How slow soever the increase of population, provided that of capital is still slower, *wages will be reduced so low, that a portion of the population will regularly die of want.* Neither can this dreadful consequence be averted otherwise, than by the use of means to prevent the increase of capital from falling short of that of population."

The passage we have marked with italics, is but the necessary logical result of the free operations of the laws of human nature and physical nature, as the latter are conceived by Malthus. Humanity recoils from it, and naturally looks for a remedy in trammelling the conduct of man. Accordingly, in the succeeding pages of his book, Mr. Mill examines the question, by which course of expedients population and capital can be made to keep pace together, whether by restraining the tendency of population to increase, or by endeavouring "to accelerate beyond its natural pace the increase of capital;" and finally arrives at the conclusion that "human happiness cannot be secured by taking forcible methods to make capital increase as fast as population," and that "the grand practical problem is, to find the means of limiting the number of births."

The ideas of Mr. Malthus have been adopted, not only by Mr. Mill, but by the great body of British Economists, down to the present day, and, crossing the Channel, they have found acceptance and approval with most of the Continental writers. Various theories, it is true, have been propounded, for the purpose of showing that the gloomy results which necessarily flow from the principles maintained by him, may be avoided, and that counteracting forces restrain the natural increase of our species. None of them, however, have recognized anything like a natural equilibrium between population and subsistence, if the former, for a long period, should expand at the rate which the native instincts of man, in their normal and healthy development, would occasion. Instead of burdening the reader with extended quotations in support of this statement, we cite the declaration of the London Times, when announcing the startling fact, proved by the census of 1851, then just completed, that the numbers of the people of Ireland had diminished by 1,659,330 souls in the preceding ten years. "For a whole generation," said the Times, "man has been a drug in this country, and population a nuisance." Repeatedly recurring to the same topic, the sentiment so bluntly expressed in this language, was represented by that journal as the prevailing one among the Economists of Great Britain.

This is not the place for us to examine the course of man's proceeding in the cultivation of the earth, which Mr. Malthus elaborated in his "Principles of Political Economy," published in 1815, as explaining why it is that subsistence increases in a less ratio than population. The doctrine in regard to rent, founded upon that theory, and more generally connected with the name of Mr. Ricardo, will naturally come under review in a subsequent chapter. It is sufficient for the present to observe, that Malthus's theory of the relations between population and subsistence is obviously founded upon the false notion, that man's consumption of food is its destruction—that having once served the purpose of supporting animal life, its capacity to contribute to that object is absolutely spent and exhausted. The failure to observe that, in the natural course of things it is returned to the earth, to be again formed into food, and resume its office of supporting animal life, is tantamount to this; and it is only in consequence of that failure, that the food-producing power of the soil can be regarded either as a fixed quantity, or as incapable of increasing in the same proportion as the food-consuming power of those who dwell upon it. It may account in part for the tacit adoption of so erroneous an opinion by an intelligent writer, that the discoveries in organic chemistry, which conclusively disprove it, have been made within the last twenty-five years, and are subsequent, by an equal period, to the publication of Mr. Malthus.

If any such exhaustion as that contemplated by Malthus takes place, in consequence of man's subjecting the earth to cultivation, it is obviously because, instead of pursuing the methods dictated by

Nature, and imitating the operations by which she maintained the fertility of the soil and the interchange of vegetable and animal life, prior to his intervention, he has sought out devices to thwart her laws. But to every law is attached the inevitable penalty of its violation, Death. It executes itself by the destruction of the offender.

Nature doubtless offers examples of what is called *special* exhaustion. Different species of plants require very unlike proportions of the several kinds of inorganic food which they derive from the soil. The oak requires much of certain kinds, the pine much of other kinds, and little of those needed by the oak. Accordingly, forests of oak and pine succeed each other alternately, or other alternations occur, depending upon the character of the soil. On the Rhine, between Landau and Kaiser-lautern, oak forests, several centuries old, are seen to be gradually giving way to the beech, while others of oak and beech are yielding to the encroachments of the pine. In our own country we have abundant opportunities of seeing that the second growth of timber differs from that of the original forest to which it succeeds. Nature thus teaches the necessity of a rotation of crops, and the greatest advances in agriculture have been since the lesson has been thoroughly learned.

But Nature nowhere teaches a system which results in continuous and permanent exhaustion, though the Economists of the Malthus school have done so. She offers no examples which should encourage a policy that would make one country the granary and another the workshop of the world. It is not among her plans, that the agriculturists of any nation should be "an exporting interest." If, as we learn from the Agricultural section of the Patent Office Report for 1849, "the farmers of Ohio, Indiana, Michigan, Illinois, and Wisconsin export a million tons of breadstuffs and provisions, where they import one ton of the atoms drawn from their virgin soil to form agricultural products," it is to perverse arrangements, for which Nature has no responsibility, and not to any tendency growing out of her laws, that the impoverishment of their territory, and the diminution of its power to sustain human life, is to be ascribed. The same document informs us how it is that Nature compels a restoration of the equilibrium, which disobedience to its laws disturbs, in assuring us that "nothing is more certain than the fact, that a District or State which exports largely the things which Nature demands to form breadstuffs and provisions, must sooner or later export also some of its consumers of bread and meat;" while the reward of obedience is "that a State can feed and clothe a population ten times larger at home than abroad." We can see no reason in the nature of things, why the disproportion should be set at so low a figure; for it is impossible to conjecture a limit to the increase of population, if man will but conform to the law which Nature exemplifies in all her processes, by which the soil regains whatever material of nutriment it has lent for the support of vegetable and animal life, and that with large interest, derived from the elements furnished by the atmosphere, and incorporated in the substance of the matter, which, on the extinction of its vitality, returns to the bosom of the earth.

Having thus cursorily stated the general laws which operate in the cycle of animal and vegetable life, independent of human agency, we are prepared to follow the steps by which the soil is prepared for the theatre of human labour, and the successive stages which mark man's progress in obtaining food, and in supplying the other wants, the pressure of which is felt, the moment the primary want of his vegetative nature is satisfied.

Those who desire to study the laws which have been the subject of this chapter, will find abundant information in the works of Liebig, and the treatise of Professor Johnston on Agricultural Chemistry. The lectures of the latter gentleman before the New York State Agricultural Society, together with the Prize Essay of Professor Norton on Agricultural Chemistry, which elucidate the subject sufficiently for general readers, may be found in the volume of its Transactions for 1849, which is widely distributed through the State, and readily accessible. Professor Emmons's work on the Agriculture of New York, forming two volumes of the series of its Natural History, is also generally accessible.

CHAPTER II.

THE FORMATION OF SOILS, AND THEIR ADAPTATION TO OCCUPATION AND CULTURE.

THE coral islands of the tropical seas present the most remarkable examples of the rapid clothing of a naked rock with vegetable life, and its preparation for the habitation of human beings. The creatures which build up these islands from unknown depths in the ocean, partake, as is indicated by the name of their species, zoophyte, or animal plant, in the characteristics of both orders of vitality. They fulfil their functions without a heart or system of circulation — the several polypi in a group have separate mouths and tentacles, and separate stomachs; but beyond this there is no individual property— and form a living sheet of animals, fed and nourished by numerous mouths and stomachs, but coalescing by intervening tissues. They possess no more power of motion than is sufficient to thrust out their arms to seize the food that drifts past them, and they propagate by buds, the bud commencing as a slight prominence on the side of the parent: the bud enlarges, a circle of tentacles grows out, with a mouth in the centre, and the enlargement goes on till the young equals the parent in size, when it begins to protrude buds itself — and the group thus continues to grow. They secrete the coral as the quadruped secretes its bones, until single reefs are formed and attain the surface of the water. But it is essential to the life of these submarine builders that they should be covered by the waves, and when they have reached low water mark they die. A new process now begins, in the accumulation of loose materials upon its summit, from coral boulder—broken off from the reef by the waves, thrown up from below, and gradually ground into fragments — coral gravel and sand. Agassiz states that all that portion of Florida known as the Everglades is only a vast coral bank, composed of a series of more or less parallel reefs, which have successively grown from the bottom of the sea up to the surface, and have been added to the main land, by the gradual filling of the intervals which separate them with deposits of the coralline sand, and debris brought thither by the action of the tides and the currents.

The cocoanut, with its husk, being well adapted to be wafted by the waves, it takes root upon the naked sand of the coral island, just lifted above the level of the ocean, and, washed by the spray, grows luxuriantly.* Nourished at first by only so much of organic aliment as the remains of the zoophytes, who built the island, supply, the decay of its leaves soon furnishes a mould which suffices for other vegetable growth. Its uses are manifold: the inhabitants, when they come, find in it material for the scanty dresses which the climate requires, drinking-vessels from the shell of its nut, and other utensils, mats, cordage, fishing-lines, and oil, besides food, drink, and building materials. In every stage, from its first formation after the fall of the blossom, to the hard, dry, and ripe nut, that has almost begun to germinate, the fruit may be seen *at the same time, on the same tree.* The pandanus, or screw-pine, another tree which soon roots itself in the scanty soil, throwing out props from the trunk, which plant themselves in the ground, and widen the supporting base as it grows, furnishes a sweetish, husky fruit, "which, though a little bitter," says Mr. Dana, in his Geology of the Exploring Expedition, from which these facts are drawn, "admits

* "How are the seeds of plants brought so immediately to these new shores?—by wandering birds, or by the winds and waves of the ocean? The distance from other coasts makes it difficult to answer this question; but no sooner is the newly-raised island in direct contact with the atmosphere, than there is found on its surface, in our *northern countries*, a soft, silky net-work, appearing to the naked eye as coloured spots and patches. Some of these patches are bordered by single or double raised lines running round the margin; other patches are crossed by similar lines, traversing them in various directions. Gradually the light colour of the patches becomes darker, the bright yellow, which was visible at a distance, changes to a brown, and the bluish-grey of the lepraides becomes a dusty black. The edges of neighbouring patches approach and run into each other; and on the dark ground thus formed there appear other lichens, of circular shape and dazzling whiteness. Thus, an organic film or covering establishes itself by successive layers; and as mankind, in forming communities, pass through different stages of civilization, so is the gradual propagation and extension of plants connected with determinate physical laws."—*Humboldt.*

of being stored away for food when other things fail." Fish and crabs from the reefs, and the large fish caught with wooden hooks from the deep waters, eke out the subsistence of the natives. "From such scanty resources," says Mr. Dana, "a population of 10,000 persons is supported on the single island of Taputeouea, whose habitable area does not exceed six square miles."

The process in this case, by which the emerging peak of the submarine mountain is fitted by the germination of vegetation for a human abode, is rapid. That by which the peaks of the land mountain have crumbled into soil involves more intermediate stages, and a much greater variety of results. Some of the rocks, such as slates and shales, decompose with such facility, that the whole process may be observed within a brief period, and we have constant opportunities of watching its progress. The granitic rocks, however, which, constituting in the view of geologists the lower and earlier strata, have been made, upon the disruption and upheaving of the crust of the earth, to occupy the highest place, are of a less frangible character. But their chemical composition is such as to favour their speedy disintegration under the action of the elements. The presence of alkalies in the feldspar and mica, which are combined with silex in granite, exerts a powerful influence in this change. Carbonic acid, the great solvent for the hardest materials, decomposes the potash with which silica is combined in the feldspar, and it is made soluble. The intensity of the frost, and the length of time during which rocks on the mountain tops are exposed to it; the suddenness of the changes of temperature to which they are subjected, and which, from their being poor conductors of heat, involve an inequality in the contraction and expansion of the surface and the interior, which induces flaking and cracking; the dampness of the air during the summer, when watery vapours condense upon their summits—are among the circumstances which hasten the destruction of rocks in these places. As disintegration is accomplished by the process of weathering, the decomposed particles fall by their own weight, and are washed by the rains into the valleys beneath, which receive in the same manner the contributions of the intermediate rocks. During this process the rocks are not merely mechanically broken into small fragments, but from their insoluble constituents, soluble salts, as those of lime, soda, &c., are generated, which may be absorbed by the roots of plants. In the decomposition of feldspar, the silicate of potassa is gradually removed by the water, and while the sand remains upon the sloping surfaces, the fine alumina or clay accumulates in the valleys, and forms a mixture of clay and sand, which is more favourable to the support of grass and grain. Thus every gradation is presented, from the naked granite of the hill-tops, through the thin, porous soils of the slopes, to the rich meadow lands of the valleys.

Vegetation of some kind, however, can find nourishment even on the surface of the rock. Lichens and algæ grow high above the line of perpetual snow; and in bleak northern climes, upon the bare face of the granite rock, a species of lichen flourishes, which the hunger-pinched Canadian voyageur seeks for food, and gives the appetizing name of "tripe de roche." Decaying vegetable matter of such kinds is swept by every shower down hill, to accumulate at the base with the deposits of mineral origin. After a sufficient period a soil is thus formed at the bottom of the slopes, which is capable of sustaining heavy timber. The first tree sheds its leaves and branches to feed the fattening soil, in a circle around its trunk, whose area is measured by the spread of its branches. The probable process from this starting point is this: Upon the outer circumference of the first circle thus nourished, and that edge of it, which, lying between the trunk and the hill-top, upon the ascending slope, is inferior to the lowest point in the collected elements of vegetable nutrition, it becomes possible for another tree to grow. This, in its turn, becomes the centre of a circle of fertilized ground, upon whose upper exterior the material to support a new growth is accumulated, by the droppings of its stem and branches. Each new plant thus manures the ground for its successor, and vegetation creeps up the hill-side, along a soil of constantly diminishing richness, and which, though made more fat and tenacious by its own growth, is always parting with some portion of its mineral and vegetable elements to fatten the valley beneath it.* The process, like so many others in the opera-

* "The plantations of the late Duke of Athol consist chiefly of white arch, and grow upon a poor, hilly soil, resting on gneiss, mica, slate, and

tions of Nature, is one of action and reaction, of a disturbance of equilibrium which sets at work the machinery for its own restoration. The elemental forces, gravitation, and the wash of running water, carry to the lowest levels the mineral and organic nutriment for vegetation; and vegetation, thus originated, carries them back again up the slopes, preparing a soil for its own progress as it goes. The slimmest and scantiest vegetation is always in the advance, like the pioneers and light troops who clear the ground for the heavy columns of an army.*

Ages roll away: dank swamps, filling the air with mists and fog, occupy the valley bottoms; tangled forests of gigantic timber surround them, at the foot of the slopes; above them the vegetable growth dwindles, from smaller and less frequent trees, to shrubs of less and less size, to weeds and plants, requiring a diminishing quantity of nutriment for their support, and finding it upon the thin, porous, sandy soil of the uplands, through which the rain filters readily, and from whose inclined surface the drenching showers run off.

Finally, man comes to begin the work of cultivation. History teaches us that he has first, everywhere, passed through a hunter

---

clay slate. In six or seven years the lower branches spread out, become interlaced, and completely overshadow the ground. Nothing, therefore, grows upon it until the trees are twenty-four years old, when the spines of the lower branches beginning to fall, the first considerable thinning takes place. Air and light being thus readmitted, grasses spring up, and a fine sward is gradually produced. *The ground, which previously was worth only 9d. or 1s. an acre, as a sheep pasture, at the end of thirty years becomes worth from 7s. to 10s. per acre.*" — *Johnston's Agricul. Chemistry, Lect.* 17, § 8.

* An analogous process is described in the following account of the banks of willows on the Mississippi, below New Orleans:—

"The growth of willows on that side of the stream where the land is gaining on the water, is often so formal and regular that they look like a young plantation. In the front row are young saplings, just rising out of the ground, which is formed of silt thrown down within the last two or three years. Behind them is an older growth, from four to eight feet high. Still farther back is seen a third row, twenty-five feet high; and sometimes, in this manner, five tiers, each overtopping the other, showing the gradual formation of the bank, which inclines upward, because the soil first deposited has been continually raised during the annual floods."— *Lyell's Second Visit to the United States, Vol.* 2, *page* 115.

state, when he subsisted upon the various spoils of the chase, and of fishing; and the nomadic, when the flesh and milk of tame flocks, cropping the spontaneous herbage, furnish him with food, and their skins with tents and clothing.

In those stages of society there is little individuality of labour or of profit. The land over which the tribe hunts, and the streams in which it fishes, the pastures over which the flocks of the wandering herdsmen browse, have no individual proprietor. They are the common stock of the tribe, and when they are exhausted, the tribe emigrates in a body to find new ones, as yet unappropriated, or engages in war, to drive off from their possessions another tribe whose territories seem worth the chances of strife. Each individual partakes in the common fortunes. The entire body obtain but a scanty subsistence; and the one who happens to have a superfluity to-day, shares with his fellow, and exchanges situations with him when less fortunate to-morrow. Individual property in land, and dependence upon individual success in gathering its products, for subsistence, only arise when the nomadic way of life is abandoned, and men settle down in fixed habitations.

But where is the man to establish himself who makes the first attempts in agriculture? Where can he? His choice is obviously controlled by his power. His implements are of the rudest description, such as Nature offers ready-made to his hand, like the shell that the South Sea Islanders use for a hoe. All the arms and tools that his forefathers had used, while the tribe was passing through its stages of hunter and shepherd life, were of this description. A flint had served for an arrow-head, and its sharp edge gave the only cutting instrument they had been able to construct. A bow fashioned by such a knife, the string of which was a thong cut from a deer-skin, was his chief weapon for the chase, or for combat at a distance—a club hardened by the fire, armed sometimes with a sharp stone, fastened to it by thongs, was the weapon for close strife. A pointed bone, from the leg of a deer, furnished his wife with a needle, and its sinews with the thread, by which she sewed together the skins that clothed her household. It is with such tools only that experience or the traditions of his tribe have made him acquainted. One has but to walk into the nearest Museum that contains a collection of savage implements, to see how imperfect they are, and at the same time, to observe with some astonishment how fully they meet the limited wants of those who use them, and through what a long tract of time generations of men make no sensible improvement upon their primitive stock.

The first planter, moreover, can have little assistance from others, for their numbers are few. "It has been computed," says Lyell, the geologist, "that eight hundred acres furnish only as much subsistence to a community of hunters, as half an acre under cultivation." Liebig gives us the scientific explanation of this fact.* It is clear, then, that the individuals of a tribe, just resolving itself into an agricultural community, would be widely scattered, and that long distances would separate them from each other. It is quite probable, indeed, that the first cultivator would be one whom physical debility had deprived of the power of accompanying his fellows in their migrations.

An individual or a community of individuals, so weak in resources, cannot undertake the tillage of land that demands great labour to prepare it for a crop. The valleys covered with heavy timber, that must be cut and removed, the swamps, suffused with water, that require only thorough drainage to convert them into fertile meadows, present insuperable difficulties to a poor and feeble people. The

* "A nation of hunters on a limited space is utterly incapable of increasing its numbers beyond a certain point, which is soon attained. The carbon necessary for respiration must be obtained from the animals, of which only a limited number can live on the space supposed. These animals collect from plants the constituents of their organs and their blood, and yield them in turn to the savages who live by the chase alone. They again receive this food, unaccompanied by those compounds destitute of nitrogen, which, during the life of the animals, served to support the respiratory process. In such men, confined to an animal diet, it is the carbon of the flesh and of the blood which must take the place of starch and sugar. But fifteen pounds of flesh contain no more carbon than four pounds of starch; and while the savage, with one animal and an equal weight of starch, could maintain life and health for a certain number of days, he would be compelled, if confined to flesh, in order to procure the carbon necessary for respiration during the same time, to consume five such animals." —*Liebig's Animal Chemistry, Part* 1, § 14.

malaria from the decay of rank vegetation upon the lowlands generates fevers, which would prevent the attempt to cultivate the rich bottoms,* even if the cultivators had the power to clear and drain them, and a sufficient supply of food in advance to wait the ripening of the crops, after those necessary preliminary operations were accomplished. But they possess neither; and the demand for food is instant and pressing. They are forced, therefore, as well as tempted, to begin the work of cultivation upon the light, thin soil of the upland slopes, which require no drainage, where there is no heavy timber for the settler to remove, which can be furrowed by a mere stick, and afford a speedy return to light labour, unassisted by mechanical contrivances or even animal power. The return is scanty, but, small as it is, it is more than the savage ancestors of the cultivator obtained, when they roamed over a thousand-fold larger space as hunters, or depastured the natural grasses with their flocks. If, while his grain is growing, he is obliged to depend in part upon fishing and hunting for food, yet, when it is gathered, there is a store for a long period, extending beyond the next harvest; a surplus which enables him to withdraw a portion of his time from the direct labour of tillage, and devote it to devising and manufacturing better tools, to improving the means of shelter for his family and stores, and to the care of such animals as he may have domesticated. It

* "The narrow plain along the seacoast"—such are the words of Murray's Encyclopædia of Geography, in describing Mexico—"is a tract in which the richest tropical productions spring up with a luxuriance scarcely to be paralleled. Yet, while the climate is thus prolific of vegetation, in the finest and most gigantic forms, it is almost fatal to animal life: two consequences which, according to Humboldt, are in this climate almost inseparable. The Spaniards, terrified by this pestilential air, have made this plain only a passage to *the higher districts, where even the native Indians chose rather to support themselves by laborious cultivation, than to descend into the plains, where every luxury of life is poured forth in ample and spontaneous profusion.*"

Humboldt, in the Aspects of Nature, infers a probability that the earlier settlers of South America came from a cool climate, because they kept, by preference, to the highlands. He says: "Throughout Mexico and Peru, the traces of a great degree of civilization are confined to the elevated plateaux. We have seen on the Andes the ruins of palaces and baths, at heights between 1600 and 1800 toises, (10,230 and 11,510 English feet)."

is always the first step that is laborious and costly. The accumula tion of one year, and the increase and improvement of tools which it enables, begets a larger increase for the next. Their owner is enabled to dig the ground more thoroughly, and therefore to obtain a richer crop. He is enabled, too, to fell the lighter timber, and thus to extend the area of his cultivation, at the same time that he brings into activity the powers of a more productive soil. As his children grow up they take part in the work, the younger and weaker doing the lighter labours, which would otherwise engross the time of the father, and the stronger uniting with him to accomplish things, which while impossible to a single man by any continuance of exertion, are easily and speedily despatched by three or four.

As the families increase in number, and new families are formed by intermarriage, they naturally cling to the neighbourhood of the soil on which the husband or the wife first drew breath. The same motives actuating men in the same situation, the grounds first subjected to tillage must have been those extending in a line along the crest of the hills, and upon the same general level. The new families can keep most neighbours in their vicinity, by occupying the next lower terrace, or an inferior level upon the slope. In doing so they take up land of a higher grade of fertility, which, by the increased facilities of association and improvement in the quantity and effectiveness of implements, they can subdue, though their fathers could not. From generation to generation the progress of cultivation is in the same direction, from the soils of inferior to those of superior fertility. This necessarily implies an increased facility of production, a greater quantity of food in return for the same quantity of labour, and consequently a greater quantity of labour disposable for other purposes than the immediate production of the materials for subsistence. The division of labour which thus results, and the vast enhancement of power *indirectly* applied to procuring nutriment for the growing society, we are not yet prepared to examine. Nor is it necessary to enlarge upon the fact, that men imitating the process of Nature, carry back the elements of fertility from the freshly subdued lowlands, to enrich the older and shallower soils. The single circumstance which at present demands our attention is, that the natural progress of society in the work of settlement, is from the less productive to the more productive soils, and of course from feebleness and poverty to wealth and power.

It is very remarkable that a fact of so striking a character, and involving so important consequences, should never have been observed, or if observed never have been announced, as universally occurring in the history of every community, until it was announced by Mr. Carey, in "The Past, the Present, and the Future," published in 1848, and marking that year as a new era in the annals of Political Economy. He establishes it as a law of Nature, a portion, and a fundamental one, of the great law of progress and improvement. It had not merely escaped the attention of all Economists previous to Mr. Carey, but for nearly forty years the whole body of them in England, and the greater portion upon the Continent, had believed, and many still continue to believe, that the fact and the law are directly the reverse of those stated by him.

In 1815, Mr. Malthus published his "Essay on the Nature and Progress of Rent." The theory there broached had indeed been several years previously presented by Mr. Anderson, and Mr. West also published a pamphlet, containing substantially the same views, so nearly contemporaneous with that of Malthus, that each is believed to have been ignorant of the ideas of the other, as well as those of Anderson. The theory has, however, become connected with the name of Malthus, and still more with that of Ricardo, who shortly afterwards made it the basis of a system, and elaborated the deductions legitimately to be drawn from it, with a skill that has dwarfed the honours of the original authors. We prefer therefore to present it in the words of Mr. Ricardo.

"On the first settling of a country in which there is an abundance of rich and fertile land, a very small portion of which is required to be cultivated for the support of the actual population, or, indeed, can be cultivated with the capital which the population can command, there will be no rent: for no one would pay for the use of land, when there was an abundant quantity not yet appropriated, and, therefore, at the disposal of whomsoever might choose to cultivate it. * * * * * If all land had the same properties, if it were boundless in quantity and uniform in quality, no charge could be made for its use, unless where it possessed peculiar advantages of situation. It is only, then, because land is not unlimited in quantity and uniform in quality, and because, in the progress of population land of an inferior quality, or less advantageously situated, is called into cultivation, that rent is ever paid for the use of it. When, in the progress of society, land of the second degree of fertility is taken into cultivation, rent immediately commences on that of the first quality; and the amount of that rent will depend on the difference in the quality of these two portions of land. * * * When land of the third quality is taken into cultivation, rent immediately commences on the second; and it is regulated as before by the difference in their productive powers. At the same time the rent of the first quality will rise, for that must always be above the rent of the second, by the difference between the produce which they yield with a given quantity of capital and labour. With every step in the progress of population, which shall oblige a country to have recourse to land of a worse quality to enable it to raise its supply of food, rent on all the more fertile land will rise.

"Thus, suppose land—No. 1, 2, 3—to yield, with an equal employment of capital and labour, a net produce of 100, 90, and 80 quarters of corn. In a new country, where there is an abundance of fertile land compared with the population, and where, therefore, it is only necessary to cultivate No. 1, the whole net produce will belong to the cultivator, and will be the profits of the stock which he advances. As soon as population had so far increased as to make it necessary to cultivate No. 2, from which 90 quarters only can be obtained, after supporting the labourers, rent would commence on No. 1; for either there must be two rates of profit of an agricultural capital, or 10 quarters, or the value of 10 quarters, must be withdrawn from the produce of No. 1 for some other purpose. Whether the proprietor of the land, or some other person, cultivate No. 1, these 10 quarters would equally constitute rent; for the cultivator of No. 2 would get the same result from his capital, whether he cultivated No. 1, paying 10 quarters for rent, or continued to cultivate No. 2, paying no rent. In the same manner, it might be shown that when No. 3 is brought into cultivation, the rent of No. 2 must be 10 quarters, or the value of 10 quarters, whilst the *rent of No. 1 would rise to 20 quarters;* for the cultivator of No. 3 would have the same profits, whether he paid 20 quarters for the rent of No. 1, 10 quarters for the rent of No. 2, or cultivated No. 3 free of all rent."

Such is the theory known as the Ricardo Doctrine of Rent, and vaunted as the greatest contribution to the Science of Political Economy since the days of Adam Smith. The only aspect of it in which we are at present interested, is that it assumes as an unquestionable fact, that the lands first subjected to cultivation are those of the highest fertility, and that in the progress of society men are continually forced to resort to those of an inferior productiveness. It furnished Mr. Malthus with a ready explanation of the supposed tendency in population to increase at a more rapid rate than the means of subsistence. If it be true, each generation must obtain food with increasing difficulty, a greater proportion of the time and labour of each must be devoted to the satisfaction of the primary want, to maintaining the mere vegetable existence of the race; and a continually decreasing proportion of the time and labour of each will be left available for the mechanic arts, or any other species of industry not aiming directly at the production of food. Such would be the effect upon the general average condition of the human family. There are other consequences equally marked, affecting the relative position and power of the different classes into which men are distributed for the purposes of Economical inquiry, which will be considered at the appropriate stage, and the absence of which, in point of fact, is a conclusive argument against the theory.

It was a very plausible notion that men, with "the earth before them where to choose," would have selected in the first instance the lands which were capable of yielding the largest returns to their labour. Its plausibility is proved by its having been so generally accepted, and so long gone without contradiction. But it manifestly rested upon the assumption that men, at the origin of cultivation, possessed equal *power* to clear and till the fertile and the thin soils, and had only to select between things equally feasible — the one offering greater advantages, and the other less.

We have already presented, in a very summary manner, an outline of those considerations by which Mr. Carey proved, that a truly sagacious conjecture would have anticipated precisely the contrary course to that imagined by Ricardo. The latter entirely overlooked that want of implements, and wretchedness in the quality of those actually possessed, which at the dawn of civilization have everywhere controlled man's choice, by limiting his power. This universal fact, about which there is no dispute, would of itself compel an hypothesis the very reverse of Mr. Ricardo's.

But the question is most satisfactorily solved by an appeal to history. It is one of *fact*. What *has* been the course of men in the occupation and cultivation of long-settled countries? What *is* their course, as exhibited by contemporaneous communities in different stages of advancement? Our reasoning from antecedent probabilities might be erroneous; for the omission of a single element would vitiate the whole calculation, and that element we may have failed to detect and allow for; but we are absolutely certain no such mistake can have occurred in the practical working of things. Every cause which can have influenced the result has certainly operated, whether its existence has been observed or not. Mr. Carey has brought the question to this test. He traces the history of settlement in the various sections of our Union, in Mexico, the

West Indies, and South America, and shows that everywhere the earliest colonists have occupied the light, dry soils of the uplands, leaving the heavy woodlands of the valleys, and the swamps bordering upon the streams, to be felled and drained by their successors. Wherever we go, we find that in proportion as the population is dense, and the mass of wealth great, the more are the best soils cultivated; while, wherever land is abundant and population sparse, it is seen to recede from the river banks, and to be perched along the crest of the ridges. In the regions sufficiently advanced to admit the construction of canals and railroads, every one has it in his power to verify the fact, by observing the contrast in the aspect of the lands bordering their course, and those which line the old highways. The latter will generally be found ascending every hill-top which lies in the neighbourhood of their general direction, even when nothing is saved in point of distance by going over the hill instead of going around it. It is usually found, indeed, that the length of a railroad, connecting two towns at any considerable distance from each other, is less than that of the old roads which formed the route of travel before it was built; although the former is necessarily under restrictions which prevent attempts to save distance at the expense of elevations in the grade, much more than the ordinary carriage-road. But the highway is lined with cultivated fields and with houses. It was made to facilitate communication between them, its track worn by the footsteps of men before it was run out by the surveyor, and its purposes compelled it to go where population went, with small regard to the labour which its steep grades would impose upon the beasts of draught that were to toil over it. The railroad, on the contrary, is constructed by engineers, whose problem it is to reduce the power to be expended in drawing heavy loads to a minimum, regard being had both to distance and to elevation. It plunges through swamps and forests, as if to hide itself from the habitations of men. They will grow up upon its edge in due season, for the road has drained the swamps, and let in the sunlight to the gloomy depths of the woods; but upon the first opening of a railroad, we ordinarily are struck with the juxtaposition of this work of highest art with those of rudest Nature.*

* "The Turtle Creek Hill lies upon the route of the central road from

Even in the prairies of the West, where hills are unknown, and which, so far from being encumbered with trees, are contra-distinguished from timber-land — the familiar division in the States in which they lie, being into timber-land and prairie—the same law of Nature which assigns the poorer soils to the first cultivators, is found to prevail. At the North American Pomological Convention, held at Syracuse, N. Y., in September, 1849, the Committee for the State of Illinois in their Report,* say,

"Many small tracts, known as 'wet prairie' fifteen years ago, and *rejected by the first settlers*, have become dry by being annually resown, and fed down by domestic animals, without any other than its natural drainage, and exposure to the sun and air, by the destruction of the impervious screen of tall 'slough grass.'

"The 'dry prairies' are generally very similar in appearance, so far as surface is concerned. Small portions of 'level prairie' are found everywhere, but to constitute dry prairie it must be 'rolling.' Between the

---

Philadelphia to Pittsburg, about fifteen miles east of the latter. Time out of mind, it has been the main impediment of that great thoroughfare; any ridge of the Alleghany chain being more easy of ascent. The road, rising from the creek, clambers the steep hill-side by doublings and windings, which evasively relieve the acclivity, but leave it still the catastrophe of the trip. But there was no help for it, for it was the proper and direct route through and by the settlements of the vicinity. Last year the Central Pennsylvania Railroad was made through that region; but, turning aside from the farm-houses and taverns on the road, as not at all in the way of its duty, and avoiding the bluff ridge as very much in the way of its progress, it made its way through the swamp, down the bank of the creek, following its course to the Monongahela River, and so, by a level track reached its terminus at Pittsburg, *lessening the distance one mile, as well as avoiding the ascent altogether.* The explanation is apparent: the public had to clamber that horrible hill for fifty years, because the earlier cultivators of the country chose the hill-sides and heads of streams, and their thinner and lighter lands, of necessity, leaving the deep, rich soil on the margin of the creek, and the narrow valley through which it ran, in its primeval state, uncultivated and untenanted, and, therefore, out of the line of travel. Here the expense of drainage has delayed the reduction of this waste land until now; though it lay directly in the nearest and best route of travel, and within marketing distance of a city demanding its products." —*Dr. William Elder, in Sartain's Magazine for June,* 1852.

* The proceedings of that Convention are published in a pamphlet; but the Report from which the above extract is made, may be found in the Patent-Office Report (Agricultural) for 1849–50, at page 430.

waves on this great ocean of God's own beautiful sod are the 'sloughs,' *the terror of the early emigrant, and the most valued possession of his successor*, as often affording water, and always an unfailing and most luxuriant natural meadow. These sloughs are the drains of the dry prairie. They are in general nearly parallel, and oftenest at about a right angle with the course of the rivers; they are from 140 to 160 rods asunder, and sometimes of many miles in length. The soil of the dry prairie is from 12 to 18 inches deep in this region; the wet prairie in general much deeper; and the alluvion (of the river bottoms), as in all countries, of irregular and often astonishing depth."

Mr. Carey extends his historical examination to Great Britain and the States of the Continent. In England, with the course of whose cultivation we are best acquainted, the existence and operation of the law which he discovered is most strongly demonstrated. The forests and swamps of the days of Richard the Lion-Hearted, are now cultivated lands of the highest fertility. The morasses, which had nearly swallowed up the army of William the Conqueror, on his return from devastating the north, are now the cornfields and meadows of South Lancashire, among the richest in the kingdom. The lands most recently taken into cultivation are the fens of Lincoln; and the counties upon the border, which two centuries ago were inhabited by moss-troopers, are now proverbial for their productiveness. In Cæsar's account of the island, as he found it, he represents the inhabitants of the southern coast as the only ones who had made any advance in the art of tillage, and that the natives were rude in their manner of life, in proportion as they receded from that coast. Those more distant, he says, never sowed their land, but followed the primitive callings of the hunter and the herdsman, clad in the skins and living upon the flesh and milk of their flocks and herds, and the spoils of the chase. The lands of the southern counties are those adapted to tillage by men possessing little capital and power, and yielding comparatively inferior returns; those recently subdued are such as require a heavy outlay of capital to prepare them for cultivation, and were therefore impracticable, until a large mass of wealth had been accumulated, and powerful machinery brought into use. The best of them were valueless until the invention of the steam-engine.*

* The Bedford level, which derives its name from the fact that the Earl of Bedford commenced its drainage by digging canals, in 1630, is a low tract of fenny country, which begins at Ely, in Cambridgeshire, and runs

It is unnecessary to follow Mr. Carey in his sketch of the history of settlement in Scotland, France, Germany, Italy, Greece, &c. It would do injustice to the very interesting outline which he has presented to attempt to condense it, and we prefer to urge the inquiring student to read it in the pages of the "Past, Present, and Future." A circumstance of more recent occurrence than the publication of that work, authorizes us to take the fact as undisputed. Mr. Carey's opinion having been adopted by Bastiat, the most brilliant and acute of the French Economists, a discussion sprung up upon the opposing

northwest into the valley of the Witham, in Lincolnshire. This tract is seventy or eighty miles in length, and from twenty to forty in width, containing nearly seven hundred thousand acres. Cromwell took an interest in its drainage. He sent great numbers of the Scotch prisoners taken at the battle of Dunbar, to be employed upon the work—unhealthy business—and afterwards he sent 500 Dutch prisoners, taken in the sea-fight between Blake and Van Tromp, in 1652; they remained ten years, when the peace enabled them to return home. They were recommended by their experience in such works in Holland, which has been wholly redeemed from the sea. In Porter's Progress of the Nation, vol. 1, page 166, it is said: "The fens in Cambridgeshire, Lincolnshire, and other eastern counties, in which the lowlands known as the Bedford level occur, were formerly very imperfectly relieved from their surplus water by means of windmills; and, to a considerable extent, they are so still. Where this is the case, the farmer has sometimes to witness the prostration of all his hopes for the year, almost at the very period of their expected accomplishment. It frequently happens, that when rain falls in large quantities near the time of harvest, there is not a breath of wind to move the sails of his mill, and the field in which the yellow grain was waving is speedily converted into a lake. Some of the land thus circumstanced is among the most fertile in the kingdom, consisting of a bed of decomposed vegetable matter, *thirty feet in depth*, and yielding crops of from four to five quarters per acre. By the substitution of steam-power for the uncertain agency of wind, the crop is now secured from the disaster we have mentioned." He proceeds to state that engines of 60 and 70 horse-power had been erected within three or four years previous to his writing (in 1836), each of which is employed in draining from 6000 to 7000 acres of land. The cost of the first establishment of the engines is stated at £1 per acre, and the expense of keeping them at work at 2*s*. 6*d*. per acre. Since Mr. Porter wrote, scientific engineering has executed works dispensing, for large districts, with both steam-engines and windmills.—*See Edinburgh Review for October*, 1847, *article on Holland.*

theories of Ricardo and Carey, in the meetings of the Politico-Economical Society at Paris, reports of which are published in the *Journal des Economistes*, a magazine which is the organ of the leading writers on this subject, of the French nation, and which is read by students in this science throughout Europe. Indeed, the savans of several continental countries have taken part, orally at the meetings of the Society, and by communications in the pages of the *Journal*, in the debate. Mr. Carey himself intervened, and in articles over his signature, in the *Journal*, has challenged any one to name a single country in which the *fact* has not been as represented by him, or a single country in which, when population and wealth have decreased, men have not abandoned the most fertile and receded to inferior lands—as in India, where once-populous districts on the plains have relapsed into jungle, tenanted by wild beasts, while their former inhabitants cluster on the hill-sides—as in Italy, where every excavation in the marshes, now sterile, and desolate from malaria, discovers the traces of ancient works for drainage, which once made them salubrious and fertile.

While the controversy has proceeded upon collateral points, and in reference to the validity of *deductions* from this fact or its opposite fiction, no one has accepted the *issue of fact*, and Mr. Carey stands uncontradicted, by enlightened and skilful disputants, who, in respect to the course of things, in France especially, have much more ample means for finding a seeming exception than he has for disproving or explaining it.

The indirect demonstration of the falsity of Ricardo's hypothesis is equally conclusive. The consequences that should infallibly attend it, if it were true, are contradicted by experience. About some of these it is as yet premature to inquire. The most obvious, however, is this. If the Ricardo doctrine is correct, we ought to find each generation less amply provided with food, and procuring it with a greater expenditure of labour than its predecessor. The more distant the periods contrasted, the more marked should be the disparity. If we assume that population proceeds at the highest rate of rapidity assumed by Malthus, and that the lands successively taken into cultivation diminish in fertility according to the scale which Ricardo gives by way of illustration, the state of things will be this: A territory producing 100 quarters (say 900 bushels, at 60 pounds to the bushel,) of wheat, and affording a supply of food for one hundred persons, may be taken as a sample of a whole country and its people. At the expiration of twenty-five years, the population will have doubled, and the hundred new recruits will require an equal territory to that occupied by the original hundred. This territory, according to the scale of progression given for the purpose of illustration by Ricardo, will produce but 90 quarters of wheat, or 810 bushels. The whole amount to be divided between 200 persons will now be but 190 quarters, or 1710 bushels. At the expiration of fifty years the population will have doubled again, and there will be 200 recruits demanding fresh land. They will have to content themselves with that of the third quality, producing but 80 quarters upon the space which formerly rendered 100, or 160 quarters instead of 200, which their two hundred forefathers obtained. In seventy-five years the population will have doubled again, amounting in the aggregate to 800 persons; and the last 400 must occupy land of the 4th quality, producing but 70 quarters instead of 100 upon an equal space, or for a space originally adequate to the support of 400 persons, 280 quarters, or 2520 bushels instead of 3600. The facts may be arranged in tabular form, as follows:

Stage.	Persons dividing.	Bushels of Wheat.	Giving to each.
1	100	900	9
2	200	1710	$8\frac{151}{1000}$
3	400	3150	$7\frac{875}{1000}$
4	800	5670	$7\frac{0875}{10000}$
5	1600	9990	6·243
6	3200	17190	5·37
7	6400	31710	4·92
8	12800	48990	3·80
9	25600	72030	2·80

Such, upon the hypothesis, would be the progress of things in two hundred years. Population would have multiplied two hundred and fifty-six times, food but eighty times; so that, upon an equal partition, each person would obtain a little less than one-third as much food as his ancestors enjoyed two centuries before. The community, to procure the same average quantity of food as its progenitors, would require three times as much land in proportion to its numbers, and thus, in the same degree be dispersed over greater spaces, and placed at greater distances from each other.

It would not be fair to insist that just such a progression as we have traced ought to be shown to have taken place somewhere, and at some time, in order to support the hypothesis of Ricardo and Malthus. But something like it should be produced; a decreasing series in the average quantity of food, the terms of which converge with less rapidity, and cover a longer period of time, but still exhibit a positive and marked law of diminution, ought to be shown to have existed in the history of some nation. The fact, however, is precisely the reverse; and that fact is not disputed by Economists who accept and inculcate the Ricardo doctrine. Mr. M'Culloch says, speaking of England: "Let any one compare the state of this or any other European country 500, or 100 years ago, and he will be satisfied that prodigious advances have been made, that the means of subsistence have increased much more rapidly than the population, and that the labouring classes are now generally in the possession of conveniences and luxuries that were formerly not enjoyed, even by the richest lords." Mr. Senior, writing in 1836, says: "Since the beginning of the 18th century the population of England has about doubled. The produce of the land has certainly tripled, probably quadrupled." It would be easy to multiply quotations to the same effect, but these suffice, in reference to a fact, which, so far at least as it relates to modern times, nobody disputes, and which we shall hereafter have occasion to demonstrate by particular statistical estimates. The farther back we go, and the longer period we embrace, the more favourable should the comparison be to the hypothesis; yet, we shall find it even more signally discountenanced by the facts. The great frequency of famines in the earlier periods of English history, and when almost the entire population was employed in agricultural labour, is conclusive evidence of the smallness of the crops. In the Saxon Chronicle, in which the occurrences of each year are given in the form of annals, they recur with startling brevity of intervals.*

* See the Pictorial History of England, Vol. I., page 266; also 579.

In regard to France, the following statement is contained in the article, Agriculture, in the Dictionnaire d'Economie Politique, contributed by H. Passy:

"The official statistics present contrasts singularly striking. If we compare the figures relating to the ten richest and most populous Departments with those relating to the ten Departments which are the least so, it will be found that in the former the average yield of a hectare (2·47 acres,) is from 15 to 20 hectolitres (the hectolitre is 2·84 bushels,) of wheat, while in the latter it is only from 7½ to 11, and that there is an equal disproportion in all the other products. In regard to consumption they offer a difference equally marked. The food is not only superior in quality in the advanced Departments, it is also superior in quantity, and, head for head, the consumption is thirty per cent. more in weight than in the less dense and poorer Departments."

This difference is attributed by Mons. Passy to the stimulant which agricultural skill derives from the greater markets in the populous Departments. This implies that there is no general diversity in the quality of the soils in the Departments compared, while it is certain that in those most densely populated, if the hypothesis of Ricardo is correct, a larger proportion of the inferior soils must be cultivated.

We may bring the question to another test, by comparing two long-settled countries. That in which the largest proportion of territory remains in forests, should, according to the hypothesis, be that whose population has, in the least proportion, been compelled to resort to soils of inferior fertility. Trying England and France by this criterion, the latter has, in proportion to its extent, a four-fold larger quantity of forest land; it constituting in England but the twenty-fourth part, while in France one-sixth of the surface is covered with woods.*

France has certainly the general advantage over England in soil and climate, and if it cultivates a less proportion of the relatively poor soil, the average gross produce per acre ought to be larger. But the reverse is notoriously true. One-third only of the population of England was engaged in agricultural labour previous to the Repeal of the Corn Laws; and when the importation of food was so trifling as not to sensibly affect the result, this one-third produced food for the whole nation. In France, on the contrary, two-thirds

* Dictionnaire de l'Economie Politique, article Forets.

of the people were agriculturists. In one country two men raised food for six; in the other, it required four to effect the same object. The diet of the French people, moreover, is greatly inferior both in quantity and quality to that of the English, sufficiently so to counterbalance any allowance that ought to be made, for an excess in its exportation of agricultural products over that of England.

The absolute failure of the facts to confirm the hypothesis, is endeavoured to be accounted for by the suggestion that greater labour, and the aid of increased capital and improved machinery, are the sources of the great return in the one instance, and their absence that of the small return in the other. Thus, J. S. Mill, (Polit. Econ., vol. 1, page 219,) finding himself compelled to admit that experience is against the doctrine, and that unquestionably a much smaller proportion of the population is now occupied in producing food than in the early times of our history, argues, "This, however, does not prove that the law, of which we have been speaking, does not exist, but only that there is some antagonizing principle at work, capable *for a time* of making head against the law. Such an agency there is, in habitual antagonism to the law of diminishing return from land; and to the consideration of this we shall now proceed. It is no other than the progress of civilization. I use this general and somewhat vague expression, because the things to be included are so various, that hardly any term of a more restricted signification would comprehend them all." He proceeds to enumerate improved processes in agriculture, improved roads and other means of communication, mechanical improvements and improvements in education, as effective elements, counteracting the law of deterioration in the productive powers of the soil. These, and others of the like nature, he regards as forces which may impede for a season the operation of the natural law; but he comes to the necessary conclusion, that a law *constantly* operating, must, surely, in the end produce its due effect — in the words of M'Culloch, that "from the operation of fixed and permanent causes, the increasing sterility of the soil is sure, in the long run, to overmatch the improvements that occur in machinery and cultivation."

When Mr. Mill, in his "System of Logic," was investigating the methods applicable to social science, he declared that,

"In order to prove that our science, and our knowledge of the particular case, renders us competent to predict the future, we must show that they would have enabled us to predict the present and the past. If there be anything which we could not have predicted, this constitutes a residual phenomenon, requiring further study for the purpose of explanation; and we must either search among the circumstances of the particular case until we find one, which, *on the principles of our existing theory accounts for the unexplained phenomenon*, or we must turn back, and seek the explanation by an extension and improvement of the theory itself."

The existence of those agencies which Mr. Mill sums up in the expression, "the progress of civilization," is such a phenomenon. When it is asserted to be coexisting with a law of Nature — as the progressive deterioration of the land taken into cultivation is averred to be—it must either be accounted for by the theory which assumes that law to exist and to be constantly active, or the theory itself must be revised.

Now, how is it possible to explain the acquisition of more extensive and improved machinery, by men who, beginning with the smallest quantity of it, and the poorest quality, are continually under the necessity of devoting more and more time and labour to procure a supply of food just adequate to maintain life? It is not enough that they should have such aid, but it must be had in a proportion increasing more rapidly than their increased numbers. The table given on page 55, will serve to elucidate this necessity. At the first stage, we have each hundred individuals in the community obtaining, upon an average, nine bushels of wheat, the quantity usually assumed as the average consumption of Englishmen. In point of fact, we know that this is a much larger quantity than fell to the share of an individual in the early periods of that country's history, or of any other country's. Habitual insufficiency and occasional famine, has always been the lot of men at the commencement of cultivation. But the quantity set down in the table may stand as the representative of that which is merely adequate to scanty subsistence. It is a question of proportion and not of absolute amount, and, therefore, one figure will serve for illustration as well as another. At the third stage, after the expiration of fifty years, the population has quadrupled, and in the meantime the average quantity of food which the deteriorating soils brought under cultivation will produce, has fallen to 7·875, a diminution of 12½ per cent., or one-eighth. If we suppose that eighty out of the hundred were able, during the first stage, to raise food for the whole, leaving the other twenty to construct and repair tools, clothing, &c., during the third stage it will require the labour of one-eighth more, or of ninety persons in the hundred, to produce food, leaving but ten available for industry of other kinds. It should require even more than ninety, for, according to the hypothesis, the ten extra husbandmen must apply themselves to worse lands than their eighty fellows cultivate. But, granting that ninety should prove as effective as eighty of their grandfathers had done, what is the warrant for anticipating that ten artizans will be able to keep ninety husbandmen as well supplied with utensils, clothing, houses, &c., as eighty were, two generations before, kept furnished by the labour of twenty artizans? Where each artizan in the first stage accomplished a mass of work represented by 4, ($\frac{80}{20}$), his successor in the third stage must perform the equivalent of 9, ($\frac{90}{10}$). Doing this, if he can, he will do his share towards maintaining a merely stationary condition of society, or rather would do so, if it were not that the law of the "increasing sterility of the soil" is constantly making greater demands upon him, as the community is carried along with the progress of time towards the fourth stage, with a still further decline in agricultural production. But his task does not end even here. As food, in point of fact, is found to have increased in a much greater ratio than population, in order that this increase should be explained, the artizan of the past must have contributed to it, either by his own direct labour, in the leisure moments remaining to him after completing the work we have just shown to be required of him, to prevent a falling off in the supply, or indirectly, by improving and adding to the quantity of the machinery of tillage.

Now, we certainly are not authorized to pronounce it impossible, that mere agricultural labour should have done all that this theory requires of it. But if it were established as an independent fact, that mechanical power has, in the progress of society, increased according to any given series of numbers, or any imaginable law of increment, it would still tend to disprove any supposed law of Nature, that instead of accounting for that increase, it creates the difficulty of accounting for it. It is manifestly against the principles of sound reasoning, to support a theory against the evidence of facts inconsistent with it, by arguing that they are the consequence of another series of facts equally inconsistent with it. The law must be broad enough to comprehend them all, and explain them all, or it must be discarded as a false conjecture, which Nature disowns; for all her laws are invariable, irresistible, and harmonious.

The theory of Mr. Carey reconciles all the facts, and explains them all. It is possible for food to increase more rapidly than population, when men begin with the inferior soils, and, as their numbers grow, pass to those of superior fertility. An increasing proportion of each community is thus released from direct employment in the raising of food, and enabled to apply its energies to the preparation of machinery and the improvement of processes. These give the ability to the husbandman to reap a larger return from his old soil, and to overcome more readily and effectually the difficulties which attend his subduing the new and richer lands. The result is necessarily a larger yield, in recompense of the same amount of labour, a further increase in the surplus of food, and the setting free of more labourers from the farm, to recruit the workshops and to undertake fresh branches of industry. Upon this theory we can comprehend the progress of civilization; it is the foreseen and certain result of a permanent law. Upon the other, it is an accidental and embarrassing fact, for which we can discover no cause in the past, no guarantee for the future.

Mr. John Stuart Mill gives the doctrine we have been examining in these terms:

"After a certain and not very advanced stage in the progress of agriculture; as soon, in fact, as men have applied themselves to cultivation with any energy, and have brought to it any tolerable tools; from that time it is the law of production from the land, that in any given state of agricultural skill and knowledge, by increasing the labour, the produce is not increased in an equal degree; doubling the labour does not double the produce; or, to express the same thing in other words, every increase of produce is obtained by a more than proportional increase in the application of labour to the land."—*Polit. Econ. vol.* 1, *page* 214.

The cautious limitations contained in this paragraph would seem to imply, that some of the difficulties we have just stated had occurred to the author of this passage. How comes it, otherwise, that the law is announced as not coming into operation until after a somewhat, if not *very*, advanced stage in the progress of agriculture, after they have applied themselves to cultivation with energy, and

6

after they have brought to it tolerable tools? Is it not because he had found it impossible to account for the possession of tolerable tools, *under the law*, and was therefore compelled to postpone the period of its taking effect, until after this difficulty had been surmounted, and the first indispensable infraction of the law taken place?

However convenient, indeed essential, this limitation may be, to make the supposed law capable of holding its place in a system of Political Economy, we apprehend it must remove the law from the canon of Nature. Her enactments are from everlasting, and have never been held in abeyance for a moment, except by the miraculous interposition of their divine author. The notion that they have been suspended from time to time among the various tribes of men, to give them an opportunity of furbishing up some tolerable tools, might not surprise us in a worshipper of Mumbo Jumbo, on the Guinea Coast, but can scarcely have presented itself in the full distinctness of its absurdity to the mind of a philosopher and a Christian.

Mr. Mill continues: "This general law of agricultural industry is the most important proposition in Political Economy. Were the law different, nearly all the phenomena of the production and distribution of wealth would be other than they are."

In reference to the importance of the proposition, we concur with him heartily. The disagreement in relation to its truth, and the consequences resulting therefrom, makes the whole difference — a sufficiently wide one—between the American system, the final issue of which, made axiomatic by the native sense of the people, is rendered in the national aphorism, "population is wealth," and the Economical system of the Old World. We have, as we think, sufficiently proved that the proposition of the Ricardo school finds no foundation in the inherent properties of land. Whether there is anything to uphold it in the laws affecting human labour, we shall now proceed to inquire. The proposition must either find its support in the latter, or it is baseless as a dream.

CHAPTER III.

THE GRATUITOUS CO-OPERATION OF THE NATURAL AGENTS WITH HUMAN LABOUR.

MAN has been defined a tool-making animal. We nowhere see him working without artificial aid. Even the rudest savages possess some simple implements, which they employ in fishing and hunting, in fabricating their raiment and building their huts. It is difficult, indeed, to conceive man as destitute of every kind of implements.

But to arrive at the laws regulating human labour — the contraction of muscular fibre — as an instrument of production, it is obviously necessary to inquire into its power and action, abstracted from all the other instruments and appliances which habitually concur with it in the execution of work. We can arrive at the laws of the combined action of two forces, only by first understanding those which control their separate action.

We see that, in point of fact, men in every civilized society perform little or nothing in the way of work, without being assisted by the natural agents, such as wood, the motion of water, the expansive power of heat in steam, and, without calling into use, to create the circumstances necessary for the development of these natural powers, a great many mechanical and chemical properties of matter, such as the hardness of steel, the polarity of the magnet, the bleaching quality of chlorine, the velocity of the electric fluid. Most of these qualities, though existing without human agency in the storehouse of Nature, require artificial combinations to exhibit them, and convert them to economic purposes, as co-workers with human muscle in labor-saving machinery. The number and variety of the agents and qualities that the intellect of a people has discovered, and the extent to which, by mastering their laws, and preparing the necessary conditions for their operation, it has reduced them into service, is the most decisive test of its civilization.

There must have been a brief period, in which our first progenitor used only his senses and his muscles to furnish himself with food.

We can conceive, now, some mariner, more hapless than Robinson Crusoe, to have been cast upon a desolate island, without clothing and without tools. To reach an idea of the process through which our race has arrived at its present power, we must conceive him as an uninstructed savage, destitute of all that knowledge, some portion of which is imbibed by the most ignorant member of a civilized community. He would gather his food in the first instance from the vines and the fruit-bearing trees, and might find shelter in a cave, or the hollow of a decayed oak.. We can imagine him running down some animals by pure swiftness of foot, throttling and killing them by main strength, tearing their flesh with his teeth, and devouring it raw. The idea would occur to him, that the skin which had kept the animal warm might protect him from the dews of night, or at least make a softer pillow than a stone or a log. He can break the limb from a tree, and use it as a club against an animal, whose claws or teeth render the attempt to subdue it by the naked hands dangerous; and by throwing it he may kill at a distance, or overtake by the missile, one whose fleetness surpasses his own. His power is thus greatly increased, and he may master three animals with as little expense of time and muscular exertion as one had cost him before. The natural agents have begun to co-operate with him — the weight and hardness of wood enable him to kill a beast which he could not have choked—the fact that he can give greater velocity to a missile than to his own body, enables him to arrest the flight of another, which his legs could not have overtaken. With the sharp edge of a shell, picked up on the sea-shore, or of a flint, he can cut and fashion his stick, and tying the flint to its end with a thong, he obtains a spear. Having found a cutting instrument in the flint, a bow and arrows are of easy acquisition. Having obtained them, he has a new natural agent for his ally, the elasticity of wood, and with it he overmatches the fleetness of the swiftest, and the strength of the most formidable beast. His power of procuring animal food is immensely enhanced. His stock of skins is increased in the same proportion, and he has leisure to fashion them into clothing and a tent. These obtained, he is no longer under the necessity of returning every night to his cave or his hollow tree, but may make extended journeys to find the best hunting-grounds, or the regions most productive in fruits, best sheltered from storms, and most inaccessible by dangerous beasts of prey, where, by the aid of his flint knife, he may build a larger house of the branches of trees, than he could conveniently carry about with him, and furnishing room to store his game and fruits, that the superfluity of one day may enable him to devote the following to the work of preparing other utensils, for cooking and preserving his meat. The great novel fact in his condition is, that a natural agent, the elasticity of wood, does a large portion of the work that formerly taxed his muscles Nine-tenths of his labour is cast upon Nature, who does it gratuitously, and gives him the time and strength thus spared to add to his comforts, without demanding any share in them. From the bow and arrow, up to Ericsson's Caloric Engine and the Electric Telegraph, the law is the same; every natural agent acts without remuneration, and co-operating with human labour makes it more effective. Each one requires, as the conditions of its activity, combinations of matter, which we call tools or machinery. Every new agent taken into partnership with human toil, facilitates the acquisition of fresh and more effective powers, and each new machine is cheaper than its predecessor—regard being had to its relative effectiveness, because it is the product in a larger degree of natural agents, which work for nothing, and in a less degree of muscular force, which, whether in man or animals, can only be exerted under the stimulus of food, and therefore must be purchased by food.

We have employed several words in the last paragraph, such as *gratuitous*, *cheap*, *purchased*, which grow out of the fact of exchange and imply its existence. They involve also the idea of Value, inseparably connected with that of Exchange. It being impossible to continue a discussion of this nature without their constant use, it is therefore important to fix their sense, that is, to inquire what are the facts they denote.

The solitary savage, whose progress we have been tracing, does everything for himself. This is the characteristic of savage life; each man hunts, fishes, bakes, builds, brings and carries, and constructs the tools employed in all these operations, for himself; while an advanced stage of civilization is marked by each person's confining himself to a very restricted routine of occupation, and depending for the supply of most, sometimes of all, his wants, upon the labours of others. A man may work a lifetime in building steam-engines without ever using them, and yet thousands of men have contributed more or less of their toil to the growth, manufacture, and transportation of the articles which he consumes in a single day. Multitudes of men and of forces are continually toiling in part for him; and his share of the products of their labour is got to him through an almost interminable series of exchanges, indirectly effected through the medium of money.

The primitive form of exchange is Barter. It presupposes a diversity of products, and, therefore, of labour. It involves a comparison of the service rendered with the service received; of the labour which it would require to obtain the thing to be parted with, and that which would be expended in procuring the thing offered in exchange.

Suppose the savage who had a bow, and with it the power to obtain as much venison in one day as he could in ten previous to owning it, to discover at the opposite extremity of his island another who has no bow, but who has made a fish-hook out of a crooked bone, and to offer deer's meat in exchange for fish—upon what terms would they barter? The fisherman has fish that it has cost him nine hours to catch; the hunter offers him for them as much venison as requires, upon the average, one hour's labour of a man armed with bow and arrows, or ten hours' labour of a man without them. The fisherman would reason — "It will take me but nine hours to replace my fish by others equal in number and quality, but to get as much venison will cost ten hours." There is a gain of an hour's labour to him in the exchange; and it is no impediment to the bargain, that he knows the bowsman effects a saving of nine hours by purchasing his fish instead of catching them. The exchange is made, to the mutual profit of the parties, and the hunter goes back to his side of the island; not, however, without having observed how easy it will be to provide himself with a hook and line, and do his own fishing when he pleases.

The fisherman is confined to the shore for lack of a boat. He sees a log floating, and the idea occurs to him that it may be hollowed by fire, and the exterior hewed into shape by a rude axe, made of a stone fastened to a stick with a thong. He accomplishes the structure of a canoe, and, no longer tied to the shore, may coast at his pleasure, or put out from land in search of larger fish in the deep water. He has the aid of one natural agent, in the capacity of water, to float his canoe, but it requires muscular power to propel it by the paddle. When he has learned to erect a sail, the labour of propelling his boat is performed by the wind. He can extend his voyages to a distance—the food which was required to support a man who paddles is saved—and the labour thus superseded can be applied directly in the production of food, or indirectly, in a larger measure, in the manufacture of boats and sails, and bows and arrows, which enable a third person to acquire food in a less time than he could by his direct efforts. We may well suppose that the power of the fisherman is increased tenfold. Having secured in a single day as many pounds of fish as formerly cost him the labour of ten, and having the ability to carry a cargo, he sails around the island and brings-to opposite the hut of the hunter, and proposes again to traffic with him for venison. The hunter finds it to his interest to exchange venison, that cost him ten hours' labour, for fish that he, without a boat, would expend ten hours in procuring, although it actually cost the fisherman but one. The boatman, under an equal disadvantage with respect to deer-killing, for lack of a bow, reasons in the same way. Each measures the value of the commodity he would purchase, by the expenditure of trouble it would require to produce it himself, and which he saves by procuring it through barter. He measures the value of the article he parts with by the labour which it will cost him to reproduce it. He would count as nothing that which cost him nothing, as being the result of the gratuitous co-operation of natural agents. Nine-tenths of the fish and nine-tenths of the venison, will be so reckoned in the case we have supposed. Each party having equally effective machinery, will exchange upon equal terms—labour for labour of equal average duration and intensity. The result will be, that one will obtain ten times the fish, and the other ten times the venison that he would have done, without the barter. The profit resulting from the gratuitous concurrence of all the natural agents brought into activity, is thus equally distributed for the common benefit.

We have thus far contemplated the case of parties to an exchange, each of whom had a practical monopoly of a particular kind of machinery, and of the natural forces which are made active by means of its possession. But such a monopoly is necessarily of brief continuance. The man who has been released from the toil of rowing, and left free to construct boats, will soon construct one for himself, and he and the original fisherman will go to the hunter to find a market for their fish. Each of them is disposed to get all the venison that he can; but each of them is willing to give the product of anything less than ten hours' labour in fishing, rather than expend that length of time in procuring for himself as much venison, as costs the huntsman the labour of but one hour. The effect of their competition is, to give the latter the entire benefit of the co-operation of the wind and water in reducing the labour cost of fish. He obtains the fish at the cost of procuring them, under the existing circumstances, and with the aids derived from natural forces, and the qualities of matter which have been brought into use, at the time they are offered for traffic.

The rule which governs a trade between savages, prevails at all times and in all places. Nothing will exchange for more labour, or for the product of more labour, than is necessary to reproduce it. The seller would fain get more, perhaps, because he expended more; but the inducement to the purchaser to obtain a commodity by exchange, is, that he may spare himself the trouble of making it, and getting it to the place where it is offered, by his own exertions.

Twenty years ago, a red paper box, containing a few sulphur matches, and a phial of acid, by which they were ignited, sold for a York shilling. Now, as many friction matches, of superior quality, in a brown paper box, are sold for a half-penny. No man doubts that, if a box of matches should chance to have lingered upon a grocer's shelf for twenty years, he would now be compelled to sell it for the half-penny, which would buy an equal quantity of a more convenient article. It would be fruitless to him to prove what it cost him. The ready answer would be, that in the meantime, by improved chemical and mechanical combinations, twenty-five boxes had come to be made by the same expenditure of human labour as his one required in its day. Out of every twenty-five, *twenty-four* may be regarded as the contribution of Nature—who gives her aid, and asks no recompense—and *one*, as the result of muscular action, which expended food in developing itself, and which cannot be renewed unless the food is replaced; which, therefore, demands pay in food, or in something that *can be exchanged* for food.

Several of the Economists have sought to establish an equation between Value, and the labour expended in the production or appropriation of commodities. They are thus compelled to attribute to human exertion, in certain cases, so much efficacy, and in others so little, in communicating value, as to render it worthless as a standard of measurement. If the case is put to them of a man who finds a precious stone while sauntering by the sea-shore, they are obliged either to deny that it has value, or to ascribe the value to the labour of stooping to pick it up. Such an accident may happen to a man who is working for a dollar a day, perfectly satisfied that such is the true value of his labour, and who would be assured by these very writers that such was the fact, if himself disposed to doubt it. One moment of his time, a single stretch of the arm, the value of which is an inappreciable fraction of a cent, suddenly becomes so valuable as to exceed a million-fold their value a moment before. It is as if one took the varying velocities of a comet as the standard for the regulation of chronometers. All such embarrassment is avoided, when we see that the cost of reproduction is the standard by which we actually compare values, and that it is equally applicable to the result of the enormously remunerated labour of the exceptional minute, and the moderate compensation for the rest of the toilsome day. The labourer who has been cracking stone to Macadamize a highway, can say, "The value of this heap of dull granite does not exceed a day's labour, for a day's labour will produce another such heap—the value of this glittering stone is a thousand days' labour, because it will cost at least a thousand days' labour to obtain another." The foundation of value is the same in both cases, and the unit of measure unchanged.*

* This doctrine is more fully elucidated by Mr. Carey, from whom it is derived, in his "Principles of Political Economy," vol. 1, page 15. Professor Ferrara, in his editorial introduction to the Italian translation of the works of Mons. Bastiat, says:—

UTILITY — the capacity a thing has to satisfy a man's wants and desires — is something more than Value, which is the sum of the obstacles to its attainment. The difference between them—between the gross amount of service, in the satisfaction of wants, that the possession of a thing will bestow, and the gross amount of labour which must be undertaken to secure it — is the sum of the effects produced by the gratuitous operation of the forces of Nature. Men differ in their estimate of the utility of objects, which is the same thing as to say that they differ in their tastes and their judgment. In proportion as this estimate is high, the demand for a commodity is urgent. In proportion as the obstacles to its production are reduced, that is, in proportion to the number and force of the natural agents, which are made to co-operate with, and to supersede muscular action, its value is diminished. PRICE is the notation *in money* of the point — a point fluctuating with every remove in time or space—at which an equilibrium establishes itself between the forces, moral, intellectual, and physical, which urge men to the acquisition of an article, and those which restrain them. There is, however,

"Carey, and after him, Bastiat, have introduced a formula, *a posteriori*, that I believe destined to be universally adopted; and it is greatly to be regretted that the latter should have limited himself to occasional indications of it, instead of giving to it the importance so justly given by the former. In estimating the equilibrium between the cost to one's self and the utility to others, a thousand circumstances may intervene; and it is desirable to know if there be not among men a law, a principle of universal application. Supply and demand, rarity, abundance, &c., are all insufficient, and liable to perpetual exceptions. Carey has remarked, and with great sagacity, that this law is the labour saved, *the cost of reproduction*— an idea that is, as I think, most felicitous. It appears to me that there cannot arise a case, in which a man shall determine to make an exchange, in which this law will not be found to apply. I will not give a quantity of labour or pains, unless offered in exchange an utility equivalent; and I will not regard it as equivalent, unless I see that it will come to me at less cost of labour than would be necessary for its reproduction. I regard this formula as most felicitous; because, while on one side it retains the idea of cost, which is constantly referred to in the mind, on the other it avoids the absurdity to which we are led by the theory, which pretends to see everywhere a value equivalent to the cost of production; and, finally, it shows more perfectly the essential justice that governs us in our exchanges."

no absolute and fixed relation between money and labour. The discovery of gold in California and Australia, is reducing the labour cost of gold every day, and raising the price, measured in gold, of every other subject of barter. Price and Value are therefore nc more synonymous than Value and Utility, in the sense we employ them. The former, Value, we are to be understood as always using to denote the relation between an object offered for exchange, and the quantity of human labour necessary to engineer the natural forces, and produce a like object.

Such is the power of habit, that ideas which, from their real correspondence with the nature of things, are essentially natural and spontaneous, come, from the forms of language, to seem strained and artificial. It has thus happened, that because we have been accustomed to denote cost by the denominations of coined metal, even sagacious and instructed men come to reason, as if the reference of value to labour was a refinement of theory, instead of a practical truth that hampers every man in his daily dealings. "Labour," says Adam Smith, "was the first price, the original purchase-money that was paid for all things." This is assented to as a truism by men, who yet habitually reason in regard to the economical policy of nations, as if money and labour were *now* convertible terms, and as if the question whether a thing is cheap or dear, was at once and conclusively settled, by the mere statement of the amount of coin standing opposite to its name in the Price Current. Professing to be disciples of the author of "The Wealth of Nations," and invoking his authority as a sanction for their dogmas, they forget that he has written what all experience confirms, "At all times and places that is dear which is difficult to come at, or which it costs much labour to acquire; and that cheap which is to be had easily, or with very little labour:" and that labour, therefore, is alone the ultimate and real standard, by which the value of all commodities can at all times and places be estimated and compared. It is their real price; money is their nominal price only.

The first general proposition in regard to Labour, is, that in the progress of society the value of all commodities tends to fall. They are continually attainable through exchange, by less and less of labour, because the gratuitous concert of natural agents, newly discovered, and made available by tools and machinery, makes less labour suffice to reproduce them. It renders labour more effective, gives it greater command over matter, greater power, more value. Since "value" is a relative term, it may as well be applied to labour, as to that for which labour is exchanged; and in so doing we come back to the original signification of the word, in its Latin primitive, *valeo*, and the English derivative, *avail*. The constantly diminishing money price of all manufactured commodities sustains the proposition; and it will be shown in the sequel that the decline of cost, measured by labour, is even greater than that denoted in coin.

The wonders of modern machinery are rehearsed so often, as to require no more than an allusion. It is impossible to estimate the extent to which it has added to animal power. Mr. Mayhew* states that the total estimated machine-power in Great Britain is that of 600,000,000 human beings, and adds that this has all been produced within the last century. This remark only serves to indicate what he had in view in using the term, "machine-power"; for machinery, in the most general sense, has been increasing in the British Islands, as elsewhere, ever since men found that fingers and nails were insufficient implements of work.

The entire population of the United Kingdom, by the census of 1851, was 27,309,346. The machine-power, according to this estimate, equally distributed among them, would give to each man, woman, and child the equivalent of the labour of twenty serfs, and would still leave a surplus, equivalent to more than twice the present population, to furnish the machines with the material necessary for developing their power, and to construct and keep them in going order. But a small fraction of the population, in point of fact, make, keep up, and feed the machines; and the result is, that for every inhabitant of the British Isles there are forces that toil and spin, without wages, and do the work of twenty-two slaves, without even the slaves' pittance of food. The entire products of this labour, mostly in the shape in which they come out of the machines, but a part transmuted by barter into other commodities, of foreign growth or make, are distributed among and enjoyed by the British people. The whole mass is bought by the labour of the kingdom. Such

* London Labour and the London Poor, page 349

grand results are often spoken of as the Economy of Power; and we speak of machinery as labour-saving. In the original sense of economy, the expression is just; in that which it ordinarily bears, an idea is conveyed as nearly true, and no more so, than the song which ascribes happiness to the soldier

> "Who lives on his pay,
> And spends half a crown out of sixpence a day."

It is the *appropriation* of power existing in Nature, and only waiting for human intellect to discover its existence and laws, and to devise the means, in accordance with those laws, of converting it to use.

Engineers inform us that there is virtue in a bushel of coals, properly consumed, to raise seventy millions of pounds a foot high. Such is said to be actually the average effect of an engine working at Hueltown, in Cornwall. This virtue is in the coal at the bottom of a mine, and was in it a thousand years ago, as well as when it lies in the furnace below a steam-boiler. It had been seen for ages exerting its power in boiling water and generating steam, without serving any greater purpose than to cook a dinner. Since the steam-engine was devised, we look at it in the concrete, and attribute power to the machine, whereas the machine is passive, the mere theatre and vehicle of power existing from the foundation of the world. Its contrivance is simply a condition of the action of certain forces in a certain direction for a certain time and with a measured intensity, which from everlasting have been passing from equilibrium to motion, and from motion back to a new equilibrium, without human direction. They laid dormant in the one condition, they ran to waste in the other, until man, by observation and thought, found how to awaken them from rest—by assaulting their equilibrium with some previously-discovered force—and to guide their motion into the direction that suits his purposes.

Now, it is obvious that the forces of Nature are inexhaustible, for no one of them is ever destroyed. Motion never stops in one direction, without creating an equal quantity in the other, or in several others, whose resultant is the opposite of its own. All that muscular effort can do is to impart motion; and this it can never do but at the expense of a waste of fibre, that must be replenished by food and by rest.

Man's office in the world is that of engineer; all his real power is mental. It is a waste of power for him to take that upon himself, which can be better and more cheaply accomplished by brute matter. He ceases to do so just in proportion as, by studying the laws which his Creator has imposed upon the material world, he rises to his Creator's design and becomes its master.*

It is manifest, too, that there is a law of constant progress in man's appropriation of natural forces, independent of the discovery of any new motive powers. Every machine facilitates the construction of new ones, for utilizing those already known. It cheapens them; it enables us to undertake those previously impossible, (without regard to cost,) for want of the necessary quantity and duration of force; and it liberates men from physical toil, to study and experiment. Each new truth discovered is the key to a whole magazine, and each new art the parent of a thousand. The motive

* "Had God intended that the work of the world should be done by human bones and sinews, he would have given us an arm as solid and strong as the shaft of a steam-engine; and enabled us to stand, day and night, and turn the crank of a steamship while sailing to Liverpool or Calcutta. Had God designed the human muscles to do the work of the world, then, instead of the ingredients of gun-powder or gun-cotton, and the expansive force of heat, he would have given us hands which could take a granite quarry and break its solid acres into suitable and symmetrical blocks, as easily as we now open an orange. Had he intended us for bearing burdens he would have given us Atlantean shoulders, by which we could carry the vast freights of railroad cars and steamships, as a porter carries his pack. He would have given us lungs by which we could blow fleets before us, and wings to sweep over the ocean wastes. But, instead of iron arms and Atlantean shoulders, and the lungs of Boreas, he has given us a mind, a soul, a capacity of acquiring knowledge, and thus of appropriating all these energies of Nature to our own use. Instead of telescopic and microscopic eyes, he has given us power to invent the telescope and microscope. Instead of ten thousand fingers, he has given us genius inventive of the power-loom. and printing-press. Without a cultivated intellect, man is among the weakest of all the dynamical forces of Nature: with a cultivated intellect, he commands them all."—*Horace Mann.*

forces of Nature first brought into use were the most gross, material, and, therefore, obvious. The weight of running water, the wind that rustled every tree—these forced themselves upon the observation of the earliest men. Steam, caloric, atmospheric pressure, are more subtle and more useful, because they can be developed on the spot where their action is required. The machinery for their use can be carried where it is wanted — can drive itself on its way. Electricity surpasses them in subtlety and power, in rapidity and intensity of action. Invisible, imponderable, of immeasurable velocity, it seems like the link between matter and spirit. So volatile is it, that it has thus far eluded the endeavours of science to make it do the work of which it is undoubtingly believed capable. It separates metals from their ores, it gilds them, it runs of errands on the telegraph wires, and finds its way back through land and water, annihilating space. But of an agent that can work such marvels what are we not authorized to expect? and once having fully mastered it, what yet more tricksy and potent spirit may we not evoke by its aid?

It is admitted by all the Economists that man begins with the worst machinery, and proceeds to the better with the growth of population, and that there is a constant tendency to its improvement in the progress of society.

A plain corollary from the proposition that the value of commodities tends to fall and that of labour to rise, with the progress of society, is that there is increased facility for accumulation. Things newly made being got by less labour, the stock of pre-existing things of the same kind, or any share of them, will be had in exchange for proportionately less of labour. The first men, without tools, found it all they could do to maintain life from day to day, without having any surplus to lay by. The moment they began to construct tools, they began to form some stock of food, clothing, and materials — some share of the products of their labour could be saved. The sum of these, belonging to an individual, we call CAPITAL; and the sum of individual capitals, the capital of the community. It is accumulated labour, the unconsumed products of man and of the natural agents he has brought to his aid. In regard to Value, some portions of it have deteriorated more and some less; as the reproduction of some has been facilitated in a greater degree than that of others. The gratuity of Nature, infused by means of improved tools, makes up a greater share in the utility of some things than of others, in any given stage of social progress. The substitution of a bronze axe for a stone one, reduces the value of canoes and houses at once and very materially, while exercising a smaller and indirect influence upon that of furs and clothing. But that share in each which has become gratuitous is common property, or, rather, has ceased to be property, and it is at the command of any one who will offer as much labour as still remains requisite for its production. The capital of the community may be likened to a warehouse of liquors, in which every cask has been reduced by water, but in varying proportions. Any one could have a cask, by paying for the spirits it contained. To make the parallel complete, the utility of the liquor must remain undiminished by its dilution. To this point Father Matthew could testify without hesitation.

A community grows by births. As every child must be fed and clothed for several years, without producing anything to contribute to the stock of food and clothing, the increase of capital must necessarily precede that of population. When the youth has attained his growth, and is fit for labour, he is destitute of tools to work with, and of materials to work upon, as well as of food to supply the waste of his muscles, whilst he is producing food, or something with which to pay for food. He is compelled to apply to somebody who has a stock of these essentials, and make a bargain, which shall promote the interests of both and set him at work. They make an association, go into a partnership, and share the benefits. It is none the less a partnership because one or the other usually assumes all the risks. The object is to change the form of the commodities contributed by the capitalist, and increase their value by combining them with a new infusion of labour. The food is to serve as fuel to maintain the animal heat of the labourer, and to be transformed into muscular fibre; for, with every manifestation of mechanical force, (employed always to produce motion,) a part of the muscular substance loses its vitality, separates from the living part, and is thrown off as waste, to be conducted out of the system. The mechanical force and the waste of fibre are mutually proportional, and the food which is to supply it must therefore be proportional to the force.*

In short, food consumed in the human body produces motion, just as does the coal consumed in a steam-engine. A given quantity of food and a given quantity of coal, are equally incapable of producing more than a fixed quantity of motion or force.

As the food is to undergo transformation, resulting in motion oı force, to be communicated or expended upon the materials, so the latter are to be changed as to form and place. If they were not, they would be let alone.

Both the capitalist and the labourer expect, therefore, to derive their respective shares in the advantages of their partnership, from some division between them of the new thing produced; and, in point of fact, do so, however long may be the series of transformations and exchanges before the division is made. The share of the iron-master in Wales may finally turn up in railroad stocks in Illinois, and that of his workman in a fustian jacket made of Georgia cotton; but both came out of the iron. Whether the miller takes toll out of the grist, or is paid in coin for grinding, or buys wheat and sells flour, comes to the same thing in the end.

If the capitalist takes the risk upon himself, the share in the product which the workman obtains is called wages; and the difference in value between the materials as turned over to the workman, the food, raiment, shelter, &c., furnished to the workman in kind, or commuted in wages, the deterioration of the tools employed, and the finished product, is termed Profits.

If the workman takes the risk upon himself, that share which he gives to the capitalist, in addition to replacing the capital he had borrowed, is called Rent. This word is usually employed to denote the compensation for the use of capital that is incorporated with land. Mr. Ricardo's definition is, "Rent is that portion of the produce of the earth which is paid to the landlord for the use of the original and indestructible powers of the soil;" and he seeks to discriminate it from that portion "paid for the use of the capital which had been employed in ameliorating the quality of the land, and in

* See Liebig on the Phenomena of Motion in Animal Organism.

erecting such buildings as were necessary to secure and preserve the produce."

This definition goes upon the notion of a fundamental difference between capital in land, and in other shapes, which we regard as altogether unfounded. Rent, in Mr. Ricardo's sense of the word, never was paid. Vegetative power, like the other natural agents, is gratuitous. But, without now discussing that point, we shall have occasion to use the word to express the fact we have indicated. When, in the place of borrowing capital in the form in which it is desired for use, money is borrowed, the compensation paid to the lender is denominated interest. It generally includes a premium, sufficient to insure the lender against the estimated risk of not obtaining the return of his principal, as is shown by the lower rates at which governments in high credit can borrow than private individuals. Our definition is intended to exclude any such premium, and to confine the meaning to the remuneration to which the lender is entitled, for having deprived himself of the advantages he might himself have derived from the aid of his capital, in adding to the efficiency of his labour, by the co-operation of the natural agents which it enables him to command.

We now want to know what effect the growth of capital, which we have seen is the result of improvement of tools, has upon the terms of the bargain to be made between the labourer and the capitalist; in other words, upon the proportion which each will respectively take in the product of labour and tools.

Let us suppose a destitute savage to go to another, who has a bow and arrows and a stone axe, and ask what share of the game he shall have, if he takes the bow and hunts, leaving the other to work without intermission at the canoe he is making. The latter offers to give half the game for wages; and if this is demurred to, as unreasonable, the ready answer is, "Chase your game on foot and kill it with a club, if you choose; you will not procure half as much as your wages will come to at my offer." He is forced to accept. The employer, becoming tired of sedentary work at his canoe, in a few days, offers to hunt for both, permitting the other to take the axe and work, on condition that he build a canoe for each. This is to the advantage of the labourer, for he obtains food, and in process of time will have a canoe for himself, and thus become a capitalist.

Suppose, now, a generation passes away, and copper axes are substituted, or, what is better than these, such an axe as Mr. Bigelow describes as in general use about the houses in Jamaica, for cutting firewood—"in shape, size, and appearance, more like the outer half of the blade of a scythe, stuck into a small wooden handle, than anything else I can compare it to. With this long knife," he continues, "for it is nothing else, I have seen negroes hacking at branches of palm for several minutes, to accomplish what a good wood-chopper, with an American axe, would accomplish at a single stroke." * With such an instrument, nevertheless, a man would do more than three times the work that he would with a stone axe. At this stage of the improvement, the son of the first labourer comes to the son of the capitalist, and wishes to hire out to make canoes. The capitalist sees that he can make six canoes in the same time that his father made two, and that if he gets two canoes out of the six, he will obtain twice as much in *quantity* for the use of his capital as his father did, though he gives the labourer two-thirds of the product of his toil, instead of one-half. But the labourer's two-thirds give him four canoes in the same time that his father obtained a single one. His share has increased both in proportion and in quantity; that of the capitalist has also increased in absolute quantity, though it has diminished in relative proportion.

Time rolls on. Mechanical skill increases; implements are improved in shape and quality. The long knife becomes an American axe—a tool as superior, for its purposes, to those used in the Old World, as the other weapon of our backwoodsman, the rifle, is to a Queen Anne's musket.† The labourer of that day comes to the

* Jamaica in 1850, page 130.

† William Vickers, of the firm of Naylor, Nicholson, Vickers & Co., of Sheffield, steel manufacturers of world-wide celebrity, was examined as a witness before the Committee of the House of Commons, on the exportation of machinery, in May, 1841. He testified, "The Americans have got the trade of making felling axes, which is a large one, employing a great deal of labour. We send more steel to make felling axes alone, than we make for all the small tools in England. It is for a plain article, *the most mecha-*

owner of the axe for work. With the improved axe he can do three times the work that was done with that which preceded it. In the time that the former wood-chopper made six canoes, the modern one will make eighteen, and so of everything else that is to be wrought by the axe. If the capitalist, hunting through the account-books of his predecessor, observes that he doubled the quantum of his profit by means of the former improvement in axes, adopts this as a rule, and thinks himself entitled to double it again, he will take four out of the eighteen of the products of the axeman's labour, and leave him fourteen for his wages. If he is tempted to insist upon a larger proportion for the use of his capital, he is restrained by the thought, that it is easier for the labourer to get the improved axe, than it was for his father to procure the poor one: for that poor one enhanced the power of labour and diminished the value of capital. The result is that, at this stage as at the preceding, both the capitalist and the labourer obtain a reward enhanced in quantity, but the proportion of the labourer has advanced and that of the capitalist receded.

The cases we have put represent the capitalist agreeing to make a fixed payment out of the product of the capital which he entrusts to the labourer, and of the mechanical force of the latter. In so doing he runs a risk that the labourer may not exert himself to his full ability, and that the residue after payment of wages, upon which he depends for profits, may be less than he calculates. To insure himself against this contingency, he naturally seeks to bargain for less wages, than he is confident that the earnest and honest exertion of the workman's strength would enable him to pay, without impairing his expected profit. The workman, on the contrary, knowing what he *can* do, and unwilling to submit to any reduction, prefers to guaranty the profit which the capitalist desires, taking upon himself the risk that the product will leave a margin, broad enough to provide for the wages which the capitalist is afraid to guaranty. The contract thus becomes one of hiring capital. What we have called Profit, and what we have called Rent, are identical; the thing bear-

---

nically and the best constructed little instrument I know; the art being that *a man can fell three trees to one,* compared with those that are ordinarily made in England."

ing one name or the other, according as it is stipulated or contingent—a fixed, determinate profit, which the borrower agrees to pay, being denominated Rent, and a rent dependent in its amount upon good faith and the success of the enterprise, in which capital and labour have associated, being styled Profit. But the substantial fact is, that Rent or Profits, and Wages, are the complements of each other, their sum making up the advantages of an association. The same circumstances which control the proportion going to one, necessarily regulate that going to the other. It can make no difference whether the transaction assume the form of a loan or hiring of labour, or of a loan of capital. The extent to which the co-operation of natural agents, through the medium of machinery, has given labour the capacity to be effective, establishes the point on the scale of facility or cheapness at which it can obtain the ownership or the use of capital; or, what is the converse of the same truth, the *dearness* of the rate at which capital can obtain *its* use. If one capitalist will not loan his capital at a rate of compensation which will give the labourer the proportion and amount of wages, to which the increased value of labour at a given stage of progress entitles him, he can obtain it by hiring his labour to another capitalist. And in any supposed conflict of interest that may exist, he has this advantage, that the capital of no individual can take on an accession of value, without being put in combination with labour; on the contrary, some portion of its value oozes from it, by the general progress of improvement and discovery, while labour is not utterly powerless if denied its aid. The one refuses association at the loss of a realized advantage, and of an advantage *in posse*, the other at the loss only of the future advantage.

We have spoken of the loan of labour. The expression implies that the labourer parts with the use of something, which is to be returned to him. What is it? The waste of muscular fibre, in producing motion, is that which he gives away. The particles of fibre that are thrown off are themselves matter, transformed by the action of the vital principle from the constituents of food, previously consumed. In the final analysis then, it is food that the labourer lends, and which is returned to him. The distinction between man and the ox, and other animals who work with him, is that they work, and obtain barely the return of the food expended in their working, while the human labourer exacts a profit—more food than supplies his muscular waste.

Men reckon their gains by a comparison between what they previously possessed and what is added to it. The capitalist reckons his profits, not by his proportion of the product which has been won by the combination with labour, but by the ratio the increment bears to the previous stock. He says he has made so much per cent. on his capital; he rents it for so much per cent. for a year. The difference is one of arithmetical notation, not of fact. When his proportion of the product is small, it being composed of the original capital and the increment, the ratio of the latter to the capital will also be small. The fact will be expressed, according to the nature of the capital of which it is predicated, by saying that Rent, Profit, or Interest, are at a low rate. The undisputed fact, that the rate of interest constantly falls with the progress of communities in numbers and wealth, is an evidence of the tendency we have sought to demonstrate.

If we conceive the course of Nature to be reversed, so that the general mass of wealth should bear a decreasing instead of an increasing proportion to population, then it is plain that the law of distribution would be reversed also. If the number of labourers increased more rapidly than the supply of materials for them to work upon, of tools for them to work with, and of food to replace the energy which they expended, then the capitalists of each succeeding generation, would find labourers competing with each other, to offer a larger proportion of the proceeds of their labour, to escape the necessity of starving in idleness. Substituting in increasing proportion the force of human muscles for the potent agencies of Nature, by reason of the deficiency of tools, and with that muscular force decreasing with the inferiority in quantity and quality of food, their labour would constantly decrease in efficiency and productiveness. Labour thus becoming more costly when measured by its results, the increased proportion of the capitalist would give him a smaller absolute quantity. His power to command men would indeed grow; he would find himself the chief of a little band of barbarians, and soon endeavour, by plundering the vassals of a neighbouring chief, to make up the leanness of his revenue. Continual strife and destruction would accelerate the common ruin; for Life is valued cheaply, where the labour of a life produces little. Disease, induced by bad food, bad clothing, and bad shelter, would rapidly thin out those who escaped the casualties of war. Population would dwindle, and society relapse into barbarism.

Social progress consists in the growth of population and capital. Both begin at zero together, and go on continually increasing. As labour becomes continually more effective, each unit of population in one generation makes a larger contribution to the stock of capital than a unit in the preceding generation. It follows that capital increases in a more rapid ratio than population. It certainly follows, unless the increasing power of man is attended with a decreasing disposition to exercise it. Such would be the case if his wants and desires were constant. But it is the characteristic of his nature, that which distinguishes him from the brute, that his desires are insatiable. The satisfaction of one creates another; and he is thus goaded by his intellectual and moral nature — the angel element in the human constitution—to ceaseless activity. The lower animals, from generation to generation, have the same uniform powers and the same wants. Nature gives them an early maturity of frame, and an instinct which makes no progress. They win from her no further powers. They are contented, and devise no machine, no art. With all the imitative faculty of the monkey, and his opportunities of seeing its great convenience to man, it is said that he has never yet learned to make a fire.

The law which regulates the distribution of the proceeds of labour, which assigns to the labourer a constantly increasing proportion, and to the capitalist a constantly diminishing one, with increased quantity to both—tending therefore to the production of equality among men—was the discovery of Mr. Carey. It was a contribution to social science, more fruitful in consequences than any made before it. It is the key to History, and enables us to understand and explain an interminable series of facts, which are incomprehensible and incredible, upon the theory of the Economists who follow Malthus and Ricardo, and, upon that of other writers, appear to be a mass of accidents, not resulting from or connected by any pervading law

Bastiat was not extravagant when, announcing it in 1850, thirteen years after Carey, he declared, "Such is the great, admirable, consoling, and necessary law of capital. To demonstrate it, is, as it appears to me, to overwhelm with discredit the declamations, with which our ears have so long been assailed, against the avidity and tyranny of the most potent instrument of civilization and *equalization*, that human faculties ever produced."

To exhibit it in its universality, the indispensable test of a genuine law, we must show that it governs capital in land. This will be more conveniently done in treating of Rent; after which we shall present historic and statistical evidence, that the course of things in the actual going-on of the world's business has been such as the law requires, and that the supposititious cases we have imagined are fair illustrations of a principle, which works unremittingly, producing its effects by slow and imperceptible gradations. Nature never acts *per saltum;* though to elucidate her laws we are obliged, for the sake of contrast, to place things and events in juxtaposition, that are separated by wide tracts of space and time, and thus to present a long series of effects in the aspect of a single and rapid change.

CHAPTER IV.

RENT.

In the United States there are rarely more than two classes of persons occupied in the cultivation of the earth, the proprietors and those to whom they pay wages. The interest of the proprietors in the soil is absolute. They own it in fee simple. The term "fee" comes from the feudal law, and imports that the land is held of a superior lord, to whom the estate, on the happening of certain contingencies, as the failure of heirs, would revert. Except as affording a basis for the right of eminent domain, residing in the State, and in virtue of which it appropriates—according to the feudal theory, *resumes*—land, when required for public purposes, the word "fee" has no practical signification in most of the States of our Confederacy. Land is allodial.

In England there are three classes concerned in the partition of the products of the soil — the landlords, the farmers, who rent of them and who furnish the capital expended in cultivation, and the labourers whom these employ. The English writers, therefore, discourse of the rent of the landlord, the profits of the farmer or capitalist, and the wages of the labourer. The separation of the proprietors and the tenants into distinct classes, undoubtedly suggested the notion, that the laws governing the remuneration received by them are different, and that there is some quality in Rent, by which it can be discriminated from other profits. It thus comes that Rent forms a distinct and prominent title in the treatises of the English Economists. They have been followed in this particular by Economists of the Continent, even where the usage upon which the English practice is founded has never prevailed. This is because the rent of land is the index of its value. In England, indeed, land is habitually valued in terms of its rent. It is said to be worth so many years' purchase, and is bought and sold at prices estimated in that way. To what circumstances is it that it owes its value? — and to what circumstances does land owe its power to produce an income or rent to its owner? are obviously the same question. We propose to inquire whether it is any original quality, or is due to subsequent causes.

Land in the Valley of the Connecticut sells for two hundred dollars the acre. Land of equal, if not superior fertility, and with advantages in point of climate, on the banks of the Genesee, can be bought for fifty dollars per acre. Land, in every respect equal in its native qualities to either, but lying in Wisconsin, can be bought for $1 25 per acre. The same laws and institutions prevail in the three localities. The settlers of the Genesee country were emigrants from Massachusetts and Connecticut. The settlers of Wisconsin were colonists from Western New York. If we proceed farther west, land can be had without asking, by any man who chooses to squat upon it. It is without value. Two hundred and thirty years ago the lands on the Connecticut—a little more than fifty years ago the lands on the Genesee, were in the same situation. What is it that has infused value into them?

A great share of the value can be traced to labour expended directly upon the land. It has been cleared of the trees which covered it — a slow and toilsome process when it was undertaken, and an expensive one, because the timber, everywhere abundant and cumbrous to transport, would bring no price. The stumps have been rooted out; ditches dug to drain it; fences, barns, and stables built; lanes made through it; the stones gathered into heaps; it has been ploughed, harrowed, manured. If it were possible to obtain an accurate account of the labour thus directly incorporated with the land, its value at present prices would be found to fall little short, if it did not equal or exceed that of the land. But this is not all. School-houses and churches have been erected in the vicinity; roads have been constructed, leading to market-towns, that have themselves been built up; bridges, canals, and railways have been made, and all of them contribute something to the value of the land. How largely improved means of transportation enhance the price of the soil, whose products are carried by them, is matter of familiar observation It is impossible, however, to assign their shares with any accuracy to each of so many causes, many of them acting simultaneously, and affecting large surfaces, and many from different periods. The removal of the overslaugh in the Hudson, below Albany, would add something to the value of every bushel of corn that passes through the Erie canal, and, of course, to that of the land on which it is grown: a break in that canal, interrupting its navigation for a week, is felt in every grain market in the Old Northwest Territory.

The only way to assign their proper influence to causes of such wide operation, is to take a large territory, and compare the price at which it is estimated, with that of the labour expended in its various improvements. Let us take the State of New York as an example. The cash value of the farms of this State, as ascertained by the census of 1850, is $554,546,642. The entire assessed value of real estate, as returned to the State Comptroller in the Fall of 1851, is $907,571,695. If we add the assessed value of the city property to that of the farms, as ascertained by the United States' census, it will exceed the aggregate valuation derived from the assessment rolls. These valuations were made by different officers, for different purposes, and in mutual ignorance of each other's ascertained results. The State assessment was made under a law passed subsequent to the taking of the census, and the information obtained by the census was not published until a year after the valuation by the County assessors. The latter is likely to be too low; the estimate of the marshals who took the census, being founded upon the statements of proprietors, not prone to depreciate their own farms, is quite likely to be high enough. That there is no greater discrepancy between the two, affords a strong presumption that neither is very remote from the truth. Nevertheless, to avoid all cavil, we propose to assume $1,200,000,000 as the value of the soil of New York, in its existing condition as to buildings and other improvements, public and private. This would pay for the labour of one million of men, working three hundred days in the year, at one dollar per day, for four years.

Let any one now picture the State as it was the day that Hendrick Hudson cast anchor in the Bay of Manhattan, and then consider whether a million of men could fell the forests, drain the swamps, make the roads, canals, and railways, quarry the stone, burn the bricks, cut and saw the timbers, erect the buildings, public and private, and execute all the work, that has made the Empire State out of the hunting-grounds of the Iroquois and the Delawares, in four years, or in ten years. No one will conclude it possible, after a deliberate survey of the multitude of things to be accomplished. Still less will he believe that the labour which has actually been expended upon the soil, can be adequately represented by as low a figure as that of a million of men for four years. The work was, in point of fact, wrought with inferior machinery and inferior mechanical skill to that which the labourer of the present day brings to his task; and, therefore, absorbed a much greater quantity of muscular exertion than would now be expended in reproducing the same effects.

We might take State after State, and exhibit the same discrepancy between the labour actually expended in the improvement of the soil, and that which its soil, covered with the improvements, would command if offered for sale. If there is anything peculiar to the States of our Confederacy, more than the fact that we can obtain more accurate statistics in regard to them than to the countries of the Old World, it is a circumstance which prevents them from exhibiting as great a deficiency in the value of their soil, compared with the cost of its improvements, as the kingdoms of Europe. The cultivation of the United States was begun and carried on by people, who were in an advanced state of civilization at the outset. If we take such a country as England, and endeavour to estimate the labour expended upon it since the landing of Julius Cæsar, we shall find that it must exceed enormously the amount of labour for which it would now exchange. The entire value of the real estate of Great Britain and Ireland, including mines, roads, &c., is estimated by statisticians at about £2,000,000,000 sterling, say, $10,000,000,000. This would purchase the labour of five millions of men for ten years, at the average wages of two hundred dollars per annum. Can any one believe this to be any approximation to the amount of labour which, during the eighteen centuries since the Roman invasion, has been devoted to the amelioration of the soil, or even to the amount of the better instructed and equipped labour of the present day, that would be requisite for reproducing the United Kingdom, if it could be set back to its condition in the days of Hengist and Horsa? The difference between the two is enormous; for the labour of the Saxons, the Danes, and the Normans, was done with wretched tools, and was therefore inefficient, compared with that of the modern Englishman.

No case can be found, which would lead to an inference different from that we deduce from the preceding. It is that land, like everything else, owes its value to the labour expended in producing its existing condition; and that its value is continually falling, because less labour is continually required to bring into activity an equal mass of vegetative power. The same labour which one generation expended upon the thin soils of the uplands, suffices, with their improved machinery, and increased co-operation of natural agents, to enable its children to subdue and till the valleys, in which Nature has accumulated the elements of fertility, that have washed for ages from the slopes above. Land, like air, the principle of gravitation, and the other natural agents, is without value; that is derived only from the accumulated labour that has been combined with it, whether by actual incorporation with its substance, or in improvements, like roads and canals, the advantages of which are spread over large districts. The drainage of one man's swampy land relieves his neighbour from the fogs which it engendered, and thereby not only promotes his health and physical strength, but increases his crops; for the mists which bring ague to man bring mildew and rust to grain.

Having established the truth that capital in land is not to be discriminated, in quality, from capital in movable things, we ought to find that the law regulating its use is the same. In the progress of improvement, Rent should constitute a decreasing proportion of the crop, though its absolute amount should increase; while, both the proportion and the absolute quantum of thē labourer who tills the land should be enlarged. The absence of facts exhibiting such a tendency, would be inconsistent with the truth of the proposition; their existence is incompatible with a contrary supposition, like that of Mr. Ricardo, that Rent is paid for certain fancied "original and indestructible powers of the soil"—for something valuable which remains in it, after all that it owes to labour has been subtracted.

Mr. Ricardo, as we have seen, has stated his theory in the following terms:—

"With every step in the progress of population, which shall oblige a country to have recourse to land of a worse quality to enable it to raise its supply of food, rent on all the more fertile land will rise.

"Thus, suppose land—No. 1, 2, 3—to yield, with an equal employment of capital and labour, a net produce of 100, 90, and 80 quarters of corn. In a new country, where there is an abundance of fertile land compared with the population, and where, therefore, it is only necessary to cultivate No. 1, *the whole net produce will belong to the cultivator*, and will be the profits of the stock which he advances. As soon as population had so far increased as to make it necessary to cultivate No. 2, from which 90 quarters only can be obtained, after supporting the labourers, rent would commence on No. 1; for either there must be two rates of profit of an agricultural capital, or 10 quarters, or the value of 10 quarters, must be withdrawn from the produce of No. 1 for some other purpose. Whether the proprietor of the land, or some other person, cultivate No. 1, these 10 quarters would equally constitute rent; for the cultivator of No. 2 would get the same result from his capital, whether he cultivated No. 1, paying 10 quarters for rent, or continued to cultivate No. 2, paying no rent. In the same manner, it might be shown that when No. 3 is brought into cultivation, the rent of No. 2 must be 10 quarters, or the value of 10 quarters, whilst the rent of No. 1 would rise to 20 quarters; for the cultivator of No. 3 would have the same profits, whether he paid 20 quarters for the rent of No. 1, 10 quarters for the rent of No. 2, or cultivated No. 3 free of all rent."—*Ricardo's Political Economy*, *chap*. 2.

Such are the necessary results of the notion, that men commence the work of cultivation on the best soil, proceeding to the worse; and that land has inherent value independent of labour. If they are true, then the proportion of the crop belonging to the landlord rises with the progress of society, and that of the labourer falls; the one becoming constantly richer and more powerful, the other poorer and more dependent.

Now, what have been the facts? Adam Smith states them thus:

"At present, in the opulent countries of Europe, a very large, frequently the largest portion of the produce of the land, is destined for replacing the capital of the rich and independent farmer, the other for paying his profits and the rent of the landlord. But anciently, during the prevalence of the feudal government, a very small portion of the produce was sufficient to replace the capital employed in cultivation. It consisted commonly in a few wretched cattle, maintained altogether by the spontaneous produce of uncultivated land, and which might be considered, therefore, as a part of that spontaneous produce. It generally, too, *belonged to the landlord*, and was by him advanced to the occupiers of the land. *All the rest of the produce properly belonged to him, too*, either as rent for his land, or as profit upon this paltry capital. *The occupiers of the land were generally bondmen*, whose persons and effects were equally his property. Those who were not bondmen were tenants at will; and though the rent which they paid was often nominally little more than a quit-rent, it really amounted to the whole product of the land. Their lord could, at all times, command their labour in peace and their service in war. Though they lived at a distance from his house, they were equally as dependent upon him as his retainers, who lived in it. But the whole produce of the land undoubtedly belongs to him who can dispose of the labour and service of all those whom it maintains. In the present state of Europe, the share of the landlord seldom exceeds a third, sometimes not a fourth part of the whole produce of the land. The rent of lands, however, in all the improved parts of the country, has been tripled and quadrupled since those ancient times; and this third or fourth part of the annual produce is, it seems, *three or four times greater than the whole had been before.* In the progress of improvement, rent, though it increases in proportion to the extent, diminishes in proportion to the produce of the land." —*Wealth of Nations, Book 2., chap.* 3.

Mr. Malthus, though fully agreeing in principle with Ricardo, admits that the facts in Great Britain correspond with the statement of Adam Smith. He says,

"According to the returns lately made to the Board of Agriculture, the average proportion which rent bears to the value of the whole produce, seems not to exceed one-fifth; whereas, formerly, when there was less capital employed and less value produced, the proportion amounted to one-fourth, one-third, or even two-fifths. Still, however, the numerical difference between the price of produce and the expenses of cultivation increases with the progress of improvement; and though the landlord has a less *share* of the whole produce, yet this less share, from the very great increase of the produce, yields a larger quantity."—*Principles of Political Economy, page* 177.

It is evident, from a comparison of these two statements, that the proportion which rent bore to the whole produce in the British Islands, has fallen, in the interval between the publication of the "Wealth of Nations," and the work of Mr. Malthus — some forty years. In a period of about equal duration, from 1790 to 1833, according to Mr. Porter, (Progress of the Nation, vol. 1, page 164,) who deduces the fact from the evidence taken in the latter year, before the Parliamentary Committee on Agricultural Distress, the revenues drawn, in the shape of rent, from the ownership of the soil, had been at least doubled in every part of Great Britain, while the condition of agricultural labourers is everywhere stated to have been visibly amended. Mr. Caird, as Commissioner for the Times newspaper, to examine the agricultural condition of England, devoted eight months, in 1850 and 1851, to an inspection of thirty-two of the forty English counties. Twenty-six of those visited by him, were also visited by the celebrated agricultural tourist, Arthur Young, in 1770. The average rent per acre, of cultivated lands in those counties, as deduced from the inquiries of Mr. Young, was

13*s.* 4*d.*, (say $3 23,) while the present average rent, according to Mr. Caird, is 26*s.* 10*d.* (say $6 52); if the other six counties visited by Caird are taken into the account, the average rises to 27*s.* 2*d.* The average rent of land in England has, according to these statements, more than doubled in the last eighty years. A very considerable difference exists between the rents of the grain-growing counties and those devoted to grazing and dairies. Mr. Caird gives as the average rent of fourteen corn-growing counties in the east and south of England, in 1851, 23*s.* 8*d.*, while that of sixteen grazing, green crop, (turnips, &c., for feeding cattle,) and dairy counties, is 31*s.* 5*d.*

The Edinburgh Review, for July, 1852, commenting upon these statements of Mr. Caird, for the purpose of exhibiting the relation between the improvements in agricultural machinery and processes, and the increase of rent, takes the case of a mixed corn, cattle, and husbandry farm, like those in the counties of Bedford and Norfolk, the average rent in which was as follows:

	1770, (Young,) per Acre. *s.* *d.*	1851, (Caird,) per Acre. *s.* *d.*
Bedford	12	25 6
Norfolk	11 6	25
Average	11 9	25 3

Supposing a farm in either of those counties to have been paying the average rent of 11*s.* 9*d.* per acre in 1770, the Reviewer proceeds to enumerate several improvements, to which an ascertained gain or saving per acre can be assigned, and estimates their value separately. The sum total amounts to 32*s.* 2*d.* But the increase of rent amounts to only 13*s.* 6*d.* The difference between the two, 18*s.* 8*d.*, goes to the farmer. If his gains stopped here, it would be apparent that the smaller proportion of the increased produce had gone to rent, and the larger to remunerate the tenant. "But," continues the Reviewer, "besides the savings and gains above described, the farmer, in all parts of the kingdom, has had his returns greatly increased by the rise in price which has taken place in farm produce during the eighty years we are considering." Upon this point he states that, "While corn will bring in the market about the same price that it did eighty years ago, an amount of dairy produce, drawn from the stiff clays of Cheshire and Lancashire, which would then sell for £100, is now worth £200; and the same is true to nearly an equal extent, of meat, wool, and butter." So far as grain is concerned, it is apparent that the increased profit of the landlord and farmer has not been gained at the expense of the consumer, since he obtains it at the same money price as before. We shall have occasion to show that the money price of labour has risen in England between the two periods taken for comparison,* and the extent of this rise diminishes in the same proportion the nominal advance in the cost of dairy produce. Any remark upon the subject is necessary here, only for the purpose of precluding an erroneous conclusion in respect to its real cost. The only question in which we are at present occupied, is that of the respective proportions in which the tenant and the landlord share the gains of husbandry. As this has to be deduced from the money prices of rent, the money prices of produce are an element in the calculation, though proving nothing as to its actual labour cost. Mr. Senior, writing nearly twenty years ago (1836), makes a statement, which coming from one of the ablest and the most generally correct thinkers of Mr. Ricardo's school, is pertinent evidence upon this point. "What changes," he remarks, "in the state of England and the southern parts of Scotland, have the steam-engine and the cotton machinery effected within the last sixty years! They have almost doubled the population, *more than doubled the wages of labour*, and nearly trebled the rent of land."

* Mr. Caird gives a table, comparing the averages of rent, of the produce of wheat per acre, of the price of provisions, and of labourers' wages per week, as ascertained in twenty-six counties by Young, in 1770, and the same counties, as ascertained by himself in 1850, and then makes a separate average of the statements of each. The general result he sums up as follows:—

"It thus appears that, in a period of eighty years, the average rent of arable land has risen 100 per cent., the average produce of wheat per acre has increased 15 per cent., the labourer's wages 34 per cent., (from 7*s.* 3*d.* per week to 9*s.* 7*d.* per week,) and his cottage rent 100 per cent., (from 8*d.* per week to 1*s.* 5*d.*); while the price of bread, the great staple of the food of the English labourer, is about the same as it was in 1770. (His average for twenty-six counties shows a reduction of about 16 per cent.) The price of butter has increased about 100 per cent, meat about 70 per cent., and wool upwards of 100 per cent."—*English Agriculture in* 1850 *and* 1851, *page* 475.

The agricultural statistics of England are so meagre and conjectural, that it is impossible to attain anything like numerical precision in inquiries of this character. They serve, however, to support that general observation of the current of affairs, in which the different writers we have quoted concur, and which proves that so far from any such tendency as the Ricardo theory requires, having been shown in the history of the British Islands, their experience establishes directly the reverse.

In respect to France we have more reliable information. Mons. Moreau de Jonnès, who for a long series of years has been at the head of the Statistical Bureau of the French Government, and has attained the highest rank in Europe as a statistician, occupied himself laboriously for years in deducing from the historical, economical, and administrative documents to which his situation gave him access, the facts bearing upon the condition and wages of the agriculturists of France. They were communicated in an extended memoir to the Institute, of which he is a member; and the general summary of the results is contained in an article contributed by him to the *Annuaire de l'Economie Politique et de la Statistique*, for 1851, pages 368 to 385. The inquiry extends back to the period of Louis XIV., embracing the experience of one hundred and fifty years, divided for the purposes of comparison into five periods. The facts as condensed in a tabular form are as follows:

The first table contains a statement of the aggregate expenditure, at different epochs, for the cultivation of the soil of France, (excluding the value of the seed,) in millions of francs—of the proportion which the sum-total of wages bore to the whole value of the product of the soil—and of the amount of such expenditure per head to the actual population of the kingdom, at each epoch, as follows:—

Epoch.	Cost of cultivation.	Proportion to the entire product.	To each inhabitant.
	Francs.	*Per cent.*	*Francs.*
1700, Louis XIV.	458,000,000	35	24
1760, Louis XV.	442,000,000	37	21
1788, Louis XVI.	725,000,000	43	30
1813, The Empire	1,827,000,000	60	61
1840, Louis Philippe ...	3,016,000,000	60	90

The following statement gives the division of wages among the agricultural families of the kingdom, at the same period, upon the estimate that they averaged four and a half persons to a family, giving the annual wages of each family, and the amount per day for each family :—

	Number of agricultural families.	Annual wages.	Daily wages of each.			
		Francs.	*Francs.*	*Centimes.**		*Sous.*
1700..........	3,350,000	135	0	37	or,	7½
1769..........	3,500,000	126	0	35	"	7
1788..........	4,000,000	161	0	45	"	9
1813..........	4,600,000	400	1	10	"	22
1840..........	6,000,000	500	1	37	"	27

M. De Jonnès compares these prices o labour with those of wheat, for the purpose of seeing how far they would go in the respective periods towards supplying the prime necessities of life. He reckons that thirteen and a half *hectolitres* (the hectolitre is $2\frac{83}{100}$ bushels) of wheat, has been about the quantity of grain needed for the consumption of a family—needed more during the earlier than the latter periods, because its want is now, in a great degree, obviated by a variety of garden vegetables, formerly unknown or very little cultivated. He constructs a table giving the mean price of wheat, deduced from an average of the market for long series of years, under each reign, as follows :—

		Mean price per hectolitre.	
		Francs.	*Centimes.*
Under Louis XIV., average of	72 years.......	18	85
" Louis XV., "	60 "	13	05
" Louis XVI., "	16 "	16	00
" Empire, "	10 "	21	00
" Constitutional Monarchy,	10 "	19	03

The result of a comparison of the annual earnings of a family of agricultural labourers, with the cost of thirteen and a half *hectolitres* of wheat, required for their annual consumption, is given in the following table :—

* The *centime* is the hundredth part of a franc, or about one-fifth of a cent: the *sou* is five centimes, or about one cent.

Period.		Wages.		Cost of 13½ hectolitres.		
		Francs.		*Francs.*		*Francs.*
1	....	135	....	254	deficit,	119
2	....	126	....	176	"	50
3	....	161	....	216	"	55
4	....	400	....	283	excess,	117
5	....	500	....	256	"	244

During the reign of the *Grand Monarque*, the rural population of France wanted bread half of the time. Under the sway of Louis XV. it had bread two days out of three. Sufficient progress had been made under Louis XVI. to give it bread three-fourths of the year; while, under the Empire and the rule of the Citizen King, wages were sufficient to supply the labourer with bread through the year, and leave a surplus towards procuring other food and clothing. Doubtless, the labouring classes at the earliest period obtained food enough, such as it was, to support animal life, and made shift to get some clothing also. But their bread was made of the inferior grains, chestnuts, and even worse materials. De Jonnès quotes the Marquis d'Argenson, one of the ministers of Louis XV., as saying, in 1739, "At the moment when I write, in the month of February, in the midst of peace, with appearances promising a harvest, if not abundant at least passable, men die around us like flies, and are reduced by poverty to eat grass." He ascribes their condition to excessive taxation, declaring that the kingdom was treated like an enemy's country, laid under military contribution. The Duke of Orleans, to bring the condition of his people to the knowledge of the sovereign, finally carried a loaf of *fern* bread to the meeting of the King's Council, and at the opening of the session laid it before his Majesty, saying, "See, Sire, what your subjects live upon." This may be regarded as an exceptional case; but a very small portion even of well-read men at the present day, have any adequate impression of the wretchedness of the food, upon which the mass of the people of Europe fed a century and a half ago, and which even now makes the subsistence of a large portion of them.* De

* According to a Report of the Central Agricultural Congress, at Paris, published in the Journal des Debats, 30th March, 1847, it appears that in 1760, only 7,000,000 of the French people lived on wheat and corn; while,

Jonnès says of his countrymen, in the year of grace, 1850, "A large part of the population of our rural districts continue, from habit and from necessity, to feed upon a detestable bread, an indigestible mixture of rye, barley, bran, beans, and potatoes, which is neither leavened nor cooked sufficiently;" and Blanqui, who, under a commission of the Institute, has for two years past been journeying through the provinces, to examine into and report upon their condition, declares that they alone who have seen it, can conceive the degree in which the clothing, furniture, and food of the rural population are slender and sorry.* An official report for 1845, of the number of houses in France subject to the *door and window tax*, shows that there are, in all, 7,519,310 houses—of which, 500,000 have only one aperture, 2,000,000 with only two, and 1,500,000 with from four to five. Two-sevenths only of the whole have six or more openings. Thus are the French people lodged.

We can obtain, however, a more complete idea of the general destitution of France, from the estimate of Michel Chevalier, that the sum-total of value annually produced in that country, if equally divided among its inhabitants, would give an average of less than

---

in 1843, 20,000,000 lived on wheat and corn, and the remainder were much better nourished than in the former period.

* Blanqui sums up his account in these terms:—

"Whatever diversity exists in the soil occupied by the people, in their customs, aptitudes, dispositions, the salient, characteristic fact of their situation is, wretchedness—a general insufficiency of the means of satisfying even the first necessities of life. One is surprised how small is the consumption of these myriads of human beings. They constitute, however, the majority of the taxpayers; and the slightest difference in their favour, of income, would not merely benefit them, but vastly advance all fortunes and the prosperity of the State. Those alone who have seen it can believe the degree in which the clothing, furniture, and food of the rural population are slender and sorry. There are entire cantons in which particular articles of clothing are transmitted from father to son; in which the domestic utensils are simply wooden spoons, and the furniture a bench and a crazy table. You may count by thousands men who have never known bed-sheets; others who have never worn shoes; and, by millions, those who drink only water, who never eat meat, or very rarely—nor even white bread."

9

63 centimes a day (12½ cents) to each. Such is the fruit of tyrannous misgovernment: that it was greatly worse than this previous to the Revolution of 1793, may serve to show how much that Revolution was needed, and how cheap a price it was, with all its crimes and horrors, for the improvement that has followed.

We were led to this digression, because the thought would naturally rise, in the mind of an American reader, that the agricultural labourers must have had bread every day, at a period when, according to the statistics of De Jonnès, their wages would only furnish it for half the time. The objection is obviated, when we see that they fed on something far different from wheaten bread, which is taken as the measure of the capacity of their wages to supply food.

Recurring now to the tables, for the purpose for which they were adduced, we see that they prove a great advance, both in the absolute amount of wages, and in the *proportion* which they bear to the entire product, and to the share of the capitalist. The proportion to the entire product has almost doubled in one hundred and fifty years, having risen from thirty-five per cent. to sixty. As between the labourers and the capitalists it was, in 1700, 35 per cent. to the former, and 65 to the latter. It is now 60 per cent. to the former, and 40 to the latter, who, instead of getting two-thirds of the product, twice as much as the labourers, now get but two-fifths, leaving the labourers three-fifths, or 50 per cent. more than the capitalists. But, although the latter get a diminished proportion, the increased efficiency of labour and capital has made the crop so much greater, that this diminished proportion yields an amount, not only absolutely greater, but greater relatively to the increased population. This is readily shown by a few figures, deduced from the tables of M. Jonnès. Taking for comparison the two extremes, we find the following results:—

	Total population.	Agricultural population.	Paid to agricul. labourers.	Total product.	Leaving for rest of population.
			Francs.	*Francs.*	*Francs.*
1700,	19,500,000	15,000,000	458,000,000	1,308,000,000	850,000,000
1840,	36,000.000	27,000,000	3,016,000,000	5,025,000,000	2,009,000,000

From this it appears that, notwithstanding the labourers are so much better paid—three and two-third times more than in 1700—

(or, rather, *because* they are so much better paid,) the remainder, left to be divided among the capitalists and non-agricultural classes, is larger than before, and they fare better also. The entire population of France lacks three millions of having doubled, while the crop has nearly quadrupled; so, that on an equal distribution, there is now twice as much for each mouth, as in 1700. But looking to the actual distribution now, and then, we see, that while the non-agricultural population has increased 100 per cent., the surplus left, after paying the agricultural labourers their increased wages and enlarged proportion, has increased 127 per cent. This is the state of the case, the comparison being made in money. If it is desired to estimate it in food, we have the necessary elements of calculation, when we know that the mean price of wheat, at the first epoch, was 18 francs 85 centimes per hectolitre, while at the latter it was 19 francs 3 centimes—a difference of less than two cents a bushel. If it should be objected, that these figures do not show how much goes to the landlord, in his quality of owner of the soil, and how much to the man who advances capital in the shape of seed, tools, &c., for its cultivation, the answer is, that the *proportion* of the crop which pays both is less than formerly; if the landlord took the whole, it would be a less share than both obtained in 1700; and if he now gets nothing in his quality of proprietor of land, leaving the whole to remunerate himself or third persons for the use of capital other than land, it is less in ratio than he originally received for the use of the land, and all the other capital employed in tilling it.

The operation of the law is indicated by a comparison of different portions of France. "It is," says Passy, "a country of contrasts. There are Departments which seem to have made no agricultural progress for a century; there are others, whose agriculture is not behind that of the most advanced countries of Europe. In the Departments most backward, the expenses of cultivation do not exceed an average of 30 francs to the hectare ($2\frac{47}{100}$ acres), and the gross revenue is about 70 francs. In the advanced Departments, on the contrary, the expenditure amounts to 200 francs and over to the hectare, and at this cost a gross product is realized of at least 320 francs, leaving the farmers, as well to pay the rent as for their own profits, about 120 francs. In the latter the excess of the produce above the cost of production, is three times that of the former but it requires nearly *seven* times the amount of advances of capital."* The capitalists who obtain for rent and profits four-sevenths of the value of the crop, have but one-third the *amount* received by those whose proportion is but three-eighths. The remaining five-eighths, which the latter expend in the wages of labourers and the improvement of the soil, is five times as much in amount, as is furnished for those objects in the poorer Departments. Decreasing proportion for the capitalists, with increasing quantity, is thus exhibited, as well by the comparison between different districts of the same country, as by that of the country at large, in different stages of its progress. The converse of the proposition must clearly hold in respect to the wages of labour; and, after better wages have been provided for the existing labourers, there is still three times the amount to be added to the capital of the advanced Departments, and to furnish wages for new labourers in the advanced Departments, that the more backward could supply. Instead of population encroaching upon the limits of subsistence, those limits recede before the advance of population.

We might multiply proofs of the same character, and extend the comparison over wider periods. The only difficulty is, that as we recede in time, the information which we are able to obtain becomes indefinite in character, and can seldom be exhibited with the precision of figures in a tabular form. It sometimes occurs that the rent of ancient times is given by the proportion to the whole produce. Thus Cato,† in his agricultural treatise, has informed us that in his day the lands of Italy, not cultivated by the owner himself, nor by his superintendent, usually a freedman or slave, were farmed out to what was styled a Politor, who retained for his personal services and those of his family, from one-ninth to one-fifth of the crop. The proprietor in this case furnished everything — the slaves, beasts, seed, and tools. Where lands in Italy are now let upon the Metairie system, or on shares, the Metayer usually has half of the crops, furnishing half of the live stock and seed; the highest pro-

* Article Agriculture, Dictionnaire de l'Economie Politique, vol. 1, p. 38.

† Chap. 136, 137, quoted by Dureau de La Malle, Economie Politique des Romains, vol. 2, page 60.

portion known is upon some of the volcanic lands of the Kingdom of Naples, where the landlord takes two-thirds.

But the great conclusive fact is, that in those countries which have attained to civilization and wealth, history shows us that at the early periods, while they were yet poor and barbarous, the actual cultivators of the land were in a condition of slavery, incapable of acquiring any property, and obtaining a bare subsistence, like the oxen that worked with them. If we look at contemporary nations, in different stages of social progress and wealth, we see the lowest in the scale are marked by the slavery of the actual tillers of the soil. The Serfs in Russia, the Fellahs in Egypt, the Peons in Mexico, the slaves of our Southern States, are ready examples. We shall necessarily recur to this point when treating of Wages.

But it is needless to multiply evidences. A single case, fairly put and fully authenticated, is decisive; for the laws of Nature admit of no exceptions, and operate equally at all times and in all places.

We have now examined all that is distinctive and consistent in Mr. Ricardo's theory of Rent, and shown that it will not bear the test either of speculative reasoning or historical experience. He has almost casually referred to "advantages of situation" as equivalent to natural fertility, in determining value and rent. By advantages of situation is meant either actual proximity to markets for its produce, or that virtual proximity which is occasioned by rapid and cheap modes of transportation. In whichever way produced, the advantage is the result of the expenditure of capital in building up towns near the farm, or in constructing roads, canals, railways, and the machines for running upon them, which, for all economical purposes, annihilate distance in the same proportion as they annihilate the cost of overcoming it. Advantages which are the product of capital must necessarily be governed, as to the value of their ownership and use, by the same laws which regulate the value of other products of capital. The cost of obtaining them diminishes with the growth of population, and that growth at the same time diminishes the necessity for them; as the number of inhabitants in a district cannot be increased without bringing them nearer to each other, and thus facilitating their exchanges. Such advantages, moreover, are not among "the original and indestructible powers of the soil," and anything paid for their use, is excluded from the denomination of Rent by Mr. Ricardo's definition.

"Though land is not the produce of industry," says Mr. J. S. Mill, "most of its valuable properties are so. Labour is not only requisite for using, but almost equally so for fashioning the instrument." Mr. Mill probably means by valuable, simply useful. In the signification we have attached to value, it would be a mere truism to say that all valuable properties of land, or any other object, are the produce of labour. He is entirely correct in calling land an instrument. It is a great machine, differing from others in the circumstance that it is immovable. But, like other machines, whatsoever of its force is due to the past operation of natural agents, having been gratuitously produced, must be gratuitously parted with, in exchange, and gratuitously lent. Such is that accumulation of organic and inorganic matter, which constitutes its fertility, and gives it what Mr. Ricardo calls its original and indestructible powers.

We have shown that, so far from there being in land any residuum of value attributable to such powers, it is, like other capital, always exchanging for less labour than has been expended in giving it value; and that all other consequences which attend this fact, are found in connection with the use of land, and the partition of its products. Henceforth we shall disregard the notion of a distinction between capital incorporated in land, and movable capital in any other shape, as to their essential laws.

CHAPTER V.

WAGES.

THE laws which govern the partition, between those who lend the capital and those who lend the muscular force, of the products which result from their combination, have been deduced in the preceding chapters. The subject, however, is so important as to justify its treatment as a separate head, and in other relations than that of proportion.

Labour is what every one has to sell. They who desire to buy it, naturally seek to obtain it at the lowest absolute price; and it is habitually called cheap or dear, by reference to the quantity of coin which is exchanged for a given number of hours of exertion. On the other hand, the man who offers it for sale compares the quantity of exertion which he intends, or is expected to give to his task, with the quantity of necessaries and comforts he is to obtain for it—things often very different in kind from those upon which his labour is to be expended. The proportion which Wages bear to Profit being practically adjusted before the latter are ascertained, it is the present and definite quantum, not the future and undetermined ratio, to which men's minds are mainly directed in the operations of business; and this fact has given the same direction, for the most part, to the inquiries of Economists. Mr. Ricardo, indeed, and some of his followers, treat wages as high or low, in reference to the proportion they bear to the entire produce. It is in this sense that he declares "There is no other way of keeping profits up but by keeping wages down;" and that Mr. M'Culloch says, "That profits vary inversely as wages — that is, they fall when wages rise, and rise when wages fall." The latter gentleman testified before a Committee of Parliament, that "The whole and only effect of a French manufacturer getting his labour for less than an English manufacturer, is to enable him to make more profit than the English manufacturer can, but not to lower the price of his goods;" and that the circumstance "would have no effect whatever on the price of the commodities produced in either country." We believe this to have been less than the truth, in the sense which Mr. M'Culloch intended to attach to the words "high wages;" for high proportional wages are the index of cheap production. The Committee, however, understood him to mean by high wages, a large amount; and, although in this sense his testimony was paradoxical, they appear to have felt so much deference for his authority and that of Ricardo, as to have wavered in their own convictions. Mr. Ricardo has not always himself succeeded in his writings, in using the words as indicative of proportion and not of quantity. There is no doubt that his authority has been supposed to be on the side of the common error, that high wages, in the ordinary sense — that is to say, a liberal amount, estimated in money or in the necessaries of life—are incompatible with high profits, and that whatever is taken from one is added to the other. There is as little doubt that this opinion has had a pernicious influence upon the policy of England. Mr. Huskisson, in his speech of April 28, 1825, on the revision of the Corn Laws, told the House of Commons, "If capital had not a fair remuneration here, it would seek for it in America. To give it a fair remuneration, *the price of labour must be kept down.*" There is no ambiguity here. When, in 1846, the views of Mr. Huskisson prevailed, and the Corn Laws were repealed, it was that the *price* of labour might be kept down. It is believed by many that their repeal was advantageous to the United States, because it enabled us to exchange our grain in the English markets for cloths and iron wrought by low-priced labour, instead of exchanging them for cloths and iron made from our native materials, and wrought by high-priced labour at home. Which is true economy, depends in part upon the question, how far low-priced labour and cheap labour are the same thing.

We mean by labour, the exertion of human powers, physical and mental; by wages, the quantity of food, clothing, and other necessaries and conveniences, actually obtained in exchange for such exertion. They are usually obtained in the first instance in the shape of money, or whatever answers as the current representative of value, which the labourer exchanges for so much as he can of material commodities, or social services, contributing to his enjoyment. We find the rate of wages, therefore, ordinarily stated at their money price. But the circulating medium is itself a standard which varies from time to time, in its relation to other commodities Great changes have taken place in the amount of labour necessary to procure a given quantity of gold or silver, by efforts directed to that immediate purpose, in mining, washing sand in California, and the like methods. Men will not consent, for a long period, to obtain a less quantity of potatoes by planting and digging them, than they could obtain by digging for gold to exchange for potatoes; nor will they saw wood for less gold than they are able to get by washing sand—all the risks, inconveniences, loss of time in removing themselves to the *placers*, and other compensating circumstances duly taken into account. We can see that, as a general fact, the improvements in machinery of all kinds, mining, transportation, &c., has had a constant tendency to reduce the amount of labour requisite for procuring the precious metals, but in a somewhat smaller degree than in the commodities of prime necessity; and, therefore, the same money-price of labour indicates a greater command of the necessaries of life at a late than at an early period. Sudden changes, like the influx of gold and silver from America soon after its discovery, and the recent one from California and Australia, require an allowance, in comparing the *prices* of labour in periods antecedent and subsequent to them, which it is difficult to estimate with any precision. Such considerations enforce the propriety of looking at the food, clothing, dwellings, and general condition of the labourers in remote periods, as the only practical test of the rate of their wages, while they justify us in regarding the ratio of money-prices in times nearly contemporaneous, as very nearly corresponding with that of the actual enjoyments of the labourer.

There is a necessary relation between the wages of labour and its efficiency, which prevents the former from being fixed at any arbitrary price. Thus, Mr. Malthus says,

"The command of a certain quantity of food is absolutely necessary to the labourer, in order to support himself and such a family as will sustain merely a stationary population. Consequently, if poorer lands, which required more labour, were successively taken into cultivation, it would not be possible for the corn wages of each individual labourer to be diminished in proportion to the diminished produce; a greater proportion of the whole would necessarily go to labour, and the rate of profits would continue regularly falling, till the accumulation of capital had ceased."

Such wages are ordinarily spoken of by the followers of Malthus and Ricardo, as *necessary* wages. It is obvious that, according to their theory, wages must continually tend to come to this limit; and they teach that wages can never exceed this rate,* except temporarily; for, if they should chance at any time to exceed it, they would stimulate an increase of population sufficient to reduce them again. In this view, the labouring population are regarded as so many animals, with definite, never-increasing wants, and doomed by eternal laws to remain in the same condition themselves, and to beget children who are never to rise above it. It draws an impassable line between the castes of labourers and of capitalists,—impassable at least in one direction, for the labourer can never climb above it, though the capitalist may possibly fall below.

Such, however, is not the necessity to which we refer. It is one more directly physical, and it regards a labourer, not as a determinate unit of force, but as a machine of varying powers, directed by an intellect of varying degrees of enlightenment, set in motion and kept in motion by a will, that varies in intensity with the attractive power of the things it aims at.

To regard first the purely mechanical nature of man. We have seen that food performs the double office of maintaining animal warmth, and of supplying the waste of muscular and nervous tissues which every exertion of force produces. Clothing also serves to maintain animal warmth; so that a man sufficiently clad requires a less amount of food than one who is not. The food that will just keep alive a man insufficiently clad, will keep a well-clothed man at a healthy temperature, and leave a surplus, which enables him to exert muscular force. Clothing being supplied, a given quantity of food can produce a fixed quantity of animal motive power, and it can produce no more. Thus it has been calculated, from the quantity of carbon, &c., consumed by an adult taking moderate exercise,

* "The permanent remuneration of the labourers depends on what we have called their habitual standard; the extent of the requirements which, as a class, they insist on satisfying before they choose to have children." —*J. S. Mill: Political Economy, vol.* 2, *page* 278.

that animal warmth, and the development of animal motive power, may be sustained in a vigorous man during a period of a year by means of ten bushels of wheat. They contain the elements which, during that period, vital chemistry transforms into motive power.

Looking upon a human labourer, then, just as we would upon a steam-engine, we see that the amount of force which he is capable of exerting, depends upon the amount of food supplied to him — a part of it answering the purpose of the coal which gives heat, another answering to the water that is converted into steam and generates motion. A sheet-iron jacket put around the boiler prevents the waste of heat in the one case, just as a woollen jacket about the body of the labourer does in the other.

But food, clothing, and shelter are supplied to the human machine in the shape of wages. To stint them, and to keep the labourer down to the lowest quantity that will induce him to live, without deterring him from propagation, is precisely the same kind of economy which would keep the steam-engines of a nation at half their working power, to save wood, and water, and sheet-iron.

The rate of wages which such considerations would demand, has been attained in very few regions of the world. Suppose it anywhere to have been just reached, the labourer is only brought up to the condition of an ox. But he has intelligence, which the ox has not, and it is the great element of his industrial power. In the lowest descriptions of labour, there is occasion for judgment in the selection of means, in the modes of exerting force most advantageously, and in the adoption of tools and simple mechanical principles, to economize time and strength. As we rise to labour in connection with more complicated machinery, the value of general intelligence becomes distinctly apparent. The Board of Education in Massachusetts procured from the overseers of factories in that State, a return of the different rates of wages paid, and of the degree of education among those who received them; from which it appeared that the scale began with those foreigners who made a mark as the signature to their weekly receipts for wages, and rose to the girls who taught school in the winter months and worked in the factories in summer. This was not the result of any concert among the proprietors of mills; as to that portion which was paid for piece-work, concert was precluded by the nature of the case. The difference in the effectiveness of American operatives, resulting from their superior intelligence, has been estimated as an advantage to our manufactories, over those of foreign countries, equivalent to twenty per cent.

But, to educate himself, a man must have more leisure from bodily toil than is merely sufficient to restore physical energy. He must be able to obtain such a subsistence as will maintain him in high animal working order, in a less number of hours than he could endure to work without impairing his health and strength. To educate his children, he must be able to support them after the period when they become capable of contributing to the support of the family, and must have the means of paying for their schooling and books. This consideration requires a further increase of wages, and repays it to the capitalist with interest and profit, in the increased efficiency of the labour which it procures. In truth, a little reflection will induce the conclusion, that intelligence is the only quality in human labour that it is good economy to employ and to pay for. So far as mere motive force is concerned, it is supplied at a cheaper rate by the natural agents, through the intervention of machinery, and therefore it is that machinery is more and more supplanting the mere animal power of man, and leaving him dependent upon his higher nature to earn him wages. Intelligence in the body of labourers, devises and perfects machinery and improved processes. It diffuses and propagates itself; that of the individual acts upon the community, improving its physical, moral, and political condition, and these in their turn react upon the individual, increasing his security, his power, and his inducements to industry, honesty, and thrift.

Muscular contraction is originated by the will, and every repetition depends upon a repetition of the mandate conveyed from the brain by the nerves. Nervous excitement cannot be maintained without a constant stimulant. Hope is a more powerful and constant stimulant than fear, because it is agreeable, and the mind loves to protract and foster it; while fear is painful, and the mind shrinks from entertaining it, and repels it as an unwelcome guest. Hope, therefore, is the great stimulant to toil, and the toil which feeds hope, by ensuring a present surplus, which may serve as the basis of future progress, and may open to the imagination a vista of indefinite advancement to the labourer, and to the children whom he may expect to start, by the aid of his savings, at a stage much beyond his own commencement, has always proved to be toil to the extremest tension, physical and mental, that our nature is capable of sustaining. It is this which makes American activity the marvel of European travellers. It is the absence of this which has ever made slave labour dear at any price, compared with that of freemen. As long ago as when Pliny wrote, it had been found out, "Coli rura ab ergastulis pessimum est, et quicquid agitur a desperantibus." An author* who has looked closely into the subject, informs us that the Greeks and Romans valued the labour of the slave at half that of the freeman; and Homer sings,

> " ——————— The day
> That makes man slave, takes half his worth away."

The conclusion to which these facts lead us, is the same as that involved in the law of Distribution, elucidated in the preceding chapters. It is that the highest wages attend the highest gross production. We contemplated them then as the result, as we have now as the cause, of a more than commensurate increase of productive power. It follows that low wages procure dear labour, and high wages cheap labour, to the capitalist and to the community.

Several of the English Economists have observed facts corroborative of this law, but without deducing any principle from them—as indeed they could not do without overthrowing the theory which lies at the basis of their system. Thus, Professor Jones, in his essay on the Distribution of Wealth, says,

> "Two Middlesex mowers will mow in a day as much grain as six Russian serfs; and, in spite of the dearness of provisions in England and their cheapness in Russia, the mowing of a quantity of hay, which would cost an English farmer half a copeck, will cost a Russian proprietor three or four copecks. The Prussian Counsellor of State, Jacob, is considered to have proved that in Russia, where everything is cheap, the labour of a serf is doubly as expensive as that of a labourer in England."

Mr. M'Culloch, writing in the Edinburgh Review, had more than once occasion to remark upon the difference between real and nominal cheapness, in comparing the current rates of wages in England and

* Dureau de La Malle: Economie Politique des Romains, vol. 1, p. 151.

France.* Mr. J. S. Mill sees that the truth may be generalized to a certain extent, but does not see that it is universal, as he would have done had he not been trammelled by his faith in the theory of Ricardo. He says,

"Nothing is more common than to say that wages are high or low, meaning only that the cost of labour is high or low. *The reverse of this would be oftener the case;* the cost of labour is frequently at its highest when wages are lowest."

---

* In June, 1827, the Edinburgh Review held the following language:—

"We very much doubt whether wages are really higher in England than in France. That wages estimated by the day are higher in the former, is, we believe, true; but the question really at issue, is not whether the wages paid to workmen employed for a particular period are higher in France than in England, but whether the wages or sums paid for executing *a particular piece of work* are higher? Now, this is obviously a radically different question from the former. A very competent judge of such matters, the late Arthur Young, gave it as his opinion, that an Essex labourer, at 2*s.* 6*d.* a day, was decidedly cheaper than a Tipperary labourer at 5*d.* And upon the same principle, though a French manufacturer may be able to hire his workmen by the day or the week, for some twenty or thirty per cent. less than an English manufacturer pays to his, yet, as the British labourers, from their better training, the greater subdivision of employments among them, and their industrious habits, are able to execute a decidedly greater quantity of work in a given space of time than the French labourers, the wages or prices of labour may really be lower in this country than in France."—*Edinburgh Review, vol.* 46, *page* 28.

He goes on to express the belief that "the English cotton, woollen, and hardware manufacturers and machine-makers, get any quantity of work cheaper and at the same time incomparably better executed than it could be done in France."

In July, 1835, the same Edinburgh Reviewer, grown somewhat more confident, says:—

"If we knew the quantity of work done in the mills of which we know the wages, we have not the slightest doubt that the stories about the greater cheapness of labour on the continent, would be found to be about as authentic as Fairy tales. Mr. Edwin Rose, who had been practically employed as an operative engineer in different factories in France and Germany, on being examined by Mr. Cowell (of the factory commission), stated distinctly that it took twice the number of hands to perform most kinds of factory work in France, Switzerland, &c., that it did in England. Wages there, if estimated by any standard good for anything, that is by the work done, were higher than in England."—*Edinburgh Review, vol.* 61, *p.* 469.

This, he argues, may arise from two causes, the first of which is, that labour, though low-priced, may be inefficient. He instances Ireland, where wages are lower than in any other country of Europe. The remuneration of an agricultural labourer in the west of Ireland is not more, he states, than half the wages of even the lowest-paid Englishman, the Dorsetshire labourer. That a difference to the same extent really exists in the efficiency of the labour, is proved, he thinks, "Not only by abundant testimony, but by the fact that, *notwithstanding the lowness of wages, the profits of capital are not higher in Ireland than in England.*" This explanation is satisfactory in the case where wages are reduced, and no increase of profit follows. But it is insufficient to account for a high rate both of wages and of profits, existing together. Such a state of facts is inadmissible, according to the theory of which Mr. Mill is a disciple. Accordingly he says, in reference to the United States:

"There the labourer enjoys a greater abundance of comforts than in any other country in the world, except some of our newest colonies; but, owing to the cheap price at which these comforts can be obtained, (combined with the great efficiency of the labour,) the cost of labour to the capitalist is considerably lower than in Europe. It must be so, since the rate of profit is higher, as indicated by the rate of interest, which is six per cent. at New York, when it is three or three and a quarter per cent. in London."—*Political Economy, vol.* 1, *page* 502.

But it is as true that the rate of wages, measured in coin, is higher in this country than in England, as it is that the rate of interest is higher. Yet, Mr. Mill is compelled to the tacit assumption that the difference of wages is not in the amount of money, but simply in the amount of comforts that an equal amount of money will command—an assumption altogether at war with the well-known fact—because his theory does not permit him to believe that high wages and high profits can coexist. The English agricultural labourer can earn, according to Mr. Kay,* from 7*s*. to 9*s*. per week, on the ave-

* Social Condition of the People, vol. 1, page 287. The estimate of Mr. Kay is somewhat lower than the average rate of agricultural wages stated by Mr. Caird, to which we have before referred. The latter remarks upon the very great and unnatural disparity of the wages paid for the same nominal amount of work in the various counties; the highest rate he met with having been 15*s*. a week in parts of Lancashire, and the lowest 6*s*. a week in South Wilts. This difference is unquestionably due in part to the operation of the Poor Law system, which ties the labourer to his parish,

rage, say 36*s.*, $8 64 per month, or less than $104 per annum. Out of this sum he has to provide himself with food, clothes, and lodging. The slaves in the States of Maryland and Virginia are hired out for similar agricultural labour, at from $60 to $80 per annum, and are boarded and sometimes clothed by their employers. Their board is estimated to cost $25 per annum.* To work upon public improve-

---

though labour be abundant and wretchedly paid, and prevents his emigration to districts where labour is in request and comparatively well paid. The Poor Laws thus prevent the equalization of wages, leaving them to be determined in the different counties by mere local causes, notwithstanding the great facilities of communication, and the very limited distance which separates any part of England from any other part.

The most effective cause of the diversity in the wages of different districts, appears to be the presence of great manufacturing establishments in some and their absence in others. Thus, Mr. Caird shows that the average rate of *agricultural* wages in the twelve northern counties of England, which include the coal region, and are the seat of manufacturing and mining enterprise, is 11*s.* 6*d.* a week, while in the southern counties it is but 8*s.* 5*d.* "The influence," he observes, "of manufacturing enterprise, is thus seen to add 37 per cent. to the wages of the agricultural labourers of the northern counties as compared with those of the south. The line is distinctly drawn at the point where coal ceases to be found." Comparing the present rates with those stated by Arthur Young, in 1770, it appears that the increase in the northern counties is about 66 per cent., while in the eighteen southern counties mentioned by Young, the increase is but 14 per cent. The greatest increase is in Lancashire and the West Riding of Yorkshire, the seats of the cotton and woollen manufacture, where it is full 100 per cent.

See Caird's English Agriculture in 1850 and 1851, p. 514, et seq.

* Patent Office Report — Agricultural — for 1849–50, page 141.

B. P. Johnson, Esq., the Secretary of the N. Y. State Agricultural Society, writes to the Albany Evening Journal, from Maryland, November 13, 1852, as follows:—

"The labour in this section of the State is mostly performed by slaves. In very many cases the slaves are hired. The practice is, as we learn, to give the slave a choice whether he will work for the applicant or not, and if he refuses to do so he is not compelled to go. This has probably led to a practice which now prevails, and may perhaps be considered so far a custom as to be nearly universal. The usual price per year for the hire of a slave suited to farm-work is about $60—the hirer taking care of him in all cases, except when the slave is sick for *more* than thirteen days at a time, when he is cared for at the expense of the master. In order to sements, they hire by the year at from $100 to $120. Their pay is about up to the English standard. The free labourer, for the lowest description of unskilled labour, is paid from 75 cents to $1 per day; or, when he hires by the year for farm work, receives from $10 to $12 a month, besides his board and lodging, which is at least twice as costly as that of the slave.

If, instead of comparing the rate of wages in countries at different stages of wealth and social progress, we trace the history of the labouring classes in any of the States of Europe, we find that they have emerged, or are emerging from a state of slavery; that this condition is uniformly accompanied by barbarism and poverty on the part of the employer; and that, from generation to generation, the advance in the rate of wages, to which there is a constant and steady tendency, has been marked by a more than corresponding increase of capital. All classes have approximated more and more to a common level, and that level has been itself constantly rising. The actual labourers of Scandinavia were thralls; the freemen employed themselves in war and piracy. When the Saxons overran Britain, they parcelled out the land among the free retainers of their chiefs, who held their farms upon the tenure of military service, and who came eventually to receive the name of "vassals," and the original British cultivators of the soil became "ceorls" or churls, and were afterwards called "villains." During the Saxon period, nearly the whole people were engaged in producing food. "The English," says Stowe, "might be said to be graziers rather than ploughmen.

cure the services of the slave, it was the practice at an early day, for the person wishing to hire him to offer to the slave, for his own benefit, from $10 to $15: this usually secured his assent. This is now usually given in cases of hiring; and the slave has thus an interest in so conducting himself as to be profitable to his employer as well as useful to himself. The slaves have many perquisites here, by which they frequently accumulate considerable property. They have a week's holiday at Christmas, at Easter also, and, usually, every Saturday afternoon, when their time is at their own disposal. They keep poultry, own a pig, gather oysters, which they often sell to their own masters, as well as to others, and frequently spend their evenings in manufacturing the husk collars for mules, straw hats, raw-hide traces, &c., and are thus enabled to secure many little comforts for themselves and families."

for almost three parts of the kingdom were set apart for cattle" Swine, who picked up their own food in the woods, and whose parings, the feet, tail, &c., were pretty much all that Gurth got for tending them, constituted a large portion of the live stock. The practice of selling their own children for slaves was common. When the Council of Armagh, in 1171, prohibited the traffic which the Norman conquerors practised, in selling English slaves to Ireland, it reminded the Saxons that they had merited such chastisements, by the former habit of their nation of selling their own kin at the first pinch of want. The author who relates this* declares, that such numbers of slaves were exported to Ireland that the market was absolutely glutted. Another states that, from the reign of William to that of King John, there was scarcely a cottager in Scotland who did not possess an English slave.

A distinction soon grew up between villains *in gross*, who were at the absolute disposal of their master, and villains *regardant*, who were annexed to the land, passing with it when the property changed hands by inheritance or purchase, and who could neither remove from it at their own will, nor were removeable at the will of their lord. Though some of them were allowed to cultivate an allotment for their own profit, just as the slaves in our Southern States are indulged with a patch of ground, on which they raise garden vegetables and poultry, yet as matter of law, they were incapable of acquiring property, and whatever money or goods they possessed belonged to the master. Such is now the position of the Russian serfs.† Many of them, in point of fact, accumulate great wealth,

* Geraldus Cambrensis, who lived in the reign of Henry II.

† "The proprietor shows his vassals the portion of land they must cultivate for him, and allots the remainder among them at his own will and caprice. Where estates, in proportion as their population increases, get almost entirely allotted out among the serfs, the owner exacts from the latter, instead of the soccage, or compulsory unpaid labour, a yearly tribute called *obrok*, whose average amount is ten or twelve rubles banco. If the lord of the soil fixes neither *obrok* nor amount of labour, the law fixes three days' work a week for every male who has attained his fifteenth year, and, for women and children, labour in proportion to their strength. * * * Many, especially young people, repair to the towns, and easily obtain permission from their master, as they are then expected to pay higher obrok." —*Jermann's Pictures from St. Petersburgh, page* 154.

and are suffered to enjoy it upon payment of an acknowledgment to their owner, by which they hire the privilege of working for themselves.

There is a natural process through which the slave works out his freedom. His toil is unproductive, because there is no heart nor hope in it. He produces little, and he gets little. The master soon sees that he can increase his profits by tempting the slave to increased *task-work*, giving him all the surplus he can earn after finishing his task. With this partial liberty of working for himself comes the stimulus of hope; he works harder for himself than when working for his master, and of course obtains higher wages. His intelligence and his power increase, and it is finally seen that more work can be got from him, and at a cheaper rate, by paying him fair wages, than in any other way. In England, as on the Continent, this change was brought about by assigning lands to the bondmen, the fruits of which they were permitted to enjoy, upon condition of performing agricultural labour upon the domain of their lord. The services thus rendered were at first arbitrary and uncertain, being such as the lord chose to demand, and at such time as he chose to demand them.

This state of things lasted, in many of the States of the Continent, until a very recent period. In Denmark the estates of the nobles, down to 1784, were cultivated by serfs, who were bound to work every day without wages, on the main farm of the feudal lord, and had cottages and land on the outskirts of the estate, to work upon for their own living. Their lord could imprison them, flog them, reclaim them if they had deserted from his land, and had complete jurisdiction over them in his baronial court. Since that period services have been rendered certain, and the slaves converted into proprietors of their holdings, rendering a fixed rent to their landlord.* In several of the provinces of Austria—Hungary, Bo-

* "About the year 1784, the spirit of the age began to make the feudal relation unprofitable as well as odious. The serfs would enlist in the army, or desert to the free towns, Hamburg and Lubeck, or emigrate and set themselves free, leaving none but the aged and infirm to labour without wages on the estate. Some nobles, among the first Count Bernstoff, emancipated their serfs, and paid day's wages for the labour they required on

hemia, Gallicia, and Moravia, a similar change was effected about 1776. Previous to that, the number of *robots* or days of forced labour, to be done on the lord's land, depended on the mere will of himself or his agent. The other dues and services were equally unlimited in fact if not in appearance; for, when defined by compact or usage, the peasant's complaint for infringement could only be heard in the court of the Herrshaft or Manor, where the lord himself, or his paid fiscal, was the sole expounder of the law. A rebellion of the peasants in 1773 led to the promulgation of a Rural Code, which defines the *robots* according to the extent of the peasant's holding.* The maximum in Bohemia and Moravia was fixed

their estates. Some valued the serf's labour, and the land with his cottage, which he had for his subsistence, and converted the amount into a debt upon the little farm, which the serf had to pay interest for and redeem, but in the meantime was full proprietor of the land. In some cases labour continued to be paid as a rent, or feudal duty, for the land; but government interfered to fix an equitable amount, to determine the number of days per week, and of hours per day which could be exacted, and to make the holding perpetual, provided the conditions were fulfilled, or a stipulated price paid for non-fulfilment. On the whole the feudal vassals and serfs became proprietors of their several holdings; some remaining subject to a few servitudes, such as certain cartages of peats, wood, or corn, certain days' work in hay-time and harvest, at certain rates, but all fixed, registered in the books of the local court, and placed beyond arbitrary exaction or oppression on the one hand, or evasion on the other."—*Laing's Denmark and the Duchies, page* 54.

Mr. Laing says at a subsequent page, (155): "Though the emancipation of the peasantry on the baronial estates was only accomplished in the beginning of this century, yet they have made greater progress in the tastes and requirements of civilized life, and in the habits of industry and accumulation of property to gratify those tastes and requirements, than the Celtic peasantry of Ireland or of Scotland have made since the earliest notice of them in history."

* See Turnbull's Austria, vol. 2, chap. 3. Mr. Turnbull says:—

"A large Bohemian proprietor, who with his brothers counted on their estates 18,000 subjects, has frequently observed to me, that he found it usually more advantageous to accept even a very small part of the legal commutation money, and to hire labour from others, than to take it in kind from those who were bound to yield it."

How much more so would it have been, when the obligations were all on one side and the benefits on the other!

at one man's labour for three days in the week. The peasant yielding the defined services was confirmed in the hereditary possession of his land, with the right of disposing of it and removing. The right of commuting the *robots* and other services in money is also secured to the peasant. In the other provinces of the Austrian Empire, the system of predial bondage has been nearly, if not wholly extinguished, by the operation of natural laws, without the interference of the government.

In Prussia, down to 1807, none but nobles or privileged persons could acquire landed property. Such parts of their estates as were not in the immediate possession of the lord, were held by occupiers in a sort of predial slavery, on condition of their paying a rent, consisting sometimes of services to be performed on the lord's land, sometimes on the delivery of a certain portion (generally half) of the produce, and, more frequently, perhaps, of both the one and the other. In 1811 the Prussian Government published an edict, by which it abolished serfdom, and enacted that the tenants who held perpetual leases should, on giving up one-third part of the land held by them, become the unconditional owners of the other two-thirds; and, with respect to those who held leases for life, or terms of years, that they should become the proprietors of half on surrendering the other half. To the remonstrances of the landlords the government replied, that the change would prove equally advantageous to the lords and the peasants; and, that if, as they alleged, they should be compelled to give better food and higher wages to their emancipated vassals, in order to obtain the labour necessary for the cultivation of their estates, it would only prove that the remuneration of the labourer had before been below its proper level. That the government was right is proved by the great increase of prosperity which followed.* Mr. M'Culloch, while protesting against such a violent invasion of vested rights, admits that its effect has been, that the country has made a greater progress since 1815 than it did during the hundred preceding years. The example of Prussia has been followed by the other States of Germany.

---

* The Prussian Minister of Statistics gives the following table of the average consumption throughout the kingdom, in 1805 and 1842:—

In England, a class of servile tenants, holding small portions of land for their own use, under the obligation of working at specified times, and rendering definite services in cultivating the domain reserved by the landlord for his immediate possession, had arisen previous to the year 1257, or within two centuries after the Norman conquest. Tenants in villanage, as these were called, soon ceased to be villains in person. They were at liberty to provide a labourer for the lord instead of working themselves, and the tenure lost the degrading character which originally attached to it. If a villain

Food and Materials.	1805. Quantity consumed per head.		1842. Quantity consumed per head.
Bushels of Wheat, Corn, &c.	4	....	4
Pounds of Flesh	33	....	35
" Rice	$\frac{3}{10}$	....	$\frac{11}{16}$
" Sugar	$1\frac{1}{2}$	....	5
" Coffee	$\frac{2}{3}$	....	$2\frac{1}{2}$
" Salt	17	....	17
" Tobacco	$1\frac{1}{2}$	....	$3\frac{1}{10}$
Ells of Cloth	$\frac{3}{4}$	....	$1\frac{1}{3}$
" Linen	4	....	5
" Woollen Stuffs	$\frac{3}{4}$	....	13
" Silks	$\frac{1}{4}$	....	$\frac{3}{8}$

The population, which was 10,000,000 in 1804, had increased to 15,000,000 in 1841. The increase in the *average* consumption proves a more than proportionate increase in that of the poorest class, who subsist upon wages; for the richer classes, having been able to indulge all their wants at the earlier period, can have increased *their* consumption in a very small degree, of such articles as are enumerated in the preceding table.

"A ministerial paper, laid before the provincial Assembly of the Rhine Province, says that the new agrarian regulations have tended to improve the cultivation of the land so much, as to have, in 1843, raised the market value of the land since 1828 about 75 per cent."—*Kay's Social Condition of the People, vol.* 1, *pp.* 137, 265.

The increase in the marketable price of the land has doubtless outrun that in its real value. Sismondi gives the reason. He says the peasant proprietor is always eager to purchase land at any price, and pays for it more than it is worth, "But what reason he has to esteem at a high price the advantage of thenceforward *always employing his labour advantageously, without being obliged to offer it cheap; and of always finding his bread wher he wants it, without being obliged to buy it dear!*"

could escape to a town, and elude the pursuit of his lord for a year and a day, he was free forever; and the rolls of Parliament, before 1350, contain the complaints of the nobility, that the facility with which they could thus emancipate themselves emboldened those who still remained in the country to behave so insolently, that their masters were afraid of exercising their powers, from fear of losing them irrevocably. The last claim of a villain, of which any record is preserved in the courts, was made in 1618; but some of the characteristics of slavery remain to this hour in the Bondagers of Cumberland;* and, down to the year 1799, when a statute was passed for their emancipation, there were colliers and salt manufacturers in Scotland, who might be bought aud sold with the collieries and salt-pans to which they were attached.

The first legislative recognition of the existence of a class of free labourers, occurs in the year 1356. The Statute of Labourers, passed in that year, recites, that since the pestilence no person would serve unless he were paid double the usual wages allowed five years before, and it proceeds to enact that they should be compelled to serve for the rates therein specified, under penalty of fine and imprisonment. It was optional with the master to hire by the year or the day, but the labourer was compelled to work by the day or the year. The rates by the day fixed in this statute are as follows:—

The wages to be paid to haymakers were 1*d.* a day. A mower of meadows 3*d.* a day, or 5*d.* an acre. Reapers of corn in the first week in August, 2*d.*, in the second, 3*d.*, and so on until the end of August, without meat, drink, or other allowance, finding their own tools. For threshing a quarter of wheat or rye, 2½*d*; a quarter of barley, beans, peas, and oats, 1½*d.* A master carpenter, 3*d.* a day; other carpenters, 2*d.* A master mason, 4*d.* a day; other masons, 3*d*, and their servants, 1½*d.* Tilers, 3*d.*, and their knaves, 1½*d.* Thatchers, 3*d.* a day, and their knaves, 1½*d.* Plasterers, and other workers of mud walls, and their knaves, in like manner, without meat or drink; and this from Easter to Michaelmas; and from that time less, according to the direction of the justices.†

To convert money of that day into its equivalent by weight of the

* Howitt's Rural Life of England, chap. 4.

† During the past year it has become known, by the publication of Mr. Hunter's "*Robin Hood, his Period, Real Character,*" &c., that this hero of

present coin, it must be multiplied by $2\frac{62}{100}$. The penny, therefore, is nearly equal to three pence sterling of modern money.

In 1388, the wages of labour were again regulated. A master hind, a carter, or a shepherd, was allowed 10*s.* a year, without clothing, or any other perquisite. This was equal in weight of silver to about $5 70 of our money. A plough-driver was allowed 7*s.*, or about $3 90, without clothing. The price of coarse russet cloth was fixed at 1*s.* a yard. The whole year's wages would buy but seven yards.

In 1444, wages were again fixed by Act of Parliament. A chief hind, carter, and chief shepherd, were allowed 20*s.* a year, with meat and drink, and clothes of the value of 4*s.* The allowance for wages and clothing would amount to about $11 16 by weight in our silver coin. The allowance of a common servant in husbandry, for wages and clothing, was 18*s.* 4*d.*, equal to $8 53. In 1496, wages of agricultural labourers were slightly raised, but not more than enough to counterbalance a debasement of the coin which had taken place in the interval. At different times, subsequently, the rate of wages was regulated by Parliament; and, as its enactments were always in the interest of the employers, to fix a maximum at which labourers should be compelled to work, every successive statute proves the tendency of wages to rise. Until a very modern period, the legislature has struggled to keep down this tendency by arbitrary regulations, either imposed by itself, or by orders of the Quarter Sessions of Justices of the Peace in the different counties, to whom it delegated the power. The efforts of the representatives of capital to fight against the "higher law," under which the remuneration of labour was increasing with the general progress of population and wealth, were not confined to the tillers of the soil, but extended to all classes of common artificers. Thus, in 1514, Parliament fixed

---

the ancient minstrelsy of England, an outlawed adherent of the Earl of Lancaster in the reign of Edward II., (about 1323,) was pardoned by that king, and, for about a year, employed as one of the porters or valets of his chamber. The situation was one of considerable confidence and respectability. Mr. Hunter finds, in a document in the Exchequer, a charge for the very wages Robin Hood was paid, *three pence per day*. Doubtless there were some perquisites in board, lodging, and livery. But such a remuneration for an attendant upon the person of the sovereign, authorizes us to infer a very great inferiority in the wages of ordinary servants.

the wages of masons, carpenters, tilers, plumbers, glaziers, carvers, and joiners, at 4*d.* a day, with diet, or 6*d.*, without, during the spring and summer months, and at 1*d.* per diem less from Michaelmas (September 29,) to Easter. Six pence were equivalent to about 18 cents of our present money, in point of quantity of metal. Its purchasing power was unquestionably greater than the same quantity of metal one hundred years afterwards, when the mines of America had swelled the circulation of the world. We cannot ascertain with any precision what allowance should be made on this account; nor is it necessary, in comparing the prices which we have thus far mentioned, for they are all equally affected by it.

During the next century and a half, great changes in the relative value of money and commodities were produced by the influx of the precious metals from America. If we jump to 1680, we shall have arrived at a period when prices had adjusted themselves to the new value of coin. We are able, moreover, from this time to obtain reliable accounts of the current prices of wheat, and to estimate wages in the amount they would procure of what is now the prime necessary of life; though wheaten bread at that time formed but a small portion of the food of the people of England, the great body living upon the coarser grains — barley, rye, and oats — for at least half a century afterwards. From a comparison of the average rates of wages of agricultural labourers with the prices of wheat, as collected by the authors who have treated on this subject, Mr. Carey has constructed the following table,* exhibiting the remuneration of an English labourer in husbandry, in the number of pints of wheat that his wages for a week would purchase.

From			Population.	Pints.
1680	to	1700	5,134,516	54
1701	"	1726	5,500,000	64
1727	"	1751	6,100,000	78
1752	"	1764	6,700,000	80
1770			7,227,586	79
1790			8,540,738	82
1824			12,500,000	89
1832			14,100,000	90

* Principles of Political Economy, vol. 1, page 63.

There is no exclusive propriety in taking wheat as the standard of wages. The main inducement for referring them to this test, is to meet the objections of those who, while admitting the increase in the money wages of the labourer, and in the quantity of all manufactured commodities which they will procure, imagine that the "decreasing fertility of the land" involves an increase in the cost of food greater than that in the price of labour. This objection is met in another way, by comparing the whole production of food in England with its population, now and at any past period; a comparison which shows that the quantity of food now grown upon its soil, if apportioned equally among the inhabitants, would give a much greater mass than at any of those Arcadian eras, which are referred to as the good old times, notwithstanding the proportion of the population engaged in agriculture has been constantly decreasing. Who is it that have increased their consumption of food? Not the landlords, surely, who have always had all that they desired; not the merchants, nor the mill-owners; not the relatives of the aristocracy and gentry, who fill the learned professions and officer the army and navy. Doubtless they enjoy a greater variety of food than formerly, or than falls to the share of the labourer at the present day; but, when we look to the great staples of subsistence, and inquire who it is that disposes of the immense increase in their weight, we must conclude that the men who live upon the wages of daily toil in the fields and the workshops are those who consume it, and that, as it is bought by their wages, their wages, estimated in food, have increased with the general wealth, and at a more rapid rate.

Those who will study the general condition of the labouring classes, the style in which they were housed and clothed, the amount and quality of their furniture, their comparative liability to disease, as shown in the number and fatality of pestilential disorders, and in the average duration of life, cannot fail to see that the labourer's ability to command the necessaries of life has been constantly advancing. Abundant, interesting, and instructive facts upon this subject may be found in the several chapters on "The Condition of the People," "The National Industry," and "Manners and Customs," in the "Pictorial History of England." We may infer what the household accommodations of the commonalty were in the days of Henry VIII., when we know what were those of a powerful nobleman, the Duke of Northumberland, who had three houses in Yorkshire, which he inhabited in turn. He had furniture for but one, and carried everything with him when he changed his residence. Beds, tables, chairs, kitchen utensils, &c., were all carried in seventeen carts and one wagon, though the family consisted of 223 persons. This is a cart-load, for the furniture of all kinds, for every twelve persons; — not very heavy nor large, we may judge, to be transported in Yorkshire, at that day, over roads whose quality may be surmised from the fact that, in 1703, Prince George of Denmark was fourteen hours in going forty miles, from Windsor, in the immediate vicinity of the metropolis, to Peterworth, and was overset more than once on the way.

We have not referred to our own country, because American readers do not require information about its brief history. It may not be amiss, however, to notice that Adam Smith, writing in 1773, when fertile lands were abundant and population small, and when wages upon the Ricardo-Malthusian theory, *ought* to have been much larger than at present, says:—

> "In the province of New York, common labourers earn 3*s*. 6*d*., currency, equal to 2*s*. sterling a day; ship-carpenters, 10*s*. 6*d*., currency, with a pint of rum worth 6*d*. sterling, equal in all to 6*s*. 6*d*. sterling; house-carpenters and bricklayers, 8*s*., currency, equal to 4*s*. 6d. sterling; journeymen tailors, 5*s*., currency, equal to about 2*s*. 10*d*. sterling. These wages are all above the London price; and wages are said to be as high in the other colonies as in New York."—*Wealth of Nations, Book I., chap.* 8.*

---

* Smith makes some errors in the comparison of York shillings with sterling: 3*s*. 6*d*. is 43¾ cents; 2*s*. *sterling*, 48 cents. His statement in respect to the wages of carpenters and bricklayers in London gives pertinence to the following extract from the Edinburgh Review, of April, 1851:

"Mr. Porter has ascertained, from the tables kept at the Greenwich Hospital, that the wages of *carpenters* had risen from 18*s*. a week, in 1800, to 29*s*. 3*d*., in 1836; of *bricklayers*, from 18*s*. to 29*s*. 9*d*.; of *plumbers*, from 19*s*. to 30*s*. In the same period the earnings of *London compositors* in the book trade had risen from 33*s*. to 36*s*. We have ascertained that they remain the same. The earnings of compositors employed on the morning papers had risen from 40*s*. to 48*s*. a week. They are now at the latter amount. From evidence published by a Committee of the House of Commons, in 1833, added to such information as we have been enabled to obtain up to the present period, we give, as fully reliable, the following

The wages of the common labourer in New York have doubled, and those of the artificers mentioned by Smith have all advanced, though not to the same extent; while the prices of the articles for which wages are expended have been on the whole reduced. The daily ration of the United States soldier—which is more than abundant food for a labouring man,* shown to be so from the fact that it is habitually unconsumed, and that at our military posts the soldiers supply themselves with a library and other conveniences by a fund, which is derived from the surplus of their rations — has been for years commuted to the officers at twenty cents per day. A dollar a bushel for the best Genesee wheat, has been a kind of normal price with the farmers who grow it for the last twenty-five years. The same price prevailed in 1791 and 1799,† when salt in the Genesee country, only sixty miles from the springs at Onondaga, was at fifty cents a bushel.

It would be interesting to trace the operation of the laws under which wages rise in the progress of population and wealth, upon the political condition of the mass of the people. About the first time that we hear of the Commons of England, is when that name was assumed in 1381, by the insurgents under Jack Straw and Walter

---

table of the earnings of a spinner of cotton yarn, No. 200, at these several dates:—

	Weekly net earnings.	Pounds of flour these could purchase.	Pounds of flesh meat these could purchase.	Hours of work.
In the year 1804............	32*s*. 6*d*.	117	62	74
" 1833............	42 9	267	85	69
" 1850............	40 0	320	85	60

"If the hours of labour had been reduced between 1833 and 1850 only in the same proportion as his wages, the spinner would work 64½ hours instead of 60 per week. If he had been paid the same wages per hour in 1833 as in 1850, he would have received 46*s*. per week instead of 42*s*. 9*d*."

* The ration is 1¼ pounds of fresh beef, or ¾ of a pound of salted pork, 18 ounces of bread or flour to each man; and at the rate of 8 quarts of beans, or 10 pounds of rice, 6 pounds of coffee, 12 pounds of sugar, 4 quarts of vinegar, 1½ pounds of tallow, or 1 pound of sperm candles, 4 pounds of soap, and 2 quarts of salt to each hundred men.

† Documentary History of New York, vol. 2, pp. 1119, 1148.

the Tyler. The immediate occasion of their rising was the capture, with an armed force, by Sir Simon Burley, of an industrious resident of the town of Gravesend, as his escaped bondman. An extravagant ransom was demanded for him, which was refused; but the Commons of Kent attacked the castle of Rochester, in which the serf had been imprisoned, and compelled his surrender. When the insurgents treated with the king, their demands were: 1. The total abolition of slavery for themselves and their children, for ever. 2. The reduction of the rent of good land to four pence an acre. 3. The full liberty of buying and selling like other men in all fairs and markets. 4. A general pardon for all past offences. The second demand, it is very probable, was nothing more than that which is now agitating Ireland — for Tenants' right, or fixity of tenure. It was the uncertainty of the rent, rather than its amount, which was felt to be a grievance. Sir T. Cullum supposes four pence an acre to have been about the average rate at which land was let, toward the close of the thirteenth century.* With this possible exception, all that was asked was personal liberty: political privilege being as yet unthought of. The insurgents failed to obtain even the abolition of personal villanage; and it was not until the time of Charles II that the obnoxious incidents of tenure in villanage were taken away. But men do not rise, with arms in their hands, a hundred thousand strong, without its operating as a caution against giving them occasion to rise again. The power of the landlord class to resist the demands of those whom they might tempt to revolt, depended upon their ability to feed hosts of personal retainers. When the lord obtains two-thirds of the entire produce of the land in the shape of rent, he can devote one-half of it to maintaining a crew of men-at-arms, equal to the whole body of cultivators, and still keep an equal quantity for himself and his family. Accordingly, the great barons had each a small army constantly at his disposal. As cultivation extended, and labour became more productive, the proportion of the rent to the entire crop fell, and the landlord was forced to curtail his retinue. The number and wages of industrious men increased, and that of military loafers diminished. Popular

* Pictorial History of England, vol. 1, p. 811: Harpers' edition.

intelligence and popular power advanced together. When the Commons rose again, under Jack Cade, in 1450, it was public abuses for which they demanded redress. No complaint was made of villanage —that was wasting away—but it was of the taking of the subject's property for the use of the Crown, without payment, under the name of purveyance; of extortion by the sheriffs; of delays in the administration of justice; of evil counsellors about the throne; of the illegal interference of the nobility, in hindering the free election of knights of the shire, the county representatives in Parliament. Wages, however, though high enough to prompt the effort for popular rights, were still too low to secure its success. Cade failed, like Wat Tyler, and England had to wait for the rebellion of 1640, before the people could obtain immunity from being plundered by the Crown, by purveyance and ship-money.

Popular liberty had its origin in the towns. The naturalization of the woollen manufacture, by Flemish weavers, brought over from the continent, creating competition for the employ of labour, is recognized as one of the most effective in the circumstances which led to the abolition of personal slavery. The Flemings brought with them the knowledge of municipal institutions and privileges, the right of local self-government, and the protection of a citizen militia. In their own country, the artizans of the towns had not only provided for their own security against marauding barons, but had created a military force in their civic organizations, which was the bulwark of their national independence. Security promoted industry, and industry accumulated the means by which security could be maintained. The exercise of self-government is the great school of popular intelligence. As the towns increased in population and wealth, they obtained royal charters, securing the personal freedom of their inhabitants, the right of legislating upon their local concerns, of representation in Parliament, and of choosing their own magistrates. The representatives of cities and boroughs, created by patent or charter, made the mass of the House of Commons. "The little men of the Commons," as they were called, thus attained the power of associating themselves with "the great men of the land" in the government of the kingdom; a power which has grown until the Peers are little more than nominal participants in its exercise—

rather an ornamental appendage than a vital part of the machinery The landlords kept the ascendency in the House of Commons and controlled its policy according to their supposed interests, down to the repeal of the Corn Laws; but that was a triumph of the representatives of machinery. The millocracy has now the upper hand of the squirearchy. Its numbers and influence are continually growing, and its property is distributing itself with a constant tendency towards equalization, as property in land would do were it permitted to obey natural laws. But the feudal instinct which struggled to prevent the alienation and division of landed property by the law of primogeniture, by the practice of entails, by withholding real estate from sale under judicial process, and permitting only its temporary use and rents to be applied to the satisfaction of debts, is still strong in the landlord class, and fences their ranks against the intrusion of those who would swell their power, if the impediments were removed, which fetter the disposition of real estate by cumbrous forms, great risks, and onerous expenses. While the ownership of land was the basis of a military aristocracy, governing the nation by the physical force of its dependants, its policy was that of a close corporation. Now that its monopoly of political power has been wrested from it, the exigencies of defence require that the number of landholders should be recruited. However long the landholders may cling to the feudal policy, and endeavour to keep the land from being marketable like other commodities, we may be sure that power goes with knowledge and capital, and that, as their progress necessarily involves the distribution of a constantly increasing proportion to the many, the many will peacefully rise to equality of political rights. As government comes to be administered by the many, it is confined to the objects in which the many can agree. Its actual power is largely increased, while the practical exercise of it is limited. It is impartial, broad-based and stable. There is scarce a nation of Europe, in which greater and more numerous changes of internal administration have not been effected in the last thirty years, than in the United States since the landing of the Pilgrims, two hundred and thirty years ago. What changes have been effected with us have been almost silent and imperceptible, without convulsion or the dread of it. No constitutional alteration in any of the old States of our Confederacy, has been comparable in magnitude to the English Reform Bill of 1832. The revolution which disconnected us from the British Empire, only affected our foreign relations, without modifying in any substantial respect the internal political system which has prevailed in the States from their earliest settlement. That system has always rested in the free States—it must rest in all the States—upon the doctrine that the labourer is worthy of his hire—that his hire should be such as not merely to nourish his vegetative life, not merely to feed animal appetites, but to enable him to cultivate the powers and affections of a *man*,—the lord and master of the natural forces, in virtue of that reason by which he ascertains their laws, conforms to them, and controls them, and valuable to his employer above all cattle, in the degree to which that reason is cultivated and active—who can be induced to the exercise of his purely human powers, by appealing to the angel in man, the sense of justice that urges him to hearty work for fair wages, and the undying affections of his better nature, which enable him to reap the richest harvest of comfort in sowing prosperity for his children—a system under which, and under no other, the design of our common Father is accomplished, and for the poor labourer as for the rich capitalist it is true, "Like as the arrows in the hands of a giant, even so are the young children; blessed is the man that hath his quiver full of them."

We have thus far spoken of wages in general, without referring to the specific differences which characterize their rate in various employments. That difference of compensation which is given for skill in a particular employment, above the current rate, may obviously be discriminated as being, in fact, the profits of capital. Time, labour, expenses, laid out in acquiring skill in any species of industry, are not the less capital to the labourer because they are inseparable from his person. They demand and obtain a higher rate of profit than is paid for the use of more enduring capital, because they die with him. The price to be paid for the rent of a machine must not only compensate its present use, but furnish a fund to keep it in repair, or renew it when it is worn out. The labourer should get for his skill, not simply the interest upon the capital which it represents, but an amount in addition which will insure his life for a sum equal to its value. Unless he can obtain that, there is nc inducement for him to make the sacrifice necessary to purchase skill. It is not necessary to suppose that a close calculation is generally made upon the basis furnished by the tables of the Expectation of Life; but that a rough approximation should be attempted, upon some balancing of known hardship and abstinence, with rewards uncertain in their duration, is not to be doubted. Man forms his expectations, lays his plans, and follows them, with some eye to their net result in his entire lifetime, and does not voluntarily expend labour without the expectation that its equivalent will be returned to him, with a profit to remunerate him for any intervening delay, within what he reckons his probable life.

This consideration serves to account for the superior wages paid to those who labour in employments requiring a long apprenticeship, as well as for the premium paid to the possessor of unusual skill in any trade over those who have it in a less degree. There are, however, many employments in which individuals obtain wages vastly higher than others, who have devoted the same amount of labour to their education, even where they have brought to it the same grade of ability. Such differences are seen in the learned professions. One lawyer accumulates a fortune, while a dozen others, of equal talent and professional learning, obtain little if anything more than a decent subsistence, and another dozen spend years in waiting in vain for the first opportunity that shall enable them to demonstrate their ability, ekeing out a subsistence by other labour, in other walks than their profession, and finally abandon it in despair. In London, a great portion of the literary labour, editorial, reporting, &c., is the work of barristers waiting for their first brief; and many of them display every day a greater amount of mental ability, than makes the stock of men receiving the highest fees. Success at the bar is said to be like success in a lottery, where the few draw great prizes, that are made up from the losses of the many. Adam Smith thought that, at his day, the prizes were not high enough and numerous enough to make the lottery a fair one; and that this and some other professions and employments, in reference to which he uses this illustration, are on the whole underpaid; that is, that the entire gains of the whole body, if equally divided among them, gave a very slender return for the expenses of their education. That men continue to embark in them, he attributes to the "absurd presumption in their own good fortune," which the majority are prone to indulge. Mr. Senior, in commenting upon the passage, remarks that "Nothing sells so dearly as what is disposed of by a well-constructed lottery; and, if we wish to sell salaries dearly, that is, to obtain as much work and knowledge as possible for as little pay as possible, the best means is to dazzle the imagination with a few splendid prizes, and by magnificently overpaying one or two, to induce thousands to sell their services at half price." It is an unmixed evil that men should run a hazard of loss in training themselves for any services which the interests of society require. Where that hazard is unavoidable, however, a plain principle of justice demands that such a compensation as would induce the effort by all whom it is needful should attempt it, be distributed among those who succeed. If a thousand able-bodied Americans are required to work every day, to construct the Panama railroad, and they are to be paid by the day, and if it be ascertained that out of three thousand men on the ground two-thirds are each day found on the sick list, the least that is fair is, that every man who works should receive treble the wages that he would demand in a healthy climate. If it should happen that the misfortune of disabling sickness fall equally upon all, so that each should be sick two days out of every three, the equity of the arrangement would be manifest. If one or two of these, however, should have the good fortune to escape disease entirely, and go home at the year's end with three years' wages in his pocket, there would be just as little ground for complaint on the part of his employers or of his fellow-workmen. He took the risk of being sick all the while, for a premium, the amount of which was contingent; whether, in the event, it prove large or small, he has equally earned it. If the workmen were the slaves of a single owner, and the contractors for building the railroad should apply to him to rebate something from the extravagant pay he was entitled, by their agreement, to receive for the services of the two lucky individuals, he would have it in his power to silence them by footing up the pay-roll, and showing that though for John and Dick he got threefold, yet, taking the whole gang together, he received no more than he would have done had he employed them at the ordinary wages in a healthy climate. The reasoning is at least equally valid in the mouths of John and Dick, when they own themselves, and when their employers, instead of being a corporation, are isolated individuals, acting without concert, and buying services or the product of services as their wants dictate.

We can account in the same way for the large wages obtained by persons having extraordinary natural advantages. Jenny Lind could get a thousand dollars for singing a single evening: she has doubtless sung at the opera, where young females who sung in the chorus received less than a single dollar. Suppose, however, that some enterprising Barnum should determine that he would train up a new Jenny Lind, or at least a tolerable rival for her, for his own profit. He would at once see it necessary to multiply his chances of success, by making the experiment with a large number of persons — some hundreds or thousands. He would be at enormous charges for years in their musical education; and if at last he produced one prodigy of song, who could earn by her vocal powers the revenue of Jenny Lind, he would also have on his hands a number of inferior songstresses, who might draw crowded houses but for the superior attractions of his Prima Donna, and scores of chorus singers, whose earnings would not repay the outlay for their board, clothing, and education, to say nothing of the scores who died, lost their voices, or came to utter failure before earning anything.*

* This illustration is borrowed — substituting Jenny Lind for Rubini — from an able article by M. Quijano, in the Journal des Económistes, for May and June, 1852, in which the imaginary capitalist who has succeeded in raising a Rubini, answers a remonstrance against the extravagant price put upon his singing, by pointing to the fact, that the average compensation of the 2043 performers of all kinds in the twenty-five Theatres, Opera-houses, and Circuses of Paris, is but $328 per annum, and would be less, but for the fact that the Government grants in aid of the Theatres amount to about one-third of the aggregate salaries of their performers.

Quijano makes use of this illustration incidentally; the main purpose of his article being to show, that the enormous value of the *Clos Vougeot*, an estate producing a famous wine, is to be accounted for in the same way, and that it does not disprove the doctrine, that land derives all its value from labour. How many fortunes have been wasted in vain endeavours to find the proper spot, and make a vineyard which will produce such wine!

One of the circumstances which Adam Smith notes, as making up for a small pecuniary gain in some employments and counterbalancing it in others, is the agreeableness or disagreeableness of the employments themselves. So far as personal danger, such as attends the workman in a powder-mill, or unhealthiness, such as that of working in a manufactory of white lead, go to stamp an employment as disagreeable, the extra wages are to be referred in part to the hazard as to their duration. When this has been compensated, however, there is yet something to be paid for the sacrifice of the workman's personal comfort—as in the trade of a butcher, which is distasteful without being unhealthy. Moral as well as physical causes make an employment agreeable, or the reverse. The trade of an opera-dancer is one to which public opinion has attached a discredit, which none can be expected to suffer, justly or unjustly, without its being considered in their wages. On the contrary, the profession of a clergyman secures respect and consideration—things which wealth is valued as a means of procuring. Among the stings of poverty, the discredit which commonly attaches to it is not the least sharp: to a clergyman, however, it is no discredit to be poor, but rather an impeachment of his fidelity that he should not be Without regard to the fact, that those who are worthy of their calling look not for their reward in this world, we see that such approximation to reward as they do get, is paid in the respect they enjoy. The majority of them, probably, receive decidedly too large a proportion of their salaries in this airy coinage. It is unnecessary to enlarge upon the application of the same considerations to the rates of remuneration for which statesmen, men of letters, and some other classes, whose objects are not merely pecuniary, are content to work.

Suppose the fact be communicated to a vine-grower, that somewhere within a district 10,000 square miles in extent, a few acres existed, which by proper cultivation would equal Clos Vougeot in the quality of its wines, and the offer to be made, either to communicate the secret of their precise location, for a sum equal to the present market value of that vineyard, or to sell the same number of acres, to be selected by himself, at the average value of the entire tract—which offer would it be wise for him to accept? In accepting the first, what is it that he pays for, except the labour saved in making a multitude of unprofitable experiments?

The constancy or inconstancy of employment in them, is another of the circumstances pointed out in the "Wealth of Nations," as affecting the comparative wages of different trades. A mason or a bricklayer, it is said, can work neither in hard frost nor in foul weather; and what he earns while he is employed must not only maintain him while he is idle, but, Dr. Smith suggests, "make him some compensation for those anxious and desponding moments, which the thought of so precarious a situation must sometimes occasion." A year is the least period that includes the vicissitudes of the seasons, and of the varying wants which they respectively involve. The expenses of subsistence, fuel, shelter, lights, &c., cannot be gauged, except by including the whole year; and the practical question about the sufficiency of wages is, therefore, not what are they per diem, but what do they amount to in the course of twelve months. The remarks already offered in respect to the element of chance, in other forms, will suggest to the student all that he requires in relation to the particular one now mentioned.

It is, however, worthy of particular notice, that the want of steadiness of employment is a prevailing evil in the early stages of society, and diminishes with its progress in the diversification of industry, and the increase of wealth. When the whole population is devoted to husbandry, it is much more than sufficient for the ordinary labours of tillage, and a great deal of time is spent in idleness. In harvest, on the contrary, there is for a few days an extraordinary demand for labourers; a demand which is pressing in proportion to that poverty of machinery, both in quantity and quality, which attend such a condition of society. The accounts of the manor of Hansted, in Suffolk, at the close of the fourteenth century, show that in one year 520 persons were hired for one day; in another year, 533; and in a third, 538; and yet the number of acres to be reaped did not exceed 200.* The wages paid for such temporary employment must obviously provide subsistence for long periods of idleness, and are no criterion of the earnings of the year. From inattention to this circumstance, very erroneous inferences have been drawn from statements of the amount paid for harvest wages in the early periods of English history, and the labourers have been supposed to be able to command

* Pictorial History of England, vol. 1, page 811.

an amount of food and clothing, which is totally inconsistent with the uncontrovertible fact of their general misery, as well as with the rates of wages in permanent employments.

The only circumstance mentioned by Adam Smith in this connection, to which we have not already referred, is the small or great trust which must be reposed in the workman. He instances goldsmiths and jewellers, as being paid higher wages than other workmen of equal or superior ingenuity, on account of the precious materials with which they are entrusted. We may account for the excess of wages due to this cause, by considering it as the reward of past efforts on the part of the workman to establish a character for honesty, which makes a part of his immaterial capital, as his mechanical skill does. To the employer, it is a premium paid for the insurance of his property against loss by fraud—differing from other kinds of insurance, in that it serves to diminish the temptations to inflict the loss. If a considerable premium is anywhere paid on this account, it proves that the general rate of wages is so low as to have demoralized the labouring class, rather than anything else; just as the payment of black-mail to the cattle-stealers of the Scotch Highlands proved that the population was sparse and the country poor.

The different circumstances which have been referred to, operate in the way of increasing or diminishing the number of persons, able and disposed to compete for employment in the different walks of industry. The doctrine sought to be established by the Economists is, that the wages paid for the various species of labour in a country, are, all the compensating circumstances taken into account, equal, or always tending to equality. They are said to be always *finding* their level; "which," in the words of Coleridge, "might be taken as a paraphrase or ironical definition of a storm." The discussion possesses little interest; nearly the whole result of it being to determine what is meant by the word "wages."

The preceding remarks have all gone upon the supposition that there are no artificial restraints, by which individuals are prevented from freely selecting that kind of labour which accords best with their capacities and inclinations. Unfortunately, such restraints are embodied in the legislation of most countries. There are very few of them in the United States. I am not aware of any vestige of them remaining in the Statutes of the State of New York. Laws fixing the period of apprenticeship to the various trades; acts incorporating the members of particular trades, and enabling them to establish by-laws, limiting the number of apprentices that an employer should take; laws prohibiting a person from engaging in more than one department of industry, such as that which in England required the wheels of a carriage to be made by one set of workmen, at one shop, while the body was made by another set at another shop, because the trades of wheelwright and carriage-maker had been erected into quasi monopolies, and their combination in the same person pronounced illegal—will serve as specimens of the kind of legislation to which we refer. It can hardly be necessary to frame an argument for their condemnation; nor can a more conclusive one be found than that of Adam Smith. He says:

"The property which every man has in his own labour, as it is the original foundation of all other property, so it is the most sacred and inviolable. The patrimony of a poor man lies in the strength and dexterity of his hands; and to hinder him from employing this strength and dexterity in whatever way he thinks proper, without injury to his neighbour, is a plain violation of this most sacred property. It is a manifest encroachment upon the just liberty, both of the workman and of those who might be disposed to employ him. As it hinders the one from working at what he thinks proper, so it hinders the others from employing whom they think proper. To judge whether he is fit to be employed, may surely be trusted to the discretion of the employers, whose interest it so much concerns."—*Wealth of Nations, Book I., chap.* 10, *part* 2.

That the interest of the community is to be promoted by everything that tends to insure the greatest industry of the greatest number; and that everything which hinders a man from working at a trade which he likes, and confines him to an employment which he dislikes, tends to cramp and limit his efficiency, are propositions, the soundness of which is, we trust, sufficiently apparent. We fully agree with Adam Smith in his earnest defence of the freedom of labour. To trammel it by voluntary combinations, is equally prejudicial to the general interest as if the same object were effected by legislative interference, and equally condemned by the great body of Economists. Mr. J. S. Mill, however, is reconciled to such combinations, for reasons which we will present in his own language. After stating that, "In several trades the workmen have been able to make it almost impracticable for strangers to obtain admission, either as journeymen or as apprentices, except in limited numbers and under such restrictions as they choose to impose;" and protesting against the acts of atrocity sometimes committed by way of personal outrage or intimidation, he declares, in regard to such combinations,

"In so far as they do succeed in keeping up the wages of any trade by limiting its numbers, I look upon them as simply intrenching round a particular spot against the inroads of over-population, and making their wages depend upon their own rate of increase, instead of depending on that of a more reckless and improvident class than themselves. And I should rejoice, if, by trade regulations, or even by Trades-Unions, the employments thus specially protected, could be multiplied to a much greater extent than experience has shown to be practicable. What at first sight seems the injustice of excluding the more numerous class from sharing the gains of a comparatively few, disappears, when we consider that, by being admitted, they would not be made better off for more than a short time; the only permanent effect which their admission would produce, would be to lower the others to their own level. * * * * * * On similar grounds, if there were no other escape from that fatal immigration of Irish, which has done, and is doing so much to degrade the condition of our agricultural, and some classes of our town population, *I should see no injustice, and the greatest possible expediency, in checking that destructive inroad by protective laws.* But there is a better mode of putting an end to this mischief, namely, by improving the condition of the Irish themselves; and England owes an atonement to Ireland for past injuries, which she ought to suffer almost any inconvenience rather than fail to make good, by using her power in as determined a manner for the elevation of that unfortunate people, as she used it through so many dreary centuries for their abasement and oppression."—*Political Economy, vol.* 1, *page* 481.

This passage shows us Malthusianism issuing in a defence of re straints upon the freedom of labour. To limit the number of labourers in any craft is to limit the production of the commodities which it furnishes—to restrict exchanges by restricting the supply of the materials of exchange—to enhance prices by the creation of a monopoly. Free trade and free labour cannot be disjoined. What reply could Mr. Mill make to an American Protectionist who should say, "The same causes which drive Irishmen to England, drive hundreds of thousands of them to the United States annually, who, if they were not here, labouring in our trades, would be in England. Instead of excluding *them,* we see no injustice, and the greatest possible expediency, in excluding from our markets the fabrics made by an equal number of Englishmen, the introduction of which would produce precisely the same amount of competition with our labour, as would the labourers themselves, if they worked on this side of the Atlantic instead of the other. This is the method by which we propose to prevent the reduction of wages." It would scarcely serve for an answer, that, by so doing the American would raise the prices of domestic fabrics; for the Protectionist might concede this—which he would not—and yet reply that Mr. Mill deemed this no objection to restrictions upon competition in labour at home. We do not intend to say that such is the argument which an American Protectionist would offer, nor to express an opinion at present in regard to its force. The object is simply to show, into what inconsistencies the necessities of a false system may compel so acute and enlightened a writer as Mr. Mill, and to leave it to the reader to judge whether the doctrines of Malthus and Ricardo conduce to freedom of trade. The answer to Mr. Mill which the reader, who has thus far concurred in our reasoning, would make, is, "That the growth of population tends to raise wages, not to lower them — that the source of the evil is to be found, not in the free operation of the laws of our beneficent Creator, but in efforts to evade or thwart them — and the remedy to be sought, by conforming to those laws instead of intrenching against them.

The effect of improvements in machinery upon wages is a problem, which is solved, so far as the permanent results are concerned, by the considerations heretofore presented. Wages steadily rise with every increase in the aid contributed by the natural agents. It is doubtless true, that the immediate and temporary effect upon those whose toil is superseded by inanimate and gratuitous workers, is sometimes distressing. Until we have examined the subject of Exchange, we shall be unprepared to describe the process through which that distress is alleviated, new employment provided for those whom machinery may expel from their old, and the general benefit to community finally apportioned so that a due share of it comes to them. Previous to 1828, when planks were prepared for flooring by manual labour, a skilful and vigorous mechanic could prepare ten or fifteen planks, equal to one hundred feet, in a day, at a cost of $2. Woodworth's planing machine prepares 5000 feet in a day, at an expense of $10, doing the work of fifty men at one-tenth the cost. Forty-five of the fifty are rendered disposable for other labour. Five are still required, to prepare materials for making the machine, to make it, to get fuel, &c., for running it, to tend it, &c.; for the whole cost of running the machinery may be resolved into the wages of present labour, or of past labour, which needs renewal. It is evident that the body of purchasers of flooring could as well afford to maintain the forty-five carpenters in idleness, paying them $2 a day, as to dispense with the machine. They have among them $90 per day, their gross savings in the cost of flooring, which is quite likely to be expended in carpentry work; since the diminution of the cost of one considerable item in house-building, enables those to build who were before unable. If not, it is expended in maintaining labour in other departments of industry, to which the superseded carpenters may resort for employment; and then, when they become purchasers of flooring, they share in the common benefit, the saving of nine-tenths in the cost of its preparation. Defective social arrangements may protract the period, in which the adjustment of things to the new circumstances would otherwise be effected. If, for instance, the forty-five men skilled in the use of the plane, the chisel, and the saw, should be shut off from working at making doors, because the door-makers were endowed by the legislature with power to confine such employment to their own apprentices; or, if these were tolerated, in the absence of legislation, in combinations for the same purpose, upon the plea that they were simply "intrenching against the inroads of over-population"; in such case we should find that population had suddenly become excessive by forty-five surplus individuals, without a single additional birth, without a particle of diminution in the means of society to feed and clothe all its members; but, on the contrary, with a positive increase in the potential labour of forty-five men, who, if they were slaves, would exchange in the market for at least 45,000 bushels of wheat, and as freemen are worth 90,000. If these men should be driven to the Poor-house, the followers of Malthus would accuse their ninety fathers and mothers of over-population; the men themselves might lay the crime at the door of Mr. Woodworth, the father of the planing machine: while we esteem them alike the benefactors of community — the first, in furnishing the State with citizens capable of a thousand things besides shoving a plane — the second, for transferring to wood and iron the toil which formerly consumed human muscle. The only error is in a false dogma, and the mischievous arrangements it helps to perpetuate.

CHAPTER VI.

PROFITS.

We have treated Profits and Wages as the shares of the Capitalist and the Labourer, in the product resulting from their combination. Each, in point of fact, contributes capital. The food of the preceding day, transformed into muscular and nervous fibre in the labourer's body, may be the whole of his part. It is a small one, and is expended in the course of a few hours; that is, is transformed, through the vital mechanism, into force, exerted upon the materials of the greater capitalist, and changing their form or location. It is necessary that it should be restored to him immediately, or his ability to exert force is exhausted; and it must be restored with some addition, bearing the same relation to the little capital that profits do to the greater, or the disposition to labour will fail, though the physical ability may continue. It is seldom, however, restored in kind. The employer of a slave, indeed, supplies him with food, raiment, and shelter; but the free labourer is ordinarily paid in money, which he transforms into materials for his physical renovation, at his own discretion. The money, moreover, from which the wages of a month or a week are paid, is not provided long in advance, but is supplied from day to day, by the sale of the commodities or the services in which the employer deals. The materials also undergo such transformations, as to prevent the direct comparison of their quantity with that of the product. Ore, limestone, coal—the grain, meat, &c., on which the labourer subsists, are virtually fused together, and run out of the furnace in the shape of a mass of iron, whose bulk and weight are many times less than those of the elements whose utilities are incorporated in it. For such reasons, the comparison between the advances of the capitalist and the return, is made, not by their quantities, but by their relative value. In practice, it is the difference between the *price* of the advances and the return, by which the profits are estimated. For the short period usually intervening between the beginning and the end of an industrial enterprise, value and price may generally be regarded as identical, or at least as differing by the same proportion at the two dates. In either case, the ratio between the price of the advance and that of the returns, will correspond with that of their values, and enable the capitalist to express his loss or gain, by the aliquot part that the deficiency or excess constitutes of the original capital. He computes that he has made or lost, as the case may be, three, six, or ten per cent. As his wants, like those of the labourer, vary with the seasons, but recur each year, and as the element of time enters into every calculation of profit — because the frequency with which operations can be repeated determines the gross amount of gain that can be realized—it is usual to denote the growth of capital by the per centage added to it in a year.

To an individual, the increase in the *value* of his capital, not in its quantity, is the point of vital concern. If he produced for the purpose of consuming in his own person and in his family the identical commodities which he produces, the annual addition to their quantity would determine his means of enjoyment. This supposition is true, however, only of the savage. Men in civilized countries produce for the sake of exchanging the products of their industry with each other. The man who makes ploughs does not use them to prepare the earth for raising his own food, and may never turn a furrow in his life. The men who grow corn eat but a small portion of their crop, and exchange the remainder for agricultural implements, for clothing, for books, &c. Each one, therefore, measures his progress in the year by the command which the increment to his capital—his profits—gives him over the labour of others, either in their future services, or as embodied in commodities — services already in the shape in which he desires them; in other words, by the value of his profits.

The capital of a society is the same as that of all the individuals who compose it. The aggregate of the additions which each has made to his capital, is the increase of the capital of the nation. It is natural enough, therefore, to jump to the conclusion, that the progress of a community in wealth is measured by the prevailing rate of profit; that when its citizens find by their annual balance-sheets that they are gaining six per cent. upon their capitals, the nation is accumulating capital twice as fast as when they gain but three per cent., and producing twice as much of the materials on which the physical comfort of its people depends. There is a fallacy in this conclusion, which lurks in the reasoning of many Economical writers, though not always distinctly expressed in their language, and which has infected the policy of nations. "To transfer," says Mr. Mill, "hastily and inconsiderately to the general point of view, propositions which are true of the individual, has been a source of innumerable errors in Political Economy." In another place he writes, "With Mr. M'Culloch, prosperity does not mean a large production and a good distribution of wealth, but a rapid increase of it; his test of prosperity is high profits." We cite this passage, not merely because it is an instance of the error to which we refer, in Mr. M'Culloch, but as showing it to be at least doubtful whether Mr. Mill himself does not regard high profits as the evidence of a rapid increase in national capital.

The fact which is overlooked in the hasty deduction, which measures the advance of national capital by the rate of profit, as individuals compute it, is, that while the individual does not personally consume his own products, the nation does consume the products of the industry and capital of its people. It is doubtless true, that some portion of the products of its domestic industry is exported, to be consumed abroad. This, however, instead of being a large, is a very small proportion of the commodities annually brought to market. The great mass of the exchanges effected by every nation, are made within their own borders, and its exports are of trifling amount compared with its internal consumption. The exports of the United States constitute but about five per cent. in value of their annual production; those of England, the greatest exporting nation in the world, are ordinarily below one-tenth of the products of its industry. The prosperity of its people is measured, not by the value, but by the *quantity* of the annual increment to its capital. In the year preceding the census of 1850, there were produced in the United States, 592,141,230 bushels of Indian corn, and 100,479,150 bushels of wheat. In the same year, 7,632,860 bushels, in corn and meal, and 7,535,901 bushels, in wheat and flour, were exported. An individual wheat-grower is indifferent whether his crop, after supplying him with seed and what is consumed in his family, leaves him 400 bushels, to be sold at 75 cents a bushel, or 300, to be sold at $1. But, to the 25,000,000 of people in the United States, the difference between a crop of 75,000,000 and one of 100,000,000 of bushels, is, that in the one case there is three, and in the other four bushels for each of them. If the crop of the next year should rise to 125,000,000, it would be a positive addition to the national capital and prosperity; though its value, or the profits of the wheat-growers, estimated by value, should prove less instead of more than in a year when the crop was but 75,000,000. What is true of wheat is true of every other product, of the growth and manufacture of the country. It is the increase in their quantity, not in their value, on which the national well-being depends—and this is not indicated by the rate of profit. We have seen, indeed, that as labour becomes more productive, and the increase of capital more rapid, the *rate* of profit declines, though the absolute quantity of commodities which the capitalist can obtain for the use of his capital is enlarged, because their value diminishes more than the rate of profit. The gratuitous co-operation of the forces of Nature adds immensely to the capital of a nation, without adding to its value. Book-keeping by double entry makes no account of this on the merchant's ledger, and the statesman must, therefore, go to other sources of information to ascertain the rate of his country's progress in wealth.

Mr. M'Culloch holds the following language:—

"As capital is nothing more than the accumulated produce of previous industry, it is evident its increase will be most rapid when industry is most productive; or, in other words, when *the profits of stock are highest.** The man who can produce a bushel of wheat in *three* days, has it in his power to accumulate twice as much as the man who, either from a deficiency of skill, or from his being obliged to cultivate a bad soil, is forced to labour six days to produce the same quantity; and the capitalist who can invest stock so as to yield him a profit of *ten per cent.*, has it equally in his power

* Mr. M'Culloch adds the following note to this passage:—

"To avoid all chance of misconception, it is necessary to observe that this refers to *net* profit, or to the sum which remains to the capitalist after all his outgoings are compensated, including therein a sum sufficient to insure his capital against risk, and to make up for whatever may be peculiarly disagreeable in his business."

to accumulate twice as fast as the capitalist who can only obtain *five per cent.* for his capital. Conformably to this statement, it is found that the rate of profit, or, which is the same thing, the power to accumulate capital, is always greatest in those countries which are most rapidly augmenting their wealth and population. * * * * * We have no hesitation in laying it down as a principle which holds good in every case, and from which there is really no exception, that if the governments of any two or more countries be equally liberal, and property in each equally well secured, their comparative prosperity will depend on the rate of profit. Wherever profits are high there is a great demand for labour, and the society rapidly augments both its population and its riches. On the other hand, wherever they are low the demand for labour is proportionably reduced, and the progress of society rendered so much the slower." — *Principles of Political Economy, Chap. ii. Sec.* 3 *of Part I.*

If we understand Mr. M'Culloch in this passage, he uses "rate of profits" in the ordinary mercantile sense, and believes that it is a true measure of the growth of a nation's capital. We have sufficiently elucidated the misconception upon which this belief rests. We cannot dismiss the quotation, however, without referring to one of the consequences of that error, which it briefly indicates. Capital, it is argued, is the fund for the support and employment of labour. The increase of labourers and of industry depends upon the increase in the quantity of capital, and is limited by it. There can be no more industry than is supplied with materials to work up and food to eat. These propositions may be freely admitted, without conceding that the demand for labour is proportioned to the rate of profit, in the mercantile sense. A barrel of flour will maintain a labourer in equal health and efficiency for no longer period when it costs him ten days' labour than when it costs him five. It will enable him to exert the same amount of mechanical force in working up a ton of iron into plough-shares, whether those plough-shares command fifty days' labour or twenty-five; and more plough-shares are likely to be demanded by farmers at the cheap rate than the dear. It is the aggregate of a country's production that measures its power to maintain and employ labour, and if the aggregate value of a given quantity is smaller at one time than another, it proves that labour is efficient, and has increased power to command the necessaries and conveniences of life. The largest amount of these is distributed to labour, and the profits of the capitalist also command the largest amount, when the *rate* of profit is low.

We have said that the fallacy of which we are treating infects the reasoning of many Economists. It lies at the ground of one of the arguments against protective duties. These, it is urged in substance, can never increase the industry of a country unless they increase the rate of profit; and this cannot be effected by transferring capital from employments in which they were securing the usual rate, to others which require protection, because without it they would give an inferior rate. If the protected employments are brought up to the current rate of profit, by giving to those who engage in them the ability to demand higher prices for their products, than those at which they can be procured from abroad, the excess is taken from the pockets of the consumers, and it is merely a transfer of capital from one body of consumers to another, without any addition to the general stock, but at a positive loss, in the substitution of a less profitable for a more profitable employment. Of the validity of the argument in other respects this is not the place to speak; but the considerations we have presented show, that it fails to disprove the alleged advantages of a protective system, in providing increased employment for domestic industry. It is pertinent, moreover, to the point under immediate discussion, to remark that a confusion of the *amount* of profits with their rate, may taint the argument in another particular. The publisher of this book will prefer to obtain a profit of five cents upon each of three thousand copies, rather than ten cents each upon a single thousand. A large part of his outlay, in type-setting, stereotyping, &c., will be the same in one case as the other; his fixed capital, in presses, buildings, &c., is the same in either event. The small amount of profit upon each copy will, I imagine, give a greater rate upon his capital, as well as a greater aggregate, and the sale of the greater number will cheapen its cost to the purchaser. In like manner, the producers of a protected commodity may be enabled to secure the rate of profit usual in unprotected employments, by having an extended sale secured to *them*, instead of its being shared by foreigners, not only without any increase of cost to the consumer, but by virtue of its diminution.

It is not to be inferred that any real conflict exists between the collective interest of a people and that of an individual. His interest, while he is engaged in the production of any commodity, is promoted by its requiring little labour, and, therefore, being able to command little labour in exchange. It is only when it is finished, and he assumes the character of a trader in respect to it, that an apparent discrepancy between his interest and that of the community of consumers begins to show itself. While, however, he is the producer of but one, or, at most, of a very few kinds of commodities, he is the consumer of a great variety. A great profit upon the sale of that one is delusive and fruitless, if it will procure him but few objects of consumption when he comes to expend it. The farmer desires that the labour he devotes to the cultivation of a field shall result in a large crop of corn. He wants cotton for clothing, and he therefore desires the crop of cotton should be large; for, when it is so, more cotton will be obtained for a given quantity of corn than when the cotton crop is small and the corn crop large. His interest requires that a large stock of all the commodities he may need should come to market, and, to this end, that labour may be everywhere efficient and in constant activity. If it be so, the share of the aggregate production coming to each member of community, will grow from year to year, unless population increases more rapidly than capital.

We have shown that, in the natural course of things, the capital of a nation increases in a more rapid ratio than its value, and, therefore, that the amount of the increase is greater than would be indicated by the rate of profit. If the latter is six per cent., then we may infer that more than six per cent. in quantity has been added in a year to the stock of good things which provide subsistence and comfort for its people. It is of so much consequence that this proposition should be thoroughly understood and established, that, at the risk of needless repetition, we may be pardoned for a further illustration. Mr. Ericsson is now testing his Caloric engine. If it succeeds according to his anticipations, it will save four-fifths of the coal which is consumed in producing the same effect in a steam-engine. Suppose its power to come up to the calculation of the inventor, and that it shall be substituted for every steam-engine now at work in the United States, the same amount of labour which now mines coal, transports it to the steam-engines, feeds their furnaces, and directs the forces they bring into productive action. will accomplish the same effect, if exerted in the same way to keep caloric engines at work; but, by the side of each of these will lie a pile of coal at the end of the year, sufficient to keep them in motion for four years longer. The industry exerted in providing the coal, and the various commodities, cloth, iron, machinery, &c., in the making of which the engines are employed, will possess no more *value* than it does at present, nor will the articles which the engines have assisted in making; but the country will be richer by the heaps of unburnt coal — by the power of running its engines for four years without any cost for fuel. It is needless to say that this is not the shape in which the facts will present themselves. The value of the coal that is saved will disappear from the articles manufactured by the caloric engine, and the purchasers of those articles will use the money which is left in their pockets, as the difference between the new and the old price, to buy the coal to warm their houses, or for other conveniences. Now, what we conjecture in this case, is actually taking place every day. It happens every time that a stream, whose waters have been running to waste for centuries, is made to turn the wheel of a mill; every time that a mechanical invention, or a discovery in practical chemistry, wrests fresh power from unpaid Nature. In every instance, the aggregate production is enlarged in a greater ratio than the sum of value, or the rate of profit. Each item in the aggregate constitutes demand for labour,* because it will reward labour — will tempt somebody to work, as the means of getting it; or, if not in the finished state and ready for consumption, requires further labour for its completion.

The ratio of increase of national capital being more than commensurate with the rate of profit, we may be sure that, if the rate of increase in population does not exceed the latter, it cannot equal the former. Every country in an advanced state of civilization takes

---

* "The demand for labour increases with the increase of stock, whatever be its profits; and, after these are diminished, stock may not only continue to increase, but to increase much faster than before. It is with industrious nations, who are advancing in the acquisition of riches, as with industrious individuals. A great stock, though with small profits, generally increases faster than a small stock with great profits."— *Wealth of Nations, Book I., chap.* 9.

measures for ascertaining periodically the rate of its progress in numbers. A registry of births and deaths is kept in England France, Holland, and other countries, which furnishes the information for each year; and the census, taken at periods of five or ten years, furnishes the corrections necessary by reason of emigration and immigration. Holland is, and long has been a country, in which the rate of profit is proverbially small—money being lent at two per cent. interest to Government, and to individuals at three, when the British Government paid three and a half and four per cent., and individuals borrowed at five per cent., and often more. In Holland, nevertheless, the rate of annual increase of the population has been but about one per cent., while in France, Belgium, and Austria, it has been somewhat less. If we go to the other extreme, we shall find that the rate of annual increase of the population in the United States, since 1790, has been about three per cent., while the rate of profit is ordinarily assumed to be six per cent. Few, perhaps, have reflected how very trifling an annual increase of capital is required, to keep it in advance of population. An advance each year upon the last, of 2·81 per cent., will double population in twenty-five years. Capital increasing in the same way, that is, at compound interest, at three per cent., will double in about twenty-two years and eleven months; and in twenty-five years will amount to 9·48 per cent. more than double the original amount. If capital increased at the rate of five per cent., it would amount in twenty-five years to 3·38 times its original sum; and, if a new division of property were made, it would give to each member of the doubled society a quantity represented by 169, in place of 100, which would have been the share of each (but half in number) at the commencement. If the process continue a second period of twenty-five years, population will have quadrupled, and capital swelled to 11·46 times its original amount; sufficient to provide each individual with a quantity represented by 286, where his father had 169, and his grandfather 100. Such calculations may serve to show how far from necessary it is that the general comfort of a people should deteriorate, or that the natural growth of the population should be restrained, to prevent its deterioration, in consequence of an imaginary tendency in the race to outgrow the means of its support.

It is not to be doubted that it is in the power of misgovernment to retard the growth of capital, and so to affect the distribution of what is accumulated, as to keep the great body of the people miserably poor, and apparently doomed to beget children to be poorer than themselves. The most effective means is, to waste capital in war, and to abstract men from industrial occupations to train them for future wars, burdening the labour of the country with the cost of their maintenance. Nearly one hundred and fifty millions of dollars are annually taken from the earnings of the people in the British Islands, to pay the interest on its national debt; and the taxes are so adjusted, that far the greater portion of this enormous charge is a burden on the wages of labour. Fifty millions more are annually taken from the accumulations of labour, and expended in paying fleets and armies, to maintain a dominion over distant colonies, that they may be compelled to abstain from the production of all those things which the mill-owners and shopkeepers of Britain desire to sell, and to bring to *them* for sale the food and raw materials they desire to buy. The great majority of the people are burdened with the support of a church establishment, whose teachings they reject, mainly because they regard themselves as taxed for them without their consent. For two hundred years the peasant has been chained to his parish by the poor-law system: for other parishes will not suffer him to gain a settlement, lest the cost of his support should increase their poor-rates. One result is, that he is in many parts of England compelled to walk four or five miles in the morning to his work, and as many more back to his bed at night. The farmers in some districts, for the purpose of economizing the strength of their labourers, furnish them with donkeys to bear them on their daily journeys. From 1765 to 1824 artizans were prohibited, under heavy penalties, from leaving the kingdom, lest the people of other countries should become instructed in manufactures, and relieved in some degree from the necessity of being customers at the workshops of the Islanders. During the same period they were prohibited from making, for exportation, nearly all the machinery and implements, in the construction of which they possessed greater skill than foreign machinists. In 1824 these prohibitions were so far relaxed, as to vest a discretionary power in the Board of Trade to permit the exportation of such machinery as it should deem proper; but it is only within the last ten years that they have been entirely removed. Various restrictions have been imposed, for the sake of the collection of the revenue, upon the modes of manufacturing articles subject to internal or excise duties, which have operated to impede and trammel industry. Under such a system it is not strange that the remuneration of labour should have been so low, as to have rendered any accumulation from wages impossible for the great body of the people, and to have confined the increase of capital, as a general thing, to the savings from profits. Nor is it strange that Economists, observing the practical state of facts, should have mistaken the results of human interference for the consequence of natural laws. Those who have convinced themselves that it is the normal and necessary condition of all old countries, that "the habitual price of labour is that which will just enable the labourers, one with another, to purchase the commodities, without which they will not consent to continue the race," will readily look to the rate of profits, as determining the increase of national capital; and a legislature which is guided by their counsels, will shape the policy of the country with a view of protecting the traders against a depreciation in the rate of profit, instead of increasing its gross production. Such for the past half century has been the policy which has controlled and still controls the legislation of Great Britain. It has, in practice, regarded the nation collectively as a gigantic trader with the rest of the world, possessing a great stock of goods, not for use but for sale, endeavouring to produce them cheaply, so that it might undersell rival shopkeepers, and looking upon the wages paid to its own people as so much lost to the profits of the establishment. If such be the true idea of a nation, then has England been wisely counselled, and done well. If, on the contrary, the true conception of a State is that of a Household, whose members have undivided interests, but whose common profit is in the increase of the general store, and the fair distribution of it, then England has much to unlearn, and in the place of it to know that, in the words of Carlyle: "Deep, far deeper than supply and demand, are laws, obligations, sacred as man's life itself: these also, if you will continue to do work, you will now learn and obey. He that will learn them, behold Nature

13 *

is on his side; he shall get work and prosper, with noble rewards. He that will not learn them, Nature is against him; he shall not be able to do work in Nature's Empire. Perpetual mutiny, hatred, isolation, execration shall wait on his footsteps, till all men discern that the thing which he attains, however golden it look or be, is not success but the want of success."

Great Britain is by no means singular either in the waste of her capital by war, or in restrictions upon the freedom of labour. France, though not now burdened with a national debt of equal magnitude, has for centuries devoted a greater proportion of the energies of her people to the work of destruction, and at the present time keeps nearly half a million of her men—picked men in point of physical ability, as the soldiers of all nations are—carrying muskets on land or exercising great guns at sea, while *women* do the work in the fields that these men ought to be doing. The extent to which her government interferes in various ways, in regulating, and thereby hampering and impeding the industry of her people, is almost incredible. About half a million civil functionaries, of all grades, are employed in the immense amount of *overseeing* which the government takes upon itself. In most of the other Continental States labour is so burdened by unproductive governmental expenditures, and by annoying and costly restrictions, as to reduce its compensation below that of England.* There is some recompense, however,

* "It has been reckoned or conjectured that on the continent in general, taking civil, military, and educational functionaries — the clergy, schoolmasters, and professors being included under the latter denomination—and taking all the financial, legal, and police officers, there are, for every thousand of the total population, men, women, and children, sixty adult men, living by office, place, or appointment under the government. This may be no exaggerated view, if we consider that, besides the regular functionaries in every parish, village, or other locality, who are paid directly by government, there is a very great class of licensed practitioners in every profession and branch of industry, such as the schoolmaster, lawyer, surgeon, apothecary, midwife, farrier, shopkeeper, who have a government license and appointment to a monopoly of their trade, or means of living, in their respective districts. They are in reality civil functionaries, paid by the people, and living on them, as if they were functionaries paid directly out of the taxes."—*Laing's Denmark and the Duchies, page* 60.

in the fact, that the Continental governments have facilitated the subdivision of the land into small parcels, and its cheap and easy transmission from one owner to another. The effect has been to render it no difficult thing for the labouring class to cease to be mere labourers for hire, and to pass, by the purchase of a small piece of land, into the rank of capitalists, working upon their own account. The small farmers cultivate their property with an assiduity, economy, and skill, that render it productive to the highest degree—a degree far surpassing that of land occupied in large masses by leasehold tenants, and worked by labourers for hire. They add each year the largest amount to the gross capital of the country. The wisdom of the Continental governments in this particular, has done much to repair the waste which their military extravagance occasions, and more than counterbalances the advantages which the superior freedom of industry, in other than agricultural employments, secures to the people of Great Britain. At all events, it effects a much more equal and just distribution of the aggregate gains of the nation.

"The peasant," says Sismondi, "who, with his family, does all the work on his little inheritance, who neither pays rent to any one above him, nor wages to any one below him, who regulates his production by his consumption, who eats his own corn, drinks his own wine, and is clothed with his own flax and wool, *cares little about knowing the price of the market;* for he has little to sell and little to buy, and is never ruined by the revolutions of commerce." The rulers over a nation of such peasants, however little of direct participation in the government the latter may enjoy, cannot avoid being

---

"In Germany every trade is exercised by privilege and license, paid for to the State, and in towns to the municipality as well as to the State. The bakers of Leipsic pay 1200 dollars each for his share of the exclusive privilege of baking bread for sale in the city. In Hamburgh every butcher pays, it is said, 10,000 dollars for his privilege to kill and sell meat in that city. * * * Every trade and handicraft, baking, butchering, shoemaking, tailoring, in short, every imaginable branch of industry, above unskilled common hand-labour, is carried on by license, paid for according to the value of the monopoly in the particular locality, and taxed to the State upon the same principle as other property is taxed, viz., by the yearly value of the protected trade."—*Laing's Denmark and the Duchies, page* 106.

affected by the general tone of their opinions and sentiments. Their policy will be dictated by the instincts of producers, and not by that of shopkeepers. They will look to the aggregate of production, not to the rate of profits in trade, as the test of national prosperity. Accordingly, the great continental nations, France, Russia, the German States — united in the Zollverein or Customs Union — have practically repudiated the idea which has so long controlled the commercial policy of England. What England has gained by that policy is thus described by one of her own learned and respected writers,* who speaks of that nation as the one "where the aristocracy is richer and more powerful than that of any other country in the world, *the poor are more oppressed, more pauperized, more numerous in comparison to the other classes, more irreligious, and very much worse educated than the poor of any other European nation, solely excepting uncivilized Russia and Turkey, enslaved Italy, misgoverned Portugal, and revolutionized Spain.*"

In the preceding remarks we have treated of capital as actually employed in production by its owner, or under his immediate personal supervision, and have spoken of a general rate of profits as if there was a uniformity in the returns received by different individuals. This is true, only in the same sense that it may be affirmed that wages in the various employments may be regarded as being, at the same time and place, all compensating circumstances taken into account, either equal or always tending towards equality. The same general considerations which were indicated in the discussion of that subject, will guide the student in his inquiries upon this head.

It has been shown in a preceding chapter that what are called Profits, when capital is put to use by its owner at his own risk, and what is called Rent or Interest, when it is borrowed by another, to be employed at his risk, are really the same thing — that a certain and liquidated Profit is called Rent or Interest, and a contingent and indeterminate Rent or Interest is called Profit. The principal circumstances which serve to obscure the perception of their identity are the following:

* Joseph Kay, of Trinity College, Cambridge, at the close of his work on National Education.

The person who devotes his own physical and mental labour to superintending the transformations which his own capital undergoes, in the processes of growth, manufacture, or exchange, earns *wages.* They are not paid to him, however, in any distinct sum, or by any particular individual or number of individuals, but result from the gross return in the whole course of his transactions. They may fail for a year, or even for a series of years, to be paid at all. To estimate what amount should be referred to the head of wages, the capitalist would consider the sum he would have to pay, upon the supposition that he should entirely abandon the care of his property to a manager. What would he have to pay an agent to secure the same skill, the same anxious vigilance and untiring pains, the same integrity to his interest that he can reckon on in himself? Nor is it simply the sum certain which would secure such services that he is to reckon as his own wages, for the latter are generally more or less uncertain. The problem is, what would the entirely competent and trustworthy manager demand, if the capitalist should make his salary contingent upon the success of his operations. Suppose him to ask for a proposal in this manner:

"I intend to commit to your charge a capital, which I can convert into $100,000 of money, and which I can lend to the State of New York at an interest of five per cent., not only with an absolute certainty that the interest will be regularly paid, and the sum lent reimbursed to me at the expiration of the term of the loan, but with the utmost confidence that I can go into Wall Street on any day in the meantime, if I should see an opportunity of making a more profitable investment, and by selling my State stock, replace my $100,000 with a premium.* Now I think your services honestly worth, say $2000 per annum; but I am determined to put myself in no worse condition in any event, than if I lent my capital to the State. How much do you require to be added to your salary, to accede to the stipulation that you shall receive it, only in case the year's profits shall afford sufficient means after paying me $5000?"

The manager might reply:

* At the time this passage is written, New York five per cent. stocks, redeemable in 1866, are selling at 115; and 4½ per cent. stocks, redeemable in 1858, 1859, and 1864, at 101.

"According to the best calculation my experience enables me to make, there will be about one year in six in which we shall get no profits at all, and do well to keep the capital unimpaired. I must obtain enough additional salary in each of those five years, to compensate for its failure in the sixth. I ask twenty per cent. to insure me, and will take $2400 a year on the terms you propose, or $2000, to be paid each year, without contingency. I reckon them to come to the same thing."

Whether the capitalist employs the manager upon terms thus adjusted between them, or employs himself, it is plain that $2400 per annum, or $2\frac{4}{10}$ per cent. upon his capital, should be charged against the gross profits, and credited as paid for wages.

Allowance for wages, so considerable in the case we have supposed, as to be nearly half what the capitalist might be willing to accept as sufficient remuneration for a loan upon absolute security, sinks in proportion, as the capital rises in amount. It is as easy, or very nearly so, to manage a bank with a capital of $1,000,000, as one of $100,000; but the compensation of a manager, which in the one instance would amount to an annual average of 2½ per cent. upon its capital, in the other would come to but a quarter of one per cent. The large bank could lend money at 5¼ per cent., while the small must obtain 7½ to pay the same dividend to its stockholders. It is one of the advantages resulting from the association of little capitals, that a great economy is effected in the expense of management. While in some modes of employing capital, the portion of gross profits which should legitimately be carried to the account of wages is so insignificant as to escape notice, in others it makes so large a portion that the idea of profit is almost lost. The man who, having worked for a dollar a day, has accumulated a sufficient surplus to buy him a horse and cart—a hundred and fifty or two hundred dollars—which enable him to earn two dollars a day, scarcely regards any portion of his gains as distinct from wages; and if he does, the wood-sawyer, whose capital is but the one-hundredth part as much, obliterates the distinction entirely.

In the imaginary colloquy we have given, the manager suggests that, for about one-sixth of the time the capital entrusted to his care is to be employed, it will probably fail to secure any profit whatever.

Every mode in which it can be used involves some chances of this description, but there is a marked diversity in the degree of risk attending different employments. The peculiar hazards attending some investments, such as the destruction of shipping and cargoes by the casualties of the sea, and of buildings and merchandise on land by fire, are so capable of strict numerical calculation, that it has given rise to the employment of capital for the purpose of insuring other capital against loss by such accidents. The cost of such well ascertained chances, when provision is made for them by the payment of an insurance, is readily seen to be a distinct item from profits, and the proper deduction is habitually made for them in estimating the latter. They go to the proper account, that of maintaining the capital, to which they belong as appropriately as the expenses of keeping machinery in repair. There are, however, a variety of risks depending upon more complicated causes, which it has as yet been found impossible to calculate with precision, and against which no system of direct insurance has been devised. The owner of a gunpowder mill is aware that it is liable to explosion. He can guard against it in some degree by extreme caution in conducting the manufacture, by improvements in his apparatus, and by separating the stores of powder, so that an explosion in one building may involve the loss of but a small portion of the stock. All these precautions involve an expense which is appreciable, and which enters into the price of his merchandise. That portion of risk which remains is sufficient to deter men from engaging in the manufacture; to limit the quantity which any given price would, but for the risk, bring to market; and thereby to enable him to secure a profit which, in a series of years, is sufficient to restore the capital destroyed by explosions. The check which tends to prevent him from obtaining a price more than adequate to maintain his capital, and increase it by a profit equal to that obtained in other employments, is the readiness of men to withdraw their capital from a business in which it increases at a slow rate, and invest it in one in which it is observed to be increasing more rapidly. The inference that profits are really higher in a business of this character, will not be hastily drawn from the experience of a single individual, nor even from that of all the gunpowder manufacturers of a nation for two or three years. It, however, it should be ascertained from inquiries into the history of a large number of them, for a sufficiently long period to exclude the probability of special good fortune, that the aggregate value of their capital had grown at such a rate as, after compensating for what may be deemed objectionable in its hazards, to much exceed the rate in other employments, it is quite certain that capital would be speedily diverted from the less advantageous investments, and so increase the quantity of powder waiting for purchasers in the market, as to bring down its price, and reduce the profit of its makers to the general level.

It is obvious that those risks which may be traced to moral or political causes produce the same effect, in requiring a fund to provide for the insurance of capital, as if they resulted from the physical properties of matter. The State of Pennsylvania contains immense beds of iron-ore, coal, and limestone, lying in the immediate vicinity of each other, and has in its canals and railroads every facility for the cheap transportation of raw materials and the completed manufacture. Food, too, is abundant and cheap. There is no reason, in the nature of things, why railroad bars cannot be made in that State, and in some of our other States, Tennessee for example, at as low a cost as anywhere else in the world. The price of British iron is subject, however, to excessive fluctuations. Between 1825 and 1843, the English price of merchant bar-iron ranged from £15, about $72, to £4 10*s.*, about $22 per ton. Within the past six months there has been an increase in the price of bars in the Glasgow market, of £3, or $14 50 per ton.* The present tariff fixing an *ad valorem* duty upon iron of 30 per cent, this advance in the foreign price involves an additional one of $4 35 in the duty; making a total rise in the price at which British iron competes with domestic, of nearly $19 per ton. The Pennsylvania iron-masters who have been able to keep their mills going, during the great reduction in the price of iron since 1847, consequent upon the cessation of the railroad mania in England, now obtain $20 per ton more than they did within a year. Such an advance will pro-

* In February, 1852, English railroad iron was sold in New York at $40 per ton; it now (January, 1853,) brings $65, and is expected to go up to $75 or $80 before a reaction takes place.

bably reopen many of the furnaces which were closed and sold by the sheriff during the depression. If it could be regarded as permanent, it would lead to the investment of sufficient capital in the manufacture of iron to provide in full for the domestic consumption; and the competition of the native and foreign manufacturers would reduce the price to the lowest limit which the natural advantages for the production in the country admits. The domestic competition alone would effect this. Domestic competition in the production of cut nails, which are of American invention and manufacture, and have never been imported, and the improvements in the methods of manufacture, which that competition has induced, have reduced their price from $6 the keg of 100 pounds, in 1839, to $2 80. Those, however, who would otherwise be tempted to engage in the manufacture of iron, are aware that a large portion of the recent advance, instead of being an addition to profits, is but the necessary insurance against the hazards of a revulsion in the foreign markets, which may, within a brief period, again reduce the price below the remunerating rate. They remember that, of the 298 furnaces in the State of Pennsylvania, 167, or 56 per cent., were out of blast in the fall of 1850; that the amount of iron made in that year was only half what it had been in 1847; and that, in the succeeding year it was still less, prices having still further declined, and failures, and sales under execution having increased. They know that, under the present tariff, every decline in the foreign price is aggravated in its effect upon them by a corresponding decline in the duty. A reduction of one dollar in the foreign price relieving the importer from thirty cents in duty, compels the domestic producer to submit to a reduction of one dollar and thirty cents. A system which thus aggravates the fluctuations in price, increasing it when it is high and decreasing it when it is low, subjects business to unnatural hazards, and to the same extent unnaturally enhances the rate of insurance, which the gross apparent profit must include and leave a margin for an adequate *real* profit beside, before it tempts sagacious calculators to a new investment of capital. It thus unnaturally limits competition, and thereby prevents the reduction of price which free competition would cause. The risk, whatever it may be, is a part of the estimated cost of production, which must be replaced out of the price, and thus fall on the consumer. If that risk which is created by the revenue system were now annihilated, by converting the amount paid upon importation at present prices into a fixed duty, with a guarantee of its continuance, the result would plainly be, to induce a large increase in the domestic production of iron, beyond what the price under existing circumstances will create. If prices should continue to rise, the fixed duty will be more advantageous to the consumer than one which should rise with it. When, on the other hand, iron shall begin to decline abroad, it will come to our market at an equivalent reduction, to compete with a number of domestic producers larger than under the present system, and either not decreasing at all in consequence of the fall of price, or at all events not decreasing so fast as they would, if a declining rate of duty were hastening their ruin. The change of system, by diminishing the risk of domestic production, and thereby contributing to a permanent increase in its quantity, would tend toward a permanent reduction of cost without a reduction of the revenue of the government. It may be said that the present system relieves the foreign producer from a portion of the risks of his business, diminishes by thirty per cent. the effective reduction of price upon so much of his commodities as comes to the American market, and thus reduces the general cost of his production. To this it may be answered, that whatever saving is effected to the American purchaser is at the expense of more than an equal loss to the treasury of his government. The fact that when the iron-masters of Wales reduce the price of rails a dollar per ton, thirty cents of that nominal reduction is virtually returned to them for every ton which goes to the United States, undoubtedly enables them to make the reduction larger than it would otherwise be. The advantage, however, is shared equally by all the purchasers of rails, as well in Europe as in America; while the rebate of duty which enables the iron-masters to concede a reduction of price, is borne by the American treasury exclusively.

As the profits of every business are amassed in fragments, some trifle destined to swell the heap being included in the price of every article offered for sale, if the seller can bring it about, it follows that an item for the benefit of the insurance fund is included also, and that the entire body of consumers contribute to it. If goods are sold upon credit, the whole body of purchasers are made mutual insurers of payment. Those who pay for what they purchase themselves, pay also for what is furnished to those who fail to pay. If the people of Illinois, for instance, tolerate a system of laws, or a laxity of social morality, maintained by public opinion, which renders the collection of debts in their State uncertain, tardy, and expensive, every one of their merchants who has occasion to make purchases in New York, or any of the Atlantic ports, will obtain his goods at a figure sufficiently advanced to cover the estimated risk and cost, not in his own case simply, but in that of the average of his fellow-citizens. Returning home he will distribute the premium of insurance he has been required to pay, with interest, among his customers. If it could in practice be thus assessed in a roundabout way upon the community, who had it in their power to remedy the evil, there would be little to regret. There is, however, a difficulty in discriminating between customers on grounds not personal to themselves; and it is much easier to require a trifling advance from the whole body than a more considerable one from a limited class. It is thus that the entire body of consumers are made insurers against every species of insecurity, and are therefore alike interested in removing the causes of insecurity, whatever may be their origin. They are bound over together to promote good faith and maintain justice everywhere.

When we have eliminated from gross apparent profits, that portion which is really the compensation for physical and mental labour or wages, and that which goes to make a fund to guaranty the employer of capital against the hazards incident to the method in which he is using it, we shall find the residue to be nearly equal, or tending to equality with Rent or Interest. Men are sufficiently fond of speculating in matters of chance: and what seems mere chance to one person is discerned by another, from more ample knowledge of all the facts upon which an event depends, to be within the limits of that high probability which is sometimes called moral certainty. This consideration will serve to account for the existence of some margin of fluctuating width, between profit and rent. Great capitalists are proverbially timid. They underbid each other for absolute security, or what approaches nearest to it; and their competition tends to depress the rate of interest, and thus to establish a margin upon which intelligent courage may lay the foundations of fortune, without any imprudence, and without levying contributions for risks which are not incurred. Men borrow capital for the purpose of associating it with their own labour; and, although it should bring them no higher rate of profit, strictly speaking, than the interest which they pay, it enables them to earn wages they would otherwise have been compelled to go without.

Rent, in the usual sense, the rent of land, is profit stripped of all accessories. The capital in this case is fixed and immovable. There is no risk of its destruction, no trouble in establishing its identity. The laws of most countries have given unusually stringent remedies to enforce its ultimate restitution, and the collection of the rent during the pendency of the lease; for the laws have been made by the landlords. It is true that it may be deteriorated by remorseless exhaustion, or by an injudicious system of cropping, in which the injury is undesigned. Against this, however, protection is sought by covenants fixing the mode of culture. That such covenants, operating as a restraint upon the tenant, which often impairs the efficiency of his labour, should be necessary, is one of the evidences that the system of tenant-culture is radically vicious; and it is abundantly certain that they fail in many cases to secure their object. Sufficient confidence in their efficacy is felt, however, in those countries where this system prevails, to reduce the rent of land to a rate even below that at which it is lent upon the security of government, bringing it as low as two and a half and three per cent. per annum, upon the value at which it sells.

The interest of money loaned to individuals varies with the degree of security with which its repayment may be counted upon. Governments have attempted to limit the rate which may be stipulated in a contract for the loan of money, and to enforce the regulation by declaring the entire contract void, so that the principal cannot be recovered in the legal tribunals; and often by superadding other penalties. They have seldom, however, interfered with the sale of an existing security, such as a mortgage or promissory note, further than to limit the amount to which recovery can be had against the seller, upon his personal guaranty of the security, to the amount which he received on the sale, with legal interest thereon. While such a transaction is not within the purview of the statute against usury in *borrowing*, it answers the same purpose, and is the mode usually resorted to by men in business, when they desire a loan and cannot obtain it at the legal rate of interest. It is not difficult to invent devices by which the usury laws can be evaded, where the interest, real or supposed, of individuals requires it. A degree of risk, however, attends the attempt, for which the lender requires and receives compensation. He has to take the chance that the borrower will repudiate his bargain, and that the ingenuity with which the transaction may have been disguised may not prove a match for the astuteness of the courts. He is ordinarily favoured by the willingness of juries to wink hard, to avoid seeing the evidence which tends to establish a defence that is commonly regarded as unconscientious. There is, however, a degree of odium which fastens upon the habitual violator, even of a law which fails to enlist the moral sense of community in its support. This odium, like the risk of pecuniary loss, limits the number of competitors for loaning money at extra-statutory interest, and enables those whom it does not deter to secure additional compensation. The principal effect of the usury laws has everywhere been to increase the cost of loans to those who are under the necessity of borrowing at usurious rates, and to weaken the respect for law, by the spectacle of their daily violation without punishment. It is probable that the latter consequence might be avoided, by diminishing the severity of the penalties; for example, by permitting a recovery against the borrower of the whole sum he contracted to pay, but confiscating the usurious excess of interest for the public charities, or some analogous provision, which should relieve the informer from the discredit of repudiating his contract for a selfish benefit. The British Parliament was so much impressed with a belief that the usury laws were ineffectual, that, in 1831, they were repealed, so far as they affected commercial paper having less than six months to run, by a temporary act, the provisions of which ceased at the end of five years. At the expiration of this period the act was renewed for five years longer, and finally was renewed without limitation.

In the beginning of the year 1837, the Legislature of New York was strongly disposed to repeal the usury laws of this State. A committee, to whom the matter was referred, embodied Jeremy Bentham's "Defence of Usury" in their report, for the purpose of having it printed in great numbers, as a legislative document—and it was sc printed. Before the expiration of the session, however, the great monetary crisis of 1837, resulting in the general suspension of specie payments by the banks of the United States, had begun; and the same Legislature, instead of repealing the usury laws, passed enactments greatly increasing their severity and the means for their enforcement. With the exception that they have been repeatedly relaxed as to some railroad corporations, who have by special act been authorized to sell their bonds in the market for such prices as could be obtained, these statutes remain in full force in the most commercial State of the Union. The great reason for retaining them is, that immense sums, loaned upon the mortgage of real estate, are always outstanding, liable to be called in at a moment's warning. It is apprehended that, if the restrictions were removed, the payment of such loans would be demanded upon the occurrence of every commercial crisis, and the borrowers be compelled to pay exorbitant interest for their renewal, or submit to an immense sacrifice of property by forced sales. Movable property can be transported from a poor market to a better one, but land cannot go in search of a purchaser. At times, when the value of money is suddenly advanced, the decline in the price of land is for this reason much greater than in property which can evade a local cause of depression. The usury laws thus serve as a barrier, to prevent the storms which strew the haunts of commerce with wrecks from wasting the rural districts. The agricultural class, whose operations never originate these convulsions, will naturally maintain all the defences which guard them against liability to share the ruin thence resulting.

Money is the sole means of preserving credit in a commercial crisis; and commercial credit depends not upon ultimate payment, with interest for delay, but on payment at the stipulated moment, whatever may be the circumstances or the cost. Its value in mercantile appreciation is such, that there is scarce a limit to the pecuniary sacrifice that will be made for its preservation. To ride out a storm in which the majority founder, is a distinction which promises great future advantage, and for its sake men will struggle, and drain themselves of the means, which might, if husbanded, have paid their creditors, if they left no surplus. The price which is paid for the use of money under such circumstances is enormous, and bears no other relation to profit, than the price of bread during famine in a besieged city does to the cost of raising it before the hostile forces sat down under its walls. If laws against usury are effectual to prevent its being borrowed, the same result can be reached, and is reached, by selling goods at auction, where no law prohibits the vendor from submitting to what sacrifice he chooses. The true remedy must be sought in efforts to obtain security against such crises—diseases in the economical condition—not in attempting to regulate the conduct of men during the paroxysm.

We find the interest of money denuded as far as possible from all premium for risk, ordinarily, in the rate of interest paid by a government to its own subjects. The security of such loans is a matter of public knowledge, while the security of a loan upon individual credit is known to but few, and that of a loan upon landed security, however ample, requires verification, attended with trouble and expense. The stock of a government in good credit is, for this reason, the most readily convertible of all descriptions of property, and furnishes a convenient means of investment for those sums which individuals have in their possession, intending to employ them after some brief interval, but without having determined upon the mode, or having not quite matured their arrangements. In the year 1848 there were 96,415 persons holding portions of the national debt of England so small, that the dividend did not exceed £5 at each payment. Such fund-holders are probably for the most part of the class to which we have referred; and no day passes without a large number selling out and a large number buying in. Persons thus circumstanced are content with the lowest rate of profit; and the existence of a numerous class of such persons in a community enables a government to borrow at the lowest interest.

The interest of money varies from one country to another with the degree of security which its institutions afford, and in the same country it is found varying at different periods for the same reason. A confidence that the fruits of labour may be securely enjoyed, is the prime stimulus to exertion, and to that abstinence for the sake of future enjoyment, which leads to accumulation. Where that confidence is weak, labour will be unproductive, and capital increase slowly. Where the aggregate of profit is small, the rate of profit is large; capital then secures a large proportion. Interest is therefore high, where, from the absence of security, production is trifling. It is high in Egypt, where the *fellah* is robbed by the agents of his government the moment he becomes worth plundering. It is high, whenever despotism, anarchy, or war, puts the rewards of industry in peril, and retards the increase of wealth. It was higher than ten per cent. in England before the Parliament of Henry VIII. legalized it at that rate, and it has continued to fall from that time with the progress of national well-being. England was getting rich more rapidly when the rate of profit had fallen, and interest was restricted by a statute, passed in the twenty-first year of James I., to eight per cent. In the reign of his grandson, Charles II., it was reduced to six per cent., and in that of Queen Anne to five, which is now the legal rate, and is from one to one and a half per cent. higher than can be obtained for permanent investments upon good security. The tendency to a fall in the rate of profit and of interest with the progress of wealth is so generally admitted, and the fact that they have everywhere fallen with that progress so well known, as to require no further illustration.

It is proper to remark that, in denying the proposition that the prosperity of a country is to be measured by the rate of profit prevailing in it, we are supported by the authority of Adam Smith. His doctrine upon this point is, that the rate of profit "is naturally low in rich and high in poor countries, and that it is always highest in the countries which are going fastest to ruin."* Mr. M'Culloch characterizes this as a most erroneous statement, and regards it as inconsistent with the opinion maintained elsewhere in the "Wealth of Nations," that those countries in which capital is increasing with the greatest rapidity, are, *cæteris paribus*, the most prosperous. It is not for the purpose of recalling attention to the distinction which reconciles these doctrines, which, though nowhere clearly expressed

* Wealth of Nations, Book I., chap. 11.

by Dr. Smith, was manifestly felt by him, that we refer to this criticism. It is because Mr. M'Culloch distinctly perceives and remarks, that another doctrine, in which nearly if not quite all the modern English Economists are at variance with the author of the "Wealth of Nations," is dependent upon that we have stated—the doctrine that individual advantage is not always a true test of the public advantageousness of different employments of capital. The successors of Smith maintain that it is, and strenuously deny what he teaches, that domestic trade is more productive, and maintains a larger industry than foreign trade. The consideration of this point will naturally occupy us in the following chapter.

CHAPTER VII.

EXCHANGE.

EXCHANGE arises from the division of labour. From the moment that men have attained the power to protect themselves and their crops from the wild beasts, agriculture begins to yield a surplus beyond the subsistence of those engaged in it. It would appear, from the prominence given by the traditions of most nations to the mighty hunter in their early history, that the struggle of man with the ferocious animals has been severe, and may for a time have seemed dubious. From Hercules down to St. George, the dragon-killer, prowess in the destruction of savage animals has been so marked a feature in the character of legendary heroes, as to afford evidence that men put a very high estimate upon services of this kind; an estimate naturally proportionate to the danger which such service averted. There are portions of the world at this day, in which carnivorous beasts divide the occupation of the earth with the human race, and greatly impair its power to multiply and find subsistence. The beasts of prey require graminivorous animals for their food, and the latter require vegetation, which is thus abstracted from the nourishment of human beings. The crisis of humanity is in the warfare by which the carnivorous animals, whose subsistence exhausts great tracts of land, are exterminated. An end once put to their joint occupation of the territory, there is no assignable limit to its power to maintain human population, and a surplus beyond the wants of its actual occupants at once rewards their toil. A portion of the community is then found withdrawing itself from the cultivation of the land, and employing its industry in the mechanic arts. The blacksmith and the weaver obtain their food by bartering their services and their wares with the farmer. Even before this stage of social advancement is reached, exchange of services is established in the domestic relations. The savage husband procures food and the wife dresses it; he hunts the fox and the beaver, and she makes their skins into clothing. Both are producers of services, which they barter with each other. Exchange in the family was organized when Adam delved and Eve spun.

To effect an exchange requires two products, two producers, and that the latter should be brought into association. What is really exchanged is a service given on the one side against a service given on the other. The one party may render a service by his present labour; as, when the blacksmith fastens a shoe upon the horse of the traveller, who stops at his door for the purpose, the other may render the service by past labour, embodied in a material form; as if, in the case supposed, the traveller were a pedlar, and should pay for his horse-shoeing with a tin pan. That which enters into the estimation of value on both sides is the service received—the amount of labour avoided by each in availing himself of the labour of the other. It is only for the sake of simplifying the discussion by dropping the human agents from consideration, that we speak of exchange as being the barter of commodities. The tin pan represents portions of the labour of various individuals: that of the miner, of the artizan who made the miner's tools, of the sailors and wagoners who transported the tin from the mines to the shop where it was made up into utensils, as well as that of the tinsmith, were all essential to its manufacture. Indeed, if we endeavour to trace the constituents of its value to their elements, we shall find that minute fragments of the labour of a host of men, of different generations, extending over long tracts of space and time, have contributed to the production of any article we may select. Each possessor of it, in the various stages of its formation, has obtained it by remunerating the labour of all his predecessors. Its ultimate labour-cost is the summation of an infinite series of fractions, decreasing as we recede into the past, as it is of another infinite series, each term of which will dwindle through a protracted future. The labour of a man who makes a hammer to-day, may be regarded as entering into every stroke of that hammer for all coming time; and the value of the hammer will thus be diffused among all the articles it shall aid to construct, and be mingled with values derived directly and indirectly from the labour of thousands. A vast multitude will share in the service which the hammer-maker is rendering to-day, who are as unregarded by him as he will be unknown to them. He looks to have his service paid once for all, by an equivalent service, or what he esteems such, received from the individual with whom he exchanges the hammer for something else. If he could construct that something else for himself with as little privation and trouble as the hammer cost him, there would be no motive for parting with it; certainly none for making hammers with the express view of parting with them. So, on the other hand, no person wanting a hammer would make something else for the purpose of getting it, if he could as easily make the hammer by his own direct exertions. Each exchange implies a double profit—an advantage on both sides; and that advantage consists in the time and labour which each saves, and which can be devoted to further production, in consequence of his confining himself to that kind of industry in which he possesses special skill and efficiency. Value, it is true, is a matter of estimation, and it is this which controls in Exchange. Each party may suppose himself to have received a greater value than he has parted with; but, whether true or not, this cannot affect the interests of the community of which both are members. The general stock of commodities in the society is no larger the moment after the exchange than the moment before; and no general advantage can be derived from exchange unless it occasions an increase of material production.

We have said that exchange requires the association of producers. The truth of this is sufficiently obvious in the case where personal services are bartered — as in the most intimate form of association, the family, or in the natural good offices of neighbourhood, as when farmers assist each other in getting in their harvests. There are a great many forms of co-operation, in which the persons who associate are brought face to face, and the advantage is palpable; because they are able to accomplish works by their united exertions in a very brief period, which are plainly impossible to a single individual, unaided by machinery, in any length of time. Every house-raising and logging-bee furnishes an example. In the exchange of services embodied in material products, there is ordinarily very much to obscure our perception of the fact. The actual producers are seldom brought into personal communication, and the products which they exchange are rarely compared directly with each other. A farmer of the town of Hamburgh brings a cheese to market, sells it for money, and with that purchases cloth, made in Oneida county from cotton grown in Tennessee, and a stove, made from Clinton county iron, melted by the aid of Pennsylvania coal. The production of the cheese was a necessary condition of the sale of the coal, iron, and cotton; and that of the coal, iron, and cotton, of the sale of the cheese. The production of the one depended upon the production of the other, since none of them were produced for the immediate use of those whose labour brought them to the market. If the cheese, in point of fact, never reaches the miners, cotton-growers, and manufacturers, for whose labour it has been exchanged, it nevertheless replaces other commodities which have been transferred to them; and until it does replace them, the cloth and stove remain clogs and incumbrances in the market, obstacles to the further production of the raw material of which they are made, and to the employment of labour in working them up into fabrics, like those which have yet to wait for the purchaser with his cheese.

The point of essential importance is, that those who furnish a market for commodities, and thereby occasion their production, are not the persons who transport the commodities from place to place, and traffic in them, but the persons who finally employ them for the satisfaction of their own wants, and who produce other commodities or services to offer in exchange. It is labour which creates the demand for labour; but labour employed in production, not labour employed in effecting exchanges. The latter only adds *value* to products, without increasing their quantity.

Mr. J. S. Mill states it as a fundamental theorem in respect to capital, "that what supports and employs productive labour is the capital expended in setting it to work, and not the demand of purchasers for the produce of the labour when completed. Demand for commodities," he adds, "is not demand for labour. The demand for commodities determines in what particular branch of labour and production the labour and capital shall be employed; it determines the *direction* of the labour; but not the more or less of the labour itself, or of the maintenance and payment of the labour. That depends on the amount of the capital or other funds, directly devoted to the sustenance and remuneration of labour." This proposition he declares is, to common apprehension, a paradox; and that even among political writers of reputation, hardly any except Mr. Ricardo and Mr. Say can be pointed out, who have kept it constantly and steadily in view. Mr. Mill illustrates the principle for which he contends in this way. He remarks that a consumer may either expend a part of his income in hiring journeymen bricklayers to build a house, or, instead of this, he may employ the same value in buying velvets and laces. In the latter case,

"He buys the finished commodity, which has been produced by labour and capital—the labour not being paid, nor the capital furnished by him, but pre-existing. Suppose that he had been in the habit of expending this portion of his income in hiring journeymen bricklayers, who laid out the amount of their wages in food and clothing, which were also produced by labour and capital. He, however, determines to prefer velvet, for which he thus creates an extra demand. This demand, however, cannot be satisfied without an extra supply, nor can the supply be produced without an extra capital. Where then is the capital to come from? There is nothing in the consumer's change of purpose which makes the capital of the country greater than it otherwise was. It appears then that the increased demand for velvet could not for the present be supplied, were it not that the very circumstance which gave rise to it has set at liberty a capital of the exact amount required. The very sum which the consumer now employs in buying velvet, formerly passed into the hands of journeymen bricklayers, who expended it in food and necessaries, which they now either go without, or squeeze by their competition from the shares of other labourers. *The labour and capital, therefore, which formerly produced necessaries for the use of these bricklayers, are deprived of their market, and must look out for other employment;* and they find it in making velvet for the new demand. I do not mean that the very same labour and capital which produced the necessaries turn themselves to producing the velvet; but in some one or other of a hundred modes, they take the place of that which does. There was capital in existence to do one of two things—to make the velvet or produce the necessaries for the journeymen bricklayers—but not to do both. It was at the option of the consumer which of the two should happen; and if he chooses the velvet, they go without the necessaries. * * * * * * * * * The detriment to the labourers would have been the same if the consumer had persisted in building a house, but instead of engaging labourers and paying them himself, had given an order to a builder, and settled the account after the work was finished. For, in this manner of proceeding, the consumer no longer himself maintains the labour, but attracts the capital of another person from some other place or occupation to do it; and, therefore, does not open a new employment for labour, but merely changes the course of an existing employment. Thus, in whatever manner the question is stated, we are brought back to the conclusion, that a demand delayed until the work is completed, and furnishing no advances, but only reimbursing advances made by others, contributes nothing to the demand for labour; and that what is so expended, is, in all its effects, so far as regards the employment of the labouring class, a mere nullity; it does not and cannot create any employment except at the expense of other employment which existed before." — *Political Economy, vol.* 1, *pages* 102–104: *Boston edition.*

The gist of this extraordinary passage is in the notion that the capital of a country is a fixed, unvarying quantity, and that all employments of it are equally productive. The object of it, and of the proposition it is intended to support, is to lay a foundation for the doctrine, that it is of no consequence in regard to its effect in furnishing employment to the industry of his countrymen, in what manner a consumer spends money for the satisfaction of his personal wants—whether in the purchase of the products of domestic labour or of foreign. The passage we have marked with italics is flagrantly inconsistent with the main proposition. It concedes that the demand for the labour of bricklayers had created a demand for the labour which produced necessaries for their use, although the person who employed the bricklayers made no advance to support the labour expended in producing the necessaries for their use, but only reimbursed, and that after at least two removes — the first to the bricklayers themselves, the second from them to the persons of whom they bought their bread and potatoes — advances made by others. Mr. Mill himself states an exception, which is quite as broad as his rule. There is a case, he observes, in which a demand for commodities may create an employment for labour: namely, when the labourer is already fed without being sufficiently employed. There is no country in the world, however, which has not a vast number of labourers, actual or potential, insufficiently employed, and who, certainly, are fed, since they continue to exist. Enforced idleness exists, to a greater or less extent, everywhere—idleness arising from no lack of the disposition and physical ability to work. Such is that of thousands, who in England are pent in the poor-houses, with a gloomy look, says Carlyle, which seems to say, "An earth all lying round, crying, 'Come and till me, come and reap me;' yet here we sit enchanted. The sun shines, and the earth calls; and by the governing Powers and Impotences of this England we are forbidden to obey." Such idlers are the operatives in the factories, as yet endeavouring to earn their bread, but working half time. Such are all those in all countries, who, pretending to work, lack the stimulus that would lead to work in downright earnest, and saunter through intermitted and inefficient labour. Where is the region to be found, after every deduction has been made for the persons who are independent of wages for subsistence, in which all or nearly all the capacity of its inhabitants for productive labour is kept in action? Where is it that all who would be glad to labour at the current rates of remuneration never want the opportunity?

Mr. Mill, in a subsequent chapter of his work, shows "of what supreme importance to the productiveness of the labour of producers, is the existence of other producers within reach, employed in a different kind of industry." He justly observes that,

"The power of exchanging the products of one kind of labour for those of another, is a condition, but for which there would almost always be a smaller quantity of labour altogether. When a new market is opened for any product of industry, and a greater quantity of the article is consequently produced, the increased production is not always obtained at the expense of some other product; it is often a new creation, the result of labour which would otherwise have remained unexerted, or of assistance rendered to labour by improvements, or by modes of co-operation to which recourse would not have been had, if an inducement had not been offered for raising a larger produce."—*Political Economy, vol.* 1, *page* 145.

The author of this quotation is of opinion that there is no inconsistency between the facts therein stated, and the doctrine that a market for commodities does not constitute employment for labour. In the case where the labour of agriculturists is stimulated to increased vigour and efficiency, by the settlement of a body of mechanics in their vicinity, he remarks, that the labour of the agriculturists was already provided with employment, and that they are not indebted to the new comers for being able to maintain themselves. Is the distinction then between employment for labour and employment for labourers? It is admitted that an additional amount of labour may be called into exercise, with a corresponding increase of remuneration, but not an additional number of labourers employed. To show how unsubstantial is this distinction, we have only to imagine the case of continued arrivals of consumers. There is certainly a supposable limit to the capacity of the existing number of agriculturists to supply the demand, and, when that is exhausted, the demand for labour still continuing becomes a demand for labourers. Three hundred thousand emigrants from Europe land upon our shores every year. Suppose that they are all non-producers of food, and that the arrivals for ten years only create such a demand for provisions, as may be satisfied by increased exertion on the part of our farmers, without any accession to the number of the latter. Can the stream of emigration continue for ever, without creating a demand for more agricultural labourers? Can the annual influx be trebled, as it easily might be, without *soon* occasioning such a demand? If this question must be answered in the negative, it is apparent that the distinction between a demand for labour and one for labourers is baseless in principle. It could only have suggested itself to those who are conversant with the phenomena of a nearly stationary population, which is nevertheless regarded as in excess, or in constant danger of becoming excessive, in comparison with capital.

Mr. Say holds to the broadest extent the doctrine that demand depends upon production. "It is production," he holds, "which opens a demand for products." "A product is no sooner created, than it, from that instant, affords a market for other products, to the full extent of its own value." "It is because the production of some commodities has declined that other commodities are superabundant." From the important truth contained in these propositions, he deduces the conclusion,

"That in every community, the more numerous are the producers, and the more various the productions, the more prompt, numerous, and extensive are the vents for those productions; and by a natural consequence, the more profitable are they to the producers; for price rises with the demand. But this advantage is to be derived from real production alone, and not from a forced circulation of products: for a value once created is not augmented in its passage from one hand to another."—*Say's Political Economy, Book I., chap.* 15.

Mr. M'Culloch, who refers with approval to the chapter of Mr. Say from which the preceding extracts are taken, remarks that the principles from which the conclusions of the latter are drawn, were stated as early as 1752, in a tract of Dean Tucker's, entitled *Queries on the late Naturalization Bill*, which has now become rare. We copy one of those queries from Mr. M'Culloch's quotation, and in the same typography which he employed, not only because it is well worthy of the most striking notation, but as an evidence that the supposed distinction between the demand for labour and for the products of labour, was not recognized either by its original author, or him who has rescued it from the obscurity of a forgotten pamphlet: "WHETHER IT IS NOT AN INFALLIBLE MAXIM, THAT ONE MAN'S LABOUR CREATES EMPLOYMENT FOR ANOTHER?"

It is the instinctive perception by the popular intelligence—wiser than the schools, though incapable of analyzing the grounds of its conviction—of the truth that this query admits but one answer, that has led to a policy of mutual protection, which the schools condemn. It was not, however, to association by express compact, to increase exchanges, by diversifying industry and thereby stimulating production, that we referred, when speaking of association as an essential condition of exchange. It is obviously necessary that the producers should be brought into some degree of proximity to each other, before they can effect the barter of their labour, either in the form of personal services or of products, by their own direct negotiation. It requires the association of producers in still greater numbers, before it can become the business of a distinct class, to arrange and conduct the exchanges of commodities which they do not produce. The want of concentration in space, between producers, is plainly an obstacle to traffic, whatever agencies may be employed to effect it. Upon this point there will be occasion to treat at some length. Something more than physical association, however, is requisite to establish the regular practice of barter. No man could withdraw himself from the labours which provide food and clothing, for more than the briefest period, without a confident assurance that others had taken upon themselves the work of providing food and clothing for him, upon well-understood conditions. It is therefore, by a real, though unexpressed concert, in the language of Mr. Wakefield, "that the body who raise more food than they want, can exchange with the body who raise more clothes than they want; and if the two bodies were separated, either by distance or disinclination—unless the two bodies should virtually form themselves into one, for the common object of raising enough food and clothing for the whole—they could not divide into two distinct parts, the whole operation of producing a sufficient quantity of food and clothes."

Some of the advantages resulting from the division of labour could not fail to attract observation in the earliest stages of society. The fact that increase in productive power resulted from it, would be noticed, before men attempted to philosophize about the reason of that increase; and success in one case, and in one kind of industry, would naturally induce experiments in others. The rules of art, and the maxims of practical wisdom, generally precede by a long time that scientific demonstration which is requisite to acquaint us with their scope and limitations, and enable us to foresee their application in untried circumstances. For this purpose we must discover the reasons of the rule, and the law upon which observed facts rest, and which they exemplify.

What then are the reasons why the division of labour occasions an increase of productive power? Without attempting to exhaust them, the following may be assigned as the principal:

1. The increased knowledge which men obtain of the properties of matter, and the natural laws which are turned to account in their respective employments. In other words, the intellectual education of producers. The division of employments is carried to less extent in the ordinary operations of agriculture than in the mechanic arts; but they are doubtless susceptible of being allotted to different classes of persons, in a much larger degree than is yet practised. This, first of the arts, however, may furnish us with an illustration of the principle under consideration. The cultivation of the grains, roots, and fruits, requires a familiarity with a large round of chemical laws, affecting soils and manures; of mechanical laws, relating to the structure and use of buildings, tools, machinery, and the motive powers; with much else that may well employ a long period of training. The breeding of animals demands a knowledge of physiological laws, of a quite different character. Mr. Bakewell, by studying those laws, and the special qualities of the various breeds of sheep, attained such skill, as to be able to produce an animal which should combine almost any desirable properties, which are not absolutely incompatible, and effected very great improvements in the flocks of Great Britain, by adopting such modes of crossing, feeding, &c., as are best adapted to secure size and fat, where these are the qualities desired—weight and fineness of fleece, where these are wanted. Other individuals have devoted themselves in the same way to perfecting the breed of cows and other domestic animals. It is quite clear that they could not have acquired such knowledge and skill in the art of cattle-breeding, if they had attempted to include in the list of their accomplishments, the same pre-eminent knowledge and skill in regard to the cultivation of the various

grains, of flax and cotton, of grasses, potatoes, and apples. Life is short, Art is long.

The mechanic arts afford examples of a still more striking diversity in the materials upon which they are employed, and the knowledge requisite for their prosecution. The workers in metals, and the dyer, for instance, avail themselves in their respective trades of properties of matter and laws of combination, which have scarce anything in common. The application of new discoveries in chemistry to the arts, is constantly requiring a greater amount of special knowledge, for the purpose of conducting their operations with economy; and the progress of knowledge necessarily tends to confine those who would be adepts, to the study of fewer departments. How very different have been the researches of Lieutenant Maury, who, by long and laborious investigation of the laws governing the winds and currents of the oceans, has been able to frame directions which very greatly reduce the length of voyages to California, China, and elsewhere: of Ericsson, the inventor of the propeller and the caloric engine, which render ships independent of winds and currents, by enabling them to carry fuel enough for the longest cruise: of Steers, who built the yacht America, and gave the model of a vessel fitted for consummate speed. The science of all three, nevertheless, is subservient to the one art of navigation.

2. The increase of dexterity — the education of the muscles of producers — is a universal and highly efficient cause of increased production. It is a well-known physical truth, that the exercise of a muscle increases its volume and strength. An operation which was difficult at first, becomes easy by its frequent repetition — that which at the beginning could only be done slowly, comes by dint of practice to be done with rapidity—that which it required close mental attention to do with accuracy, is done at length without any conscious watchfulness, and with a precision that rivals the action of machinery. It is said that there are boot-closers so skilful that they can begin to close a boot with a thread a yard long in each hand, throw out each arm at once to the extent of the thread without making a second pull; and, at each successive pull, contract the swing of their arms, so as to allow for the diminished length of the thread each time that it passes through the leather. Delicacy of

touch, as well as rapidity of movement, are susceptible of indefinite cultivation. In some manufacturing operations, children repeat a hundred times in a minute, and for hours in succession, motions involving the action of several muscles. As an instance of the economy obtained by training the muscles, it is stated, that "a sort of twist or gimp," made in England, "which cost three shillings for making when first introduced, is now manufactured for a penny; and this solely through the increased dexterity of the workmen, without the intervention of any new machine."*

It is plainly impossible for a person to acquire the same dexterity in a great number of distinct processes that he could in a single one; and, if it were practicable, the time spent in learning them must be withdrawn from productive labour. It is sometimes mentioned under this head, as an advantage, that from the increased simplicity of operations, children can be put to them at an earlier period of life. This, however, is of very questionable utility. The years of childhood are with most profit to the community devoted to their *general* education: the fireside, the school, and the play-ground, are the places where immature bodies and minds can earn most for the commonwealth, by accumulating power instead of expending it.

3. The division of labour makes it possible so to distribute different processes, as that each shall be assigned to the persons whose capacity is adequate to their performance, and best fitted for it. Great bodily strength is necessary for some kinds of industry; very little suffices for others, in which rapidity of movement and delicacy of touch are the chief recommendations. So of skill. Anybody can, in a very few days, learn to feed the fires of a steam-engine, while the qualifications of an engineer require an education of months and years. It would be a great waste of power for the latter to make the fires. Economy in productive force is secured, when some employment is found for every person, whatever may be his peculiarities of physical constitution or education. A blind man can turn a grindstone; a lame one can throw a shuttle; one who is dumb can set type. Different parts of a series of operations necessary to a common purpose, may be performed with equal success by

* Edinburgh Review, January, 1849.

individuals, in whose faculties, original and acquired, there is as great a difference as in those of the dumb, the blind, and the cripple. If there are four operations, in but one of which the possession of the five senses and sound legs is necessary, three persons labouring under the above-mentioned infirmities, and one who is free from them, can do the same work as four of the latter description could do; whereas, but for such a distribution, the productive power of three of them would be lost to society, while their subsistence would remain a charge upon its energies. The same truth holds with regard to minor differences of capacity, though the gain may be less in degree.

4. Economy of tools. Different operations being facilitated by tools and machinery of like diversity, the man who should undertake to perform a variety of operations, would need a stock of tools of corresponding magnitude. Three individuals, each of whom should attempt to be carpenter, blacksmith, and weaver, by turns, must have three times the quantity of tools that would suffice, if each confined himself to a single trade. Three times as much labour would be expended in the accumulation of aids to production, and abstracted from production itself.

Such appear to be the most general advantages of the division of employment. Another, which is enumerated by Adam Smith, is that gained by saving the time commonly lost in passing from one sort of work to another. "A country weaver," he observes, "who cultivates a small farm, must lose a good deal of time in passing from his loom to the field, and from his field to the loom. When the two trades can be carried on in the same workhouse, the loss of time is no doubt much less. It is even in this case, however, very considerable. A man commonly saunters a little in turning his hand from one sort of employment to another. When he first begins the new work, he is seldom very keen and hearty; his mind, as they say, does not go to it, and for some time he rather trifles than applies to good purpose." Mr. Babbage remarks, that "when the human hand or the human head has been for some time occupied in any kind of work, it cannot instantly change its employment with full effect. The muscles of the limbs employed have acquired a flexibility during their exertion, and those not in action a stiffness during rest, which renders every change slow and unequal in the commencement. Long habit also produces in the muscles exercised a capacity for enduring fatigue to a much greater degree than they could support under other circumstances. A similar result seems to take place in any change of mental exertion; the attention bestowed on the new subject not being so perfect at first as it becomes after some exercise." On the other hand it is observed, and with justice, that a change of occupation will often afford relief, where complete repose would otherwise be necessary; the employment of different muscles and faculties of the mind allowing some to rest and be refreshed while others labour. This consideration is undoubtedly entitled to some weight, and renders it impossible to assign any uniform rule, in regard to the degree of sameness in bodily or mental occupation which is most advantageous. In respect to the time necessarily involved in passing to and from the places where different descriptions of work must be carried on, it was omitted in our enumeration, because the object was to ascertain the causes from which division of labour increases production, upon the supposition that the producers really employ the whole of the time in work that is nominally given to it.

Another of the advantages enumerated by Adam Smith is, that "the invention of all those machines by which labour is so much facilitated and abridged, seems to have been originally owing to the division of labour." The man whose attention is confined to a single and simple object, is much more likely to devise improvements in the tools and methods for accomplishing it, than if he were distracted by a variety of objects. This advantage, however, appears to be consequential rather than direct. The division of labour in this way prepares the means for making future labour vastly more productive; but the invention, however admirable, is not that immediate increase of production of which we are in quest.

Mr. Senior has remarked another advantage arising from the circumstance "that the same exertions which are necessary to produce a single given result, are often sufficient to produce many hundred or many thousand similar results." He instances the Post-office establishment as furnishing a familiar illustration. It is as easy to carry fifty letters from New York to Chicago as a single one, and nearly as easy to carry a thousand. If each individual attempted to transmit his own correspondence, every man of any considerable business would have a large number of messengers constantly on foot. All the inhabitants of the United States, acting independently, would be unable to effect, what, by their association and concert in making the carrying and distribution of the mails the work of a particular class, is accomplished by the labour of a few individuals. There are other functions performed by governments and their agents, which would afford examples of the same character. Its provision for the public defence, for the detection and punishment of crime, and for the administration of private justice, have been instanced by Mr. Senior. The same principle is a main source of the economy resulting from conducting industrious operations of any kind upon a large scale, and is doubtless capable of indefinite extension. It is ordinarily treated under the head of association, and often in connection with ideas and schemes with which it has no necessary relation. The very word "association" has thus become suggestive of the visionary and impracticable, if not of the revolutionary and dangerous, to a class of men who hear and read of exchange and of the division of labour, without the slightest shock to their conservatism : though at bottom the ideas are the same. It is not within our province to discuss the direction or the limits, towards which the application of this principle may be profitably extended. This is matter of detail. The principle itself comes within the considerations in regard to economy in the distribution of labour, which has been stated as the third of the most general advantages arising from its division.

Exchange and the division of labour are, as we have seen, coextensive and mutually dependent. The former owes all its capacity to benefit the individual, and the community of which he is a member, to the increase of production resulting from the latter. A. and B. each need both hats and boots, and it requires, we may assume, the same amount of labour to make the one that it does to make the other. We may assume, too, for the sake of illustration, that by reason of his devoting himself exclusively to the manufacture of hats, A. attains the power of producing a hat by the labour of four days; while B., who confines his efforts to the production of boots and shoes, can produce a pair of the former by working the same number of days. If, on the contrary, each of them had attempted to combine both trades, and half a dozen others, in his own person, he would have been occupied, we may safely say, eight days in the manufacture of a hat, and as many more in that of a pair of boots. Four days' labour of the two, when they co-operate in production by diversifying their industry, accomplishes the same result that would have demanded eight under the opposite system. The hatter provides a covering for his own head in four days; by making a hat for his neighbour, the shoemaker, in four days more he provides himself with a covering for his feet. The shoemaker does the same. In eight days each has a hat and a pair of boots; whereas, but for the division of labour and exchange, one would have been hatless and the other bootless. Thus far the benefit may seem to be confined to these two persons: but let them continue working eight days longer, and the community is the richer by two new pairs of boots, and two new hats, for other persons to wear, who, without the association of the producers, must have gone without those essentials to personal comfort and health, which contribute to invest them also with increased productive power. The combined gain of the individuals who produce and exchange, is the gain of the community to which they belong. What the shoemaker has gained is the time saved to him — the four days which he did not expend in half-making a hat, and which enabled him to contribute an extra pair of boots to the general stock. What the hatter gained is the additional hat he obtained the power of making, by being relieved from wasting his productive force. The community in which both reside gains a hat and a pair of boots, which it otherwise would have lost.

Suppose that, instead of being members of the same community, the hatter lives in Connecticut and the shoemaker in England, and suppose that an exchange of their respective fabrics is effected, without any cost for transportation, and the services of merchants in managing the barter. What then? The American hatter undoubtedly gains the equivalent of a hat as before, and his country also gains it, but does not gain the extra pair of boots which the British shoemaker is enabled to make. These are lost to Connecticut, and are a gain to England. There is an advantage, undoubtedly, to both communities (the expenses of transportation, &c., being left out of the calculation), but it is only half as great as the advantage to either would have been, if both parties to the exchange and both profits had belonged to itself.

If the English shoemaker can be induced to emigrate, and to pursue his craft in Connecticut, exchanging with the hatter as before, it is manifest that a double benefit accrues to that State. The community is enriched by what enriches him—the enhanced productiveness of his labour, which results from his having the capacity to exchange it with that of the native citizen, enures to the advantage of the State, in the tangible form of an increased supply of boots and shoes.

No possible estimation of value in the commodities exchanged, no variation of price between boots in Liverpool and boots in New Haven, can in the least degree affect this grand fact; though a reasoning based upon values and prices may obscure the perception of it. Value and price may, indeed, in connection with other circumstances, furnish indications in respect to the limit of cost at which the advantage of domestic exchange may be purchased, with profit to a community; but this does not impair the conclusion that internal exchange, other things being equal, and looking only at the essential foundation of all exchange, is more advantageous than foreign trade.

If there be a single individual in Connecticut who sits idle—able to make shoes, but incapable of any other species of productive industry — it presents a case where the advantage of a system of domestic exchanges which shall secure him the opportunity, is readily appreciable. Idle or busy he must be fed, and in either case his subsistence must be provided from the labour of the other members of society. Suppose that it requires twice the labour for him to make a pair of boots, and, consequently, that he must be paid twice the price, to enable him to procure the subsistence which the public would otherwise be compelled to furnish, that the Englishman demands, it is evident that the community may as well pay him that price, as feed him in idleness and obtain its boots from

England. Its total expenditure and total acquisition are the same in one case as in the other.

We are now prepared to appreciate the justice with which Adam Smith insisted upon the superior advantage of internal over foreign trade. The following extract exhibits his views:—

"The same capital will, in any country, put in motion a greater or smaller quantity of productive labour, and add a greater or smaller value to the annual produce of its land and labour, according to the different proportions in which it is employed in agriculture, manufactures, and wholesale trade. The difference, too, is very great, according to the different sorts of wholesale trade in which any part of it is employed. * * *

"The capital which is employed in purchasing in one part of the country in order to sell in another, the produce of the industry of that country, generally replaces by every such operation two distinct capitals, that had both been employed in the agriculture or manufactures of that country, and thereby enables them to continue that employment. When it sends out from the residence of the merchant a certain value of commodities, it generally brings back in return at least an equal value of other commodities. When both are the produce of domestic industry, it necessarily replaces by every such operation two distinct capitals, which had both been employed in supporting productive labour, and thereby enables them to continue that support. The capital which sends Scotch manufactures to London, and brings back English corn and manufactures to Edinburgh, necessarily replaces by every such operation two British capitals, which had both been employed in the agriculture or manufactures of Great Britain.

"The capital employed in purchasing foreign goods for home consumption, when this purchase is made with the produce of domestic industry, replaces, too, by every such operation, two distinct capitals; but one of them only is employed in supporting domestic industry. The capital which sends British goods to Portugal, and brings back Portuguese goods to Great Britain, replaces by every such operation only one British capital. The other is a Portuguese one. Though the returns, therefore, of the foreign trade of consumption should be as quick as those of the home trade, it will give but one-half of the encouragement to the industry or productive labour of the country."—*Wealth of Nations, Book II., chap.* 5.

Mons. Say concurs with Smith, holding the following language:—

"The internal commerce of a country, though from its minute ramification it is less obvious and striking, besides being the most considerable is likewise the most advantageous. For both the remittance and returns of this commerce are necessarily home products. It sets in motion a double production; and the profits of it are not participated with foreigners."—*Say's Political Economy, Book I., chap.* 9.

In a subsequent chapter, commenting with disapprobation upon the policy which induced the British Government, in its anxiety to enlarge the foreign vent for its manufactures, to grant bounties upon exportations, the same author observes,

"The British Government seems not to have perceived that the most profitable sales to a nation, are those made by one individual to another within the nation; for these latter imply a national production of TWO values—the value sold and that given in exchange." — *Say's Political Eco nomy, Book I., chap.* 17.

The language employed by Dr. Smith in the preceding extract, does not appear very well calculated to convey the true grounds upon which its doctrine rests. The idea of an intermediate capital, employed in replacing two other capitals, introduces a needless complexity, inasmuch as the whole question turns upon the advantage of an exchange of a product, or quantity of products, or a given amount of capital, if that term is preferred, for another capital, like it in the circumstance of being the result of domestic industry, or unlike it, as being the result of the industry of strangers. It is one of these which replaces the other. The capital employed in effecting the exchange, may, if the products are in adjacent warehouses, consist only of money in coin. If the distance between them is two or three miles, it will consist in part of wagons and horses. If they are separated by a distance of a hundred miles, it may include also a railway, with its engines and cars; or a canal, with its boats and the animals who tow them. The capital which is the instrument of exchange has no influence upon the result, except that it requires pay for the services it has rendered, and thus abstracts some share of the products from those whose toil brought them into the sphere of exchange. It is difficult to see in what sense it can be said to replace anything, since, while it adds to value—that which measures the difficulty of obtaining a commodity—it adds nothing directly to the quantity of commodities, but trenches upon the quantity that would otherwise be shared by the producers. It does not follow that such services are unprofitable to a community. A certain amount of them is absolutely indispensable; and a class of men devoting themselves to the business of effecting exchanges, can do so with a saving to the community, resulting from the general principle by which the division of labour secures economy of labour. It is obvious, nevertheless, that the smaller the amount of capital and of labour required for the purpose of conducting the traffic of a community, the greater will be the amount left free for the work of production.

We shall have occasion to refer to other passages of the "Wealth of Nations," from which the grounds of the proposition under dis cussion may be inferred more clearly and satisfactorily. That which has been cited above, was selected for the purpose of presenting, in connection with it, the contradiction which it has met from Mr. Ricardo and his followers. It is a place where the paths divide—and they lead to irreconcilable differences. Mr. Ricardo quotes at full length the proposition of Adam Smith, and comments as follows:

"This argument appears to me to be fallacious; for, though two capitals, one Portuguese and one English, be employed, as Dr. Smith supposes, still a capital will be employed in the foreign trade double of what would be employed in the home trade. Suppose that Scotland employs a capital of £1000 in making linen, which linen she exchanges for the produce of a similar capital, employed in making silks in England: £2000, and a proportionate quantity of labour, will be employed in the two countries. Suppose, now, that England discovers that she can import more linen from Germany for the silks that she before exported to Scotland, and that Scotland discovers that she can obtain more silks from France in return for her linen than she before obtained from England, will not England and Scotland immediately cease trading with each other? and will not the home trade of consumption be changed for a foreign trade of consumption? But, although two additional capitals will enter into this trade—the capital of Germany and that of France—will not the same amount of Scotch and English capital continue to be employed? and will it not give motion to the same quantity of industry as when it was engaged in the home trade?" —*Principles of Political Economy, chap.* 26.

These questions may be safely answered in the affirmative, without conceding the fallacy of Dr. Smith's argument. The answer would only admit, that if at the same time that Scotland lost a market in England she found a better in France, and England also found a market in Germany in the place of that she lost in Scotland—that is, were TWO foreign exchanges substituted for the single domestic exchange—exchanges involving the value of £4000, £2000 supplied by Great Britain, and £1000 each from Germany and France, instead of an exchange at home comprehending values on both sides, amounting to but £2000—then the same quantity of industry would be put in motion as if the silk and linen had been exchanged within the island. The form of the interrogatory admits, by necessary implication, that both the contingencies specified should concur, before the industry of Great Britain can be compensated for the suspension of its internal commerce; and this is admitting that commerce to be equivalent to double the amount of foreign trade, in its contributions to the support of domestic labour. This, however, is the very proposition the fallacy of which was to be shown. We are under no obligation, therefore, to inquire whether the supposed contingencies are likely to occur at the same time. If we were, a mere probability would not suffice. It ought to be shown that the one had a necessary tendency to bring about the other—that the fact that Scotch linen would not pay for English silk, afforded a positive reason why it should be received in payment for French silk—that because English silk was rejected by Scotchmen, *therefore*, Germans would be anxious to obtain it. It is cheapness, unquestionably, that must be supposed to recommend an article to purchasers, other things being equal. Mr. Ricardo's illustration implies, that German linen is found to be cheaper to the English, who pay for it with silk, than the linen of Scotland: why then should the people of France, who also pay in silk, purchase the dear Scotch commodity instead of the cheap German? The supposition involves a state of things which would naturally lead to the destruction of the linen manufacture in Scotland, because of its inability to produce as cheaply as Germany, and of the silk manufacture in England, from inability to compete with France. The entire industry of Great Britain, in both species of manufacture, must either be thrown out of employment, or that disaster averted by means which Mr. Ricardo does not suggest, and which are inconsistent with the belief that foreign trade is equally advantageous with internal exchange.

Mr. M'Culloch, in a work on Commerce, quotes the proposition of Adam Smith, and reasons upon it as follows:—

> "If, when Scotch manufactures are sent to Portugal, the same demand for them continues in England as before they began to go abroad, an additional capital and an additional number of labourers will be required, to furnish supplies for both the English and Portuguese markets."

This requires no comment. He then puts the other case.

> "If, at the same time that the Scotch began to export manufactured goods to Portugal, the Londoners also found a foreign market, where they could be supplied at a cheaper rate with the goods they had formerly imported from Scotland, all intercourse between Scotland and London would immediately cease, and the home trade would be changed for a foreign trade. It is obvious, however, that this change would not occasion any embarrassment, and that it would not throw a single individual out of employment."

We pause here to remark, that, as in the illustration of Mr. Ricardo, we have *two* foreign markets, supposed to have been acquired, in the place of one internal exchange suppressed. The quotation continues:

"On the contrary, a fresh stimulus would be given to the manufactures both of Scotland and the metropolis, inasmuch as *nothing but their being able to dispose of their produce to greater advantage, could have induced the merchants to change the home for a foreign market.* The fact is, that when a home trade is changed for a foreign trade, an additional capital, belonging to the nation with which it is carried on, enters into it; but there is no diminution whatever either of the capital or industry of the nation which has made the change. So far from this, they are plainly diverted into more productive channels, and are employed with greater advantage."

It will not escape observation, that while the argument in the first of the above passages is *conditional*, the conclusion drawn from it in the second is absolute. To make them homogeneous, the latter should read — "The fact is, that when a home trade is changed for a DOUBLE foreign trade, an additional capital," &c.

In regard to the passage we have italicised, it may be remarked, that if we grant the sole inducement of the Scotch merchants, in sending their goods to Portugal instead of London, to have been the ability to dispose of them to greater advantage, yet it is by no means clear in respect to the London traders. They have lost the domestic market, which the exchange of their merchandise for that of Scotland furnished—lost it, not because they saw any advantage in the withdrawal of their Scottish customers, but because of the supposition that the latter could do better elsewhere. It is no longer a matter of choice whether they will sell to Scotland or to France, but a matter of necessity that they sell abroad or make no sale. The question is not one of the greatest profit, but of the least practicable loss. The goods already produced must be sold; and, as the purchasers no longer come for them, they must go in search of purchasers. If, when the existing stock is exhausted, the trade stops, then the labour which produced it is thrown out of one employment, to which it has been trained, and in which it has acquired knowledge and skill, to take its chance of finding another, and beginning a new apprenticeship to acquire the knowledge and skill necessary for its prosecution. If, on the contrary, the trade continues, and the producers are kept in their former employment, it proves, not that it is as advantageous to them as before the change, but only that it is less unprofitable than to starve in idleness, or to throw away the capital which they have accumulated through their skill, by betaking themselves to employments for which they are unfitted.

The radical error in Mr. M'Culloch's argument is, that the pro ducers, the ultimate and real parties to every exchange, are left out of view, and merchants are substituted for them — a class whose profits depend simply upon the price at which they can vend commodities abroad; while, in respect to its internal exchanges, it is the quantity of commodities that is of consequence to a nation, and their price is immaterial. If price and value always corresponded, then, so far as the interests of the nation in the aggregate are concerned, the less the price of any given quantity of the products of its own labour, the better. It is evidence that those products are attainable with little labour, and that the community has a large stock of conveniences at its command—at its command if its available labour is actually employed, but not otherwise. Price and value correspond in respect to the aggregate interest, only when the actual labour of the community is equal to its potential labour, when the entire productive ability of the community is exerted, under the most advantageous extension of the division of labour; for the associated people is burdened with the support of all its constituents, whether productive or unproductive. The private trader has no such burden; if he increase its amount by throwing an individual out of employment and rendering him a pauper, to subserve an immediate personal interest, he derives all the profit, while, of the accompanying loss, but an infinitesimal portion falls upon himself, and the rest is levied upon the guiltless. A profit in dollars and cents, on the day-book, is the consummation and end of a transaction with him, though a debit to a hundred times its amount in the ledger of a county poor-house may be its consequence. The moment we begin to talk of merchants, or to permit their notation of profit to mix itself up with our tacit transitions of thought, these vital considerations fade from our view, unless a strenuous effort is made to retain them. An author writing deliberately in his study, may avoid any absurdity from this cause sufficiently flagrant to be startling, while it escapes a practised debater, who is delivering the same ideas with less cautious premeditation, and who only exposes by pardonable inadvertence, what lurked undetected in the reasoning of his teacher. Thus, Sir Robert Peel, in a speech in Parliament in defence of the repeal of the Corn Laws, on the 6th July, 1849, endeavoured to support the doctrine of Ricardo and the modern British Economists, by the following illustration:

"Let us suppose the case of two artizans or dealers, resident in the same town—a shoemaker and a tailor. The one wants clothes, the other shoes: they think it right to encourage the domestic industry of their own town—to deal with each other and not with strangers. The shoemaker gives ten shillings to the tailor for a certain quantity of clothes, which he could get for seven shillings if he bought them in a neighbouring town. But, by way of compensation, the tailor gives him his custom, and pays ten shillings for shoes, which he could buy from a distant shoemaker for seven. Is there not a loss of six shillings to the town in which they live, as the result of this dealing between these tradesmen?"

It is very remarkable, that an intelligent man could bring himself to suppose that this question could be answered otherwise than in the negative. The transaction is a barter of shoes for clothes, and nothing more. How can it possibly affect the interest of the town whether one price or another is put upon them, the same being put upon both? To take an extreme case, let us suppose that the clothes are exhibited in the tailor's window, with a ticket marked £1000 upon them, and the shoemaker is obliged to borrow the money from a banker in order to purchase them. The next day, the tailor seeing a pair of shoes, also ticketed £1000, purchases them with the identical money he had received of the shoemaker, and the latter takes the money back to the banker in payment of his debt. The town was possessed of shoes, clothes, and £1000, in coin, before the exchange: it is possessed of the same afterwards. What is true of a town is true of a larger territory. To those who are exchanging labour, the prices affixed to its products are immaterial, so that the price bears the same proportion to labour in one case as in the other.

Sir Robert Peel explains the application of this passage, by treating the shillings as representing each an hour's labour; and the exchange between the shoemaker and tailor, as the giving of ten hours' labour by each for that which might have been procured in seven. "Could not each party," he asks, "have procured that for which he gave the labour of ten hours by the labour of seven, and thus have had three hours at his disposal?" That evidently depends upon the question, whether he could obtain employment or not. Each has condemned the other to idleness, and each has, unhappily, *ten* hours at his disposal, with no customer for them. The problem is, how is a man to obtain seven shillings by ten hours of idleness? Doubtless, it is easier to obtain seven shillings than ten, by working at the same rate of wages, but when wages cease they are equally unattainable.

While the illustration presented by Peel serves to show that reasoning, based upon the relations of price, really determines nothing in regard to the aggregate interest of a community, it nevertheless suggests a question which has something substantial in it. We may assume it to be satisfactorily proved, that domestic exchange, other things being equal, maintains twice the amount of productive industry that a foreign trade to the same extent would support. Two labourers, however, whose toil only suffices to procure their own subsistence, add no more to the capital of the nation than does one. Whether one of them or two are merely provided with food, the surplus stock of the community is stationary. If they should cease to exist, the nation would be no poorer than before, except in a military point of view. If, however, they produce a surplus, however small, beyond their own wages, the national wealth is increased, and the loss of one of them would be a positive injury. We must inquire, therefore, whether domestic exchange has any advantage over foreign trade, in rendering a given amount of labour more productive, as well as in supporting a greater quantity of labour.

It has been shown that the advantage of exchange, foreign or domestic, arises from its increasing production, by causing the division of labour. All the instances employed for the purpose of illustration, have been those of labour devoted to adapting materials for the use of consumers. The hatter, the shoemaker, the tailor, take cloth made of wool, flax, or cotton, and the skins and furs of animals, and change their form, converting them from the shape in which they came from the hands of the original producer, into manufactured fabrics, ready for wear. If the result of either system of exchange is to render their labour more efficient, it must be either by the saving of materials, that is, by producing the same quantity and quality of fabrics from less material — or by enabling them to work up a greater amount of material by the same quantity of labour. The latter is obviously of no benefit, unless a greater quantity of material is produced. Unless more wool, flax, and cotton are raised, the skill which converts them into clothing by a smaller expenditure of toil would be fruitless, but for the fact, that the labour which is saved from the work of conversion can be applied to that of producing materials. In the other case, where the advantage obtained is that of saving a waste of material, we find the same ultimate profit. Under all circumstances, the benefit exhibits itself in a given utility produced, with a surplus of materials, which are the basis of a further utility. The question, then, is reduced to this: Which system is most favourable to the production of primary materials; that under which the materials are wrought into the shape adapted for final consumption in the immediate vicinity of the producers, and there exchanged for the labour of those who are engaged in changing the shape of materials, and getting them in the hands of the persons to whose wants they are ultimately to minister, or the system which sends them abroad, for the use of other communities?

The grand divisions of the arts are those of Production, Conversion, and Exchange, Agriculture, Manufactures, and Commerce. The first includes Mining, and every mode of industry by which the elemental wealth, contained in the bosom of the earth, is brought to the surface and severed from the place of its formation, to be transported and modified for human use. The second comprehends all the arts which effect mechanical or chemical alterations in the form and composition of materials, whether carried on in extensive establishments, and with vast and complicated machinery, or by the solitary workman, with the simplest tools. The third includes all those employments, the object of which is to change the location and ownership of products, by transportation, or simple purchase and sale. Agriculture is the first in order and importance; the others are only subsidiary to it—their advantages being summed up in the fact, that they enable communities to devote a larger share of their energies to the first pursuit of man, and measured by the proportion in which they secure the power to do so.

We are thus brought to consider the influence which the vicinity or remoteness of manufacturing consumers exerts upon the productiveness of agricultural industry; that vicinity or remoteness depending, as is sufficiently apparent, upon the degree in which the system of domestic exchange prevails or is superseded by foreign trade. This will involve a discussion of the obstacles to exchange, which are obviously the constituents of its cost, and limit the value which the operations incidental to barter can communicate to the articles in which it takes place. The great obstacle to association is distance in space between the producer and consumer; the great charge upon both is the cost of transportation. This subject cannot be better introduced, than by the following quotation from the "Wealth of Nations;" which will serve also to show the accordance between the principles which have been maintained in this chapter, and those of the author of that great work:

"The great commerce of every civilized society, is that which is carried on between the inhabitants of the town and those of the country. It consists in the exchange of rude for manufactured produce, either immediately or by the intervention of money, or of some sort of paper which represents money. The country supplies the town with the means of subsistence and the materials of manufacture. The town repays this supply by sending back *a part* of the manufactured produce to the inhabitants of the country. The town, in which there neither is nor can be any reproduction of substances, may very properly be said to gain its whole wealth and subsistence from the country. We must not, however, upon this account, imagine that the gain of the town is the loss of the country. The gains of both are mutual and reciprocal; and the division of labour is, in this as in all other cases, advantageous to all the different persons employed in the various occupations into which it is subdivided. The inhabitants of the country purchase of the inhabitants of the town a greater quantity of manufactured goods, with the produce of a much smaller quantity of labour than they must have employed had they attempted to prepare them themselves. The town affords a market for the surplus produce of the country, or what is over and above the maintenance of the cultivators; and it is there that the inhabitants of the country exchange it for something else which is in demand among them. The greater the number and revenue of the inhabitants of the town, the more extensive is the market which it affords to those of the country; and the more extensive that market, it is always the more advantageous to a greater number. The corn which grows within a mile of the town, sells there for the same price with that which comes from twenty miles distance. But the price of the latter must generally not only pay the expense of raising it and bringing it to market, but also afford the ordinary profits of agriculture to the farmer. The proprietors and cultivators of the country, therefore, which lies in the neighbourhood of the town, gain in the price of what they sell, over and above the ordinary profits of agriculture, the whole value of the carriage of the like produce that is brought from more distant parts; and they save, besides, the whole value of this carriage in the price of what they buy."

The great importance of the truth set forth in the closing sentences of the above extract, will justify our dwelling upon it, and presenting the facts which prove that it depends in no wise upon any considerations of value or price. This may be done by a statement of the course of things, verified by daily experience, in a great trade, which is the main support of costly artificial channels of communication. The figures given for the prices of transportation, are those which have actually ruled during the past year. A cargo, say 4000 bushels of wheat, collected in the interior of Ohio, at the distance of 120 to 150 miles from Cleveland, is carried to that city by canal at a cost of 7 cents a bushel; thence by Lake Erie, 206 miles, for 8 cents; thence to New York, 365 miles, by the Erie Canal, and 143 by the Hudson River, for 13 cents. The whole cost of transportation to New York amounts to 25 cents a bushel; and the wheat may be sold at that place for $1. It consequently requires one-fourth of the whole quantity, or 1000 bushels, to defray the expenses of getting it to market. For all practical purposes, the owner who started with a boat-load of 4000 bushels, is possessed of but 3000 when he has arrived at his journey's end. The result is the same, whether the wheat is actually consumed by the various persons, whose capital in boats and horses, and whose personal services in managing them, have effected the transportation, or those services are paid in coin, advanced by the farmers who grew the wheat, and replaced upon its sale. The latter will have but 3000 bushels, or the price of 3000 bushels, with which to buy such commodities as they may desire. If, however, they should expend the whole of the 3000 bushels in exchange for cotton goods from Lowell, cutlery from Connecticut, and whatever else their wants may demand, the difficulty arises, that the latter have yet to undergo a transportation of 800 miles, before they arrive at the farms in Ohio where they are to be used. Enough wheat, or its price, must be reserved, to defray the charges of the return voyage. Fortunately, manufactured fabrics condense a greater value in a smaller bulk than agricultural products, and the cost of their transportation is therefore greatly inferior. Two hundred bushels of wheat, or even a less quantity, may suffice to carry back all that is received in return for what it cost 1000 bushels to bring to the place of exchange. If the cost of transporting the cotton and cutlery, instead of being retained from the wheat, is paid in those articles, or in coin obtained by the sale of a portion of them, the final issue is not altered. So much the less of them will find its way to the farms; and the upshot, under any arrangement as to the modes of payment, or any state of prices, must be, that the cost of transportation both ways falls upon the agriculturists.

We may find abundant evidence of this truth, by comparing the prices of any agricultural staple at varying distances from any great market. Let the reader look into the commercial article of any daily newspaper, published in any of the large cities on the great routes of transit from the West to the seaboard, and he will generally see the prices of wheat, corn, &c., at New York, Albany, Buffalo, Toledo, Chicago, &c., reported by the telegraph, for the same day, or, at all events, the prices given which they bore at the different points at intervals of but two or three days. He may follow, if he will, a bushel of corn from the interior of Illinois, where it sells for 25 cents a bushel, to Lancashire, or Ireland, where it may sell for $1; and if at any stage of its progress he inquires the price which corn grown at that point bears — at Rochester, New York, for instance, where it may be 60 cents — it will appear that the farmer at the intermediate place obtains a price, increased by the whole cost of transportation upon the produce of the more distant soil. The notations of price are used, because it is by means of such notation that the information is communicated through the press. It is easy, however, to avoid any chance of error from this circumstance, and to show that the proposition is as true in regard to labour-value as to price. It is plain that the utmost which can be obtained for a given quantity of grain, is the labour which its nutritive powers will sustain, or the product of that labour; and it is equally plain, that no increase of nutritive power is gained by a change of location. A bushel of wheat will repair the same amount of muscular waste, and can be transmuted by vital chemistry into the same quantity of mechanical force, in Illinois, as in an English workshop. The artizan who eats it at the latter place cannot, by possibility, execute any more work in consequence, than if he fed upon it close by the soil where it grew, and, therefore, can give no more work in exchange. So long as it will leave any surplus, after paying the services of those who carry it, it is doubtless better that it should be transported, than that it should be suffered to rot on the ground; but when the comparison is made between an exchange at or near the place of production and one at a distant point, it is clear that the entire cost of transportation is wasted, and at the expense of the producer. The same reasoning applies to materials as to food. Cotton will make no more cloth in Manchester than in Tennessee. All that can be obtained in return for a bale of it, is the cloth into which it is made, *minus* what must be retained as a compensation for the labour expended in spinning and weaving. This might be had if the cotton-mill were by the side of the cotton-field. If, however, the former be 4000 miles distant, in Manchester, or 1000 miles, in Lowell, the cotton-grower must suffer a further deduction for the cost of carrying the cotton to the mill, and bringing the cloth back again. It is worth noting, because it is easy to remember, that the cost of transporting cotton from Tennessee to Manchester, and that of converting it into cloth, are as nearly as possible equal. It would be absolutely cheaper to make the cloth, to carry it to Manchester and bring it back again, than to carry the cotton and bring back the cloth, as the latter occupies less bulk.

Any improvement in the means of transportation which diminishes its expense, produces the same effect as a shortening of distance. The substitution of a plank-road for the common earth road, of an iron track in place of a wooden one, and, in a still higher degree, the construction of a canal, reduces the cost of carrying the products of agriculture to market; and it is matter of familiar observation, that the whole difference of cost is immediately added to the value of those products at the place of their growth. In 1817, a committee of the Legislature of the State of New York, in a report urging the construction of the Erie Canal, stated, that "the expense of transportation from New York to Buffalo is about $100 a ton, and the ordinary length of the passage about twenty days." The price of wheat in the Genesee country was at that time thirty-one cents a bushel. Immediately after the construction of the canal, it rose to $1 a bushel, and has ever since maintained about that price. The average cost of transporting a ton of produce from Buffalo to New York, for the last twenty years, has been about $8 80. In this case the difference between the present price of wheat, and that previous to the opening of the canal, is very much less than the difference in the cost of transportation. It is to be remembered, however, that in the mean time cultivation has been extended to the great West, which now sends about 500,000 tons of wheat and flour per annum to the Hudson; and that the price of Genesee wheat is that which it can maintain, in the face of this competition from the region bordering the great lakes. The test case is, that of opening a new and cheap route of transportation to market, in the place of a slow and expensive one. Such cases are of so frequent occurrence, and the result, in giving to the producer the whole saving in the cost of carriage, so uniform, and so generally known, as to require no illustration.

At any given price for agricultural produce, there is obviously a certain distance from market, at which its whole value will be exhausted in the cost of reaching it. It varies, of course, with the bulk and weight of the commodity, and with the mode of transportation. We may take fifteen cents a ton as about the average cost of carriage upon the ordinary earth roads of this country. Thirty-three bushels of wheat or corn may be taken as the equivalent of a ton. If we estimate wheat at the price of one dollar, and corn at fifty cents a bushel, the value of the former will disappear, or become equal to zero, at 220 miles, and the latter at 110 miles from market, if they must be drawn by teams on the common highways. Beyond those distances they will respectively become worthless for the purpose of sale, and the producer can have no pecuniary inducement to raise any larger quantity than suffices for his own consumption. The bulkier products, like potatoes, cabbages, &c., of course become valueless at a smaller distance. At twenty-five cents a bushel, potatoes would cease to afford any remuneration to the grower fifty miles from market, even if land were gratuitous, and the labour devoted to their cultivation could be procured for nothing. Other products, like peaches, strawberries, and lettuce, do not admit of carriage for any considerable distance, in consequence of their delicate character, or the necessity of their being eaten in a fresh condition. Milk can be transported but a short distance; butter, a somewhat longer; cheese, a longer still. Considerations of this nature obviously make the kind of cultivation to which land can be profitably applied, dependent upon its vicinity or remoteness from the persons by whom its products are to be ultimately consumed. When the distance is reached at which the value of corn is absorbed in the expenses of reaching the consumer, the difficulty may be overcome by converting it into pork. Five pounds of grain, it is said, are sufficient, under a judicious system of feeding, to make one pound of meat. There is no reason why it should require any less quantity in the vicinity of the market; nor is there any difference in the comparative nutritive power of meat and grain at the two points. Their actual relative value in maintaining the ability to labour in the human frame — the quantity of heat and of muscular and nervous energy they can respectively supply—must be the same at one place as at another. The pork, however, into one pound of which the value of five pounds of grain has been compressed, can be transported at one-fifth the cost, and, therefore, leave something to remunerate the grower. Turnips and pumpkins will bear less carriage than grain, and lose all value in their original shape at a much shorter distance from market: but turnips may be converted into mutton, and pumpkins into beef. The circle in which sheep and cattle husbandry are resorted to, is therefore a more limited one than that in which the raising of grain, or animals fattened upon grain, will prevail. At a certain distance the value of meat disappears. In Brazil immense numbers of cattle are slaughtered merely for their hides, their flesh being abandoned to the carrion birds. The same practice prevailed in California before the American conquest. The agriculturist is everywhere subjected to the necessity of adapting his modes of tillage and grazing, not simply to the capacity of the soil which he cultivates, but to its distance from the abodes of the men who are to eat, and wear, and fabricate its products. He is controlled in regard to the kinds of crops and stock that he shall raise, not by the quantity it is in his power to obtain in return for a given amount of labour, but by the quantity that he must sacrifice in conveying them to his customers. He can consult his inclination and judgment, and exert his powers productively — his trade, the great trade of civilized man, is free—in inverse proportion to the space he is compelled to traverse in effecting his exchanges.

It needs, we think, no farther demonstration that foreign trade, by abstracting labour from production to expend it in fetching and carrying products, necessarily involves a positive waste of power, as compared with domestic exchange. The nearer the parties to barter are to each other, the greater, other things being equal, will be the amount of products they can bring to the market, which each proffers to the other, and the greater, therefore, the amount and value of the exchanges which will be effected between them. It is plain, that in proportion to the number of inhabitants in any given district or country, will be their proximity to each other. When the population of the State of New York, now a little over 3,000,000, shall have become 6,000,000, the intervals which now separate New Yorkers will be reduced one-half in their dimensions. No greater amount of transportation will be necessary to accomplish the aggregate traffic of the 6,000,000, than is now required for that of 3,000,000. Their products, however, in the natural course of things, will have more than doubled, as well because a less proportion of labour will be withdrawn from production, as because the greater proportionate quantity of labour which will be employed in production, will be made more effective by an increased degree of subdivision and specialization. In regard to the consideration last mentioned, we shall content ourselves for the present with a citation from Mr. Mill, which contains the evidence of its own truth, as well as testimony to the general concurrence of Economical writers:—

"The division of labour, as all writers on the subject have remarked, is limited by the extent of the market. If, by the separation of pin-making into ten distinct employments, 48,000 pins can be made in a day, this separation will only be advisable, if the number of accessible consumers is such as to require every day something like 48,000 pins. If there is only a demand for 24,000, the division of labour can only be advantageously carried to the extent that will every day produce that smaller number. This, therefore, is a further mode in which an accession of demand for a commodity tends to increase the efficiency of the labour employed in its production. The extent of the market may be limited by several causes: too small a population; the population too scattered and distant to be easily accessible; deficiency of roads and water-carriage; or, finally, the population too poor—that is, their collective labour too little effective, to admit of their being large consumers. Indolence, want of skill, and want of combination of labour among those who would otherwise be buyers of a commodity, limit, therefore, the practicable amount of labour among its producers."—*Political Economy, vol.* 1, *page* 158.

We have treated the question of the comparative advantage of domestic and foreign exchange, as if the former could be substituted for the latter, only by inviting the foreign producer to emigrate, and take his place by the side of the domestic producer, with whom he formerly exchanged labour across the boundary of their respective countries, and the intervening tracts of land and sea by which their countries may be separated. The reason for instituting the comparison under this restriction is, that the Economists who maintain that both modes of exchange are equally advantageous, argue that it can never be profitable to naturalize a new species of industry, if it requires any domestic producer to change his employment. That he is employed in making hats, for instance, in Connecticut, which he exchanges for shoes made in England, is, they conceive, evidence that his labour is more effective in hat-making than in shoe-making, and that the change must consequently be to a less productive, in the place of a more productive industry. Among other objections to the force of such reasoning, it has been mentioned that it obviously involves the supposition that there is nobody idle, though willing to work, in the country to which it may be proposed to transfer the new industry—and, moreover, ignores the fact that people are being born every day, and every day arriving at an age fit for labour, whose employment in any imaginable mode, abstracts no person from any other department. We avoid, however, all controversy upon these points, and all risk of error from a possible mistake in regard to them, by stating the question as if the naturalization of a new industry necessarily involved the naturalization of the men who labour in it. Let the case be treated as if it were like that of the introduction of the woollen manufacture into England, in its early history, by the emigration of the weavers from Flanders; or that of the silk and other manufactures, at a later period, by the settlement of the Huguenot refugees, who fled from France upon the revocation of the Edict of Nantz. If the reader will refer to the language of Mr. Mill, last quoted, he will see that such an accession of artizans tends to obviate or to diminish *all* the impediments which are enumerated as preventing the division of labour in the *existing* employments, by limiting the extent of their market. Is the population too small? Every emigrant makes it larger. Is it too scattered and distant to be easily accessible? The addition of a body of recruits renders it more dense. Is the difficulty in a deficiency of roads and water-carriage? The necessity of transportation diminishes with the density of population. Men who are a mile apart must have a mile of road. Bring them within half a mile of each other, and there are two men to make and keep up that half mile of road, where there was but one before; and each of them has more leisure to devote to keeping the highway in order, because he has but half as much travelling to do as formerly. The ability to defray the cost of transportation in a given district, increases as the square of the number of inhabitants. Where there is one inhabitant to the square mile, he toils over the hill-tops on a mule-track, with an insignificant load, and at enormous expense: where there are a hundred, they dart through the valleys on a railroad. Is the population too poor to admit of their being large consumers? The saving in the cost of exchanging their products, and the increased effectiveness of their labour, by reason of its greater division, consequent upon extending their market through the increase of customers in the new-comers, make them all richer.

The power of a people to regulate the extent of its domestic markets, exceeds its capacity to control those in foreign countries. It can, by agreement, expressed in the shape of legislative enactment, or otherwise, secure whatsoever market its internal consumption may afford to the industry which supplies it, while it can only conjecture, and experiment upon the extent of market which that same industry may find, if its products are driven abroad for disposition, and is liable to have such markets reduced, not only by free competition but by restrictive enactments. This circumstance is worthy of consideration; but we can here give it no more than a passing allusion.

We have thus compared the influence of foreign and domestic exchange, in regard to the amount of production, only so far as production depends upon the quantity and quality of human labour available, under the contrasted systems, for its increase. We have found that internal trade is the more advantageous, because it admits of a greater saving in the labour required to be applied to conversion and transportation, and thus increases the quantity that may be given to production. It sets free an additional number of persons, who may devote themselves to obtaining materials from the earth, the only source from which such products can be drawn. The number of agriculturists and miners is increased. If the land within the territory of the nation is not already entirely occupied and cultivated, it follows that more land must be subjected to tillage; if already tilled, a greater amount of labour must be expended in its cultivation. Such would be the case, even if the substitution of domestic exchange for foreign trade did not lead to the introduction of new inhabitants from abroad; for a greater proportion of the native citizens are left free for agricultural labour. It would be the case in a still higher degree if the change should induce immigration. And here we encounter the objection from the followers of Ricardo, of "the decreasing fertility of the soil." They argue that the superior lands having first been taken into use, the new labourers must be obliged to resort to lands which yield an inferior return. We have thus come round, in the circle of our inquiries, to the point at which we started, and can now see that the doctrines of Malthus and Ricardo, in regard to Population and Rent, lie at the root of their difference with Adam Smith. If they are correct, then it is possible that the disadvantages resulting from an increase of population, which compels more labour to be devoted to cultivation, may counterbalance the advantage of having a larger share of labour available for that purpose.

The doctrines which suggest the objection under consideration, have been examined in the first and second chapters of this treatise, and shown, as we think, conclusively, to be absolutely without foundation, and directly the reverse of the fact. If the conclusions at which we there arrived are sound, and men uniformly proceed in the work of cultivation from lands of inferior to those of superior productiveness, then the new agricultural labour set in motion, by the substitution of domestic exchange and production in the place of foreign trade, must be relatively more effective, and yield a larger return in proportion to its amount, than that already in operation. The new producers will open the mines, in which Nature has been storing up the elements of fertility for a longer time, and in greater profusion than in those previously opened. The addition which they will contribute to the aggregate production of their country, will be a greater quantity than an equal number of their predecessors in agricultural labour have been able to make, because they obtain more liberal assistance from the accumulated vegetative forces, on which no draft has yet been made. The additional work which the community has obtained by the transfer of power from exchange to production, is done under more favourable circumstances and with better machinery.

We do not design to renew the discussion of the Ricardo doctrine of Rent. Trusting that the reader is satisfied of its incorrectness, and concurs in the belief that the last labour spent upon the land is, so far as it depends upon the laws of Nature, the most profitable instead of the least, we, nevertheless, invite his attention to some considerations, the validity of which does not depend in any degree upon the truth of that doctrine or of its opposite. It is proper, however, to remind him, that Mr. Ricardo recognises "advantages of situation" as equivalent in all respects to fertility of soil. Advantages of situation consist in nothing else than greater facility, or smaller necessity, for transportation. Mr. Mill is explicit in the admission, that such is the meaning of the words. "Land may be inferior," he remarks, "either in fertility or in situation. The one requires a greater proportional amount of labour for growing the produce; the other for carrying it to market." He repeats, after a few sentences: "Inferior lands, or lands at a greater distance from the market, of course yield an inferior return; and an increasing demand cannot be supplied from them unless at an augmentation of cost, and, therefore, of price." * Again, after the interval of a page, the same idea is reiterated: "Only when no soils remain to be broken up, but such as, either from distance or inferior quality, require a considerable rise of price to render their cultivation profitable, can it become advantageous to apply the high farming of Europe to any American lands; except, perhaps, in the immediate vicinity of towns, where saving in cost of carriage may compensate for great inferiority in the return from the soil itself." Now, it will not escape observation, that one of these causes of diminished return from land is directly antagonistic to the other. The same increase in agricultural population which drives the last comers to inferior lands diminishes the intervals between them. This is a general

* Political Economy, vol. 1, page 215.

objection to the doctrine. In regard to its application to the particular question in dispute, it is enough to remark, that however distant the producers from the consumers *within* their country, they will at all events be nearer than if the latter were in another country, and will therefore have gained advantages of situation by the transfer.

There is, however, no necessity of determining how far one of the conflicting elements, which, according to the Ricardo hypothesis, affect production, may counterbalance the other. The system of foreign trade, of itself, necessarily tends to impoverish the land already under cultivation, to reduce it to a lower grade of fertility, or, what is the same thing, to require a greater outlay of labour and capital, in order to maintain its rate of production. We have seen that the process of growth is but a part of the process of circulation; that no new material is created under the action of the vegetative forces; but that they simply elaborate one form of matter out of others. The soil continues to produce, only upon the condition that whatever is taken from its surface shall be returned to it in some form or another. Every crop is made from matter furnished by its predecessors; and whatever is lacking in the manure will surely, sooner or later, disappear in the product. Exhaustion and renovation must reciprocate in equal measure. If any element, however minute in quantity, is constantly withdrawn and removed from the soil, the product of which it is a constituent must finally cease to reappear. If animals are fed upon the land, their excrements restore a large portion of the inorganic matter, of which the plants on which they feed have robbed the soil. But the richest pasture will, after a time, show signs of exhaustion, if the young cattle that grow upon it are sent to distant markets. Let the cattle remain, and their manure be faithfully restored: if they are cows, a considerable quantity of phosphate of lime is contained in their milk; and if this is sent away in its original form, or in the shape of butter and cheese, the soil must cease to furnish pasture which will make milk. The grass lands of Cheshire, in England, famous for its dairy husbandry, were thus impoverished. They were restored by the application of ground bones—human bones, in a great measure, imported from the battle-fields of the continent—which contain essentially the same substances as the milk. The importance of what might seem insignificant loss to the land, is shown by the fact stated by Prof. Johnston, that lands which paid but five shillings an acre of rent, have been, by restoring the bone phosphates, of which they had been ignorantly robbed, made to yield a rent of forty shillings, besides a good profit to the dairyman. Different crops take away the inorganic substances of the soil in different proportions; the grains, for instance, take chiefly phosphates; potatoes and turnips, mostly potash and soda; but all crops, natural or artificial, deprive the land of some essential ingredient, and, in whatever shape the ingredient is finally removed, in animal or human muscle and bones, in cloth made from the cotton, the wool, or the flax, boots or hats made from the skin or the fur of the animals, no matter how many transformations the elements may have undergone, the vegetative power of the earth from which they were withdrawn has been diminished to an equivalent extent. Nature is an easy creditor, and presents no bill of damages for exhausted fertility. We are, therefore, little accustomed to take account of what is due to the earth. An idea, however, of the great pecuniary magnitude of the debt, may be gained from the fact, that the manure annually applied to the soil of Great Britain, at its market prices, was estimated in 1850* at £103,369,139, a sum much exceeding the entire value of its foreign trade. In Belgium, which sustains a population of 336 to the square mile—one to every arable acre in the kingdom —which, according to Mr. M'Culloch, "produces commonly more than double the quantity of corn required for the consumption of its inhabitants," and where immense numbers of cattle are stall-fed for the sake of their manure, the liquid excrements of a single cow sell for ten dollars a year. The people of Belgium are able, by making their own population, animal and human, the most dense of any country in the world, to raise beef, mutton, pork, butter, and grain, cheaply enough to admit of their exportation to England, to feed people who believe in over-population.

The necessity of taking into account the comparative exhaustion resulting from the growth and removal of different crops, as well as their comparative cheapness of transportation, modifies considerably

* Macqueen's Statistics, page 12

the inferences which would otherwise be made in regard to their value. A work in which all the circumstances which can affect the economy of different modes of cultivation, are subjected to rigorous mathematical calculation* — the necessary elements being derived from exact accounts, kept by its author during fifteen years of superintendence of an agricultural school and model farm in Germany—supplies us with this illustration. Three bushels of potatoes, it is said, have been ascertained to possess the same amount of nutritive power as one bushel of rye—the standard with which all crops are compared by this writer. It is also stated that ground, equal in extent and of equal quality, will produce nine bushels of potatoes where it would yield but one of rye, while one bushel of the latter demands as much labour as $5\frac{7}{10}$ of the former. A given quantity of nutriment could therefore be obtained upon one-third the area of land, and with half the amount of labour, by the cultivation of potatoes, which would be required to produce it in the shape of rye. But in order to keep the soil in heart, so that it will continue to grow either rye or potatoes, a certain portion of the farm must be devoted to pasturage, that manure may be made. Taking into account the requirements in this respect of the two crops in question, it is found that the same area which suffices for the production of 39 measures of nutritive matter in rye, instead of producing three times that number in potatoes, yields but 64. The actual value of the two crops, instead of bearing the proportion of 100 to 300, has that of 100 to 164.

The above calculation proceeds upon the assumption, that the farm must manufacture and save its own manure. Every town, however, every hamlet where artizans are congregated, is a place whence the refuse of crops, after subserving human nutrition, may be removed with great advantage to the health of the inhabitants, and no detriment to the productiveness of their industry. The

* De Thünen: "RECHERCHES sur l'influences que LE PRIX DES GRAINS, LA RICHESSE DU SOL, ET LES IMPOTS exercent SUR LA CULTURE," page 178. The work is only known to the writer in the French translation, made from the original German, under the auspices of the National and Central Agricultural Society of France.

sewer-water of large towns contains its refuse in a state of dilution highly favourable to the growth of plants and the increase of fertility. "From every town of a thousand inhabitants," says Professor Johnston, "is carried annually into the sea, manure equal to 270 tons of guano, worth, at the then current price of guano in England, $13,000, and capable of raising an increased produce of not less than 1000 quarters of grain." It is alleged by competent engineers, that liquid manure can be distributed at a much less cost than that of carting an equal fertilizing value in a solid form. The drainage-water from a large portion of the city of Edinburgh has been conducted into a small brook, and made to overflow some three hundred acres of flat land, which is thus rendered so productive as to be sometimes mown seven times in a season. A portion of it, held under a long lease at £5 per acre, is sub-let at £30, and some of the richest meadows at even higher rates. Advantages of this character are the result of combination upon a large scale. The centres of population, however, supply manures which may be made immediately available by the individual farmer, with no other assistance than that of his own carts and horses. Whether it is more profitable to manufacture manure upon the farm, by devoting to that object portions of the land, which might otherwise grow crops for sale, or to procure the manure from town, depends upon the price which must be paid for it, and the distance to which it has to be carried. The German agriculturist, to whom we before referred, has deduced the relation between the prices the farmer can afford to pay for fertilizing material at the town—for the purpose of growing potatoes with the same economy as if it were made from other crops upon the farm—and the distance it is to be transported. The result at which he arrives is, that a quantity of manure which would be worth $5 40, for the purpose of applying to land in the immediate suburbs of the town, or where the expense of cartage is so trifling that it may be disregarded, is worth $4 20, if the farm be one German mile (4·60 English miles) distant—$3 10, if the distance be two German miles—$1 90, at three miles—83 cents at four; and that at the distance of 4¾ German, or about 22 English miles, he can pay nothing for it: though he may still carry it away as cheaply as to give up the growing of potatoes upon that portion of his land, which must otherwise be devoted to the growth of crops for restoring the fertility which the tubercles exhaust.

It follows, from considerations which in the preceding paragraphs it has been sought to elucidate, in scant proportion to their importance, that the vicinity of the producer to the place where conversion and exchange are effected—in other words, to the consumers—is an indispensable condition of his being able to grow those crops which the earth yields most abundantly. The same space which, sown with wheat, gives what has been termed muscular matter — that is, muscle-sustaining power—to the amount of two hundred pounds, if planted with cabbages gives fifteen hundred pounds; in turnips, a thousand pounds; in beans, four hundred.* It is, however, as we have seen, but a limited circle around the centres of population, in which the agriculturist has the capacity to determine freely to what object he will consecrate his land and his labour. In proportion to his distance from the consumer, two causes act in concert to contract his power. The first is the cost of transporting the crop to market, which compels him to select those whose bulk is small compared to their value, because they require much land and much labour for their production. The second is the difficulty of bringing back, over the increasing distance, the refuse of the crop; in default of which the crop itself runs out. Whatever may be the quality of soil cultivated, these conclusions are equally valid. They hold good, without reference to the truth or falsehood of the theory of Ricardo, in regard to the occupation of the earth; while they are fatal to that of Malthus, as showing that density of population is essential to the plenitude of subsistence.

The illustrations which we have employed have generally supposed the existence of towns, from which the fertilizing elements remaining in the refuse of vegetable and animal products, after all has been extracted from them which is useful for the food and clothing of human beings, as well as what the body rejects after the process of digestion, can be gathered up to stimulate further production. There is a visible tendency in those who devote themselves to the work of conversion and exchange, to agglomerate in towns. The

* Professor Johnston, in Edinburgh Review, October, 1849.

stage of industrial progress at which any community has arrived, is denoted by the proportion subsisting between its rural and civic population. It is an unavoidable tendency; for population attracts population. Wherever a blacksmith sets up his forge and anvil, he creates a demand for the presence of the baker, the tailor, the carpenter, and every other artizan whose labour can contribute to his comfort. Their children require the presence of the schoolmaster; and with him comes the demand for the bookseller and the printer A single tailor may perhaps make the clothing for a hundred men; if so, the advent of one individual calls for only that minute fraction, the hundredth part of a tailor. He requires, however, some fraction of the labour of a hundred other craftsmen; and when the fractions are combined, as by the accession of three hundred persons to the population of a town, their value amounts to one or more units. Let a factory be erected upon the bank of any stream, and a hundred weavers or spinners be collected, it is evident at once that butchers, bakers, shoemakers, &c., must also come, and that the latter invite still further accessions, by furnishing a market for the labour of others. If there are only enough carpenters to supply the wants of the operatives in the factory, in making machinery, buildings, &c., another is necessary, to saw and plane for the blacksmith and his fellow-mechanics, for the grocer, the doctor, and the clergyman. With every one that comes, the necessity of sending to a distant town for some product or service, diminishes, the advantages of combination increase, and the town becomes more attractive. People gravitate towards it in proportion to its mass—to the number who have already been collected.

The argument, however, derives none of its force from the supposition that the consumers are assembled in large numbers in villages or cities, and loses none if that supposition is negatived. On the contrary, the more equally the inhabitants are diffused throughout their territory, the less is the aggregate of transportation which substracts from their productive power. The natural course of things is towards the growth of a multitude of little centres of exchange, for the reasons thus indicated by Adam Smith. After remarking that, "According to the natural course of things, the greater part of the capital of every growing society is first directed to agricul ture, afterwards to manufactures, and, last of all, to foreign trade," he declares "that order of things is in every country promoted by the natural inclinations of man;" and, giving the reasons why man retains, in every stage of his existence, a predilection for the primitive employment of the race, he continues:

"Without the assistance of some artificers, indeed, the cultivation of land cannot be carried on, but with great inconveniency and continual interruption. Smiths, carpenters, wheelwrights and ploughwrights, masons and bricklayers, tanners, shoemakers, and tailors, are people whose service the farmer has frequent occasion for. Such artificers, too, stand occasionally in need of the assistance of one another; and as their residence is not, like that of the farmer, necessarily tied down to a precise spot, they naturally settle in the neighbourhood of one another, and thus form a small town or village. The butcher, the brewer, and the baker soon join them, together with many other artificers and retailers, necessary or useful for supplying their occasional wants, and who contribute still further to augment the town. The inhabitants of the town and those of the country are mutually the servants of one another. The town is a continual fair or market, to which the inhabitants of the country resort, in order to exchange their rude for manufactured produce. It is this commerce which supplies the inhabitants of the town, both with the materials of their work and the means of their subsistence. The quantity of the finished work which they sell to the inhabitants of the country, necessarily regulates the quantity of the materials and provisions which they buy. *Neither their employment nor subsistence, therefore, can augment, but in proportion to the augmentation of the demand from the country for finished work; and this demand can augment only in proportion to the extension of improvement and cultivation.* Had human institutions, therefore, never disturbed the natural course of things, the progressive wealth and increase of the towns would, in every political society, be consequential, and in proportion to the improvement and cultivation of the territory or country."

The great cities, which grow up to proportions outrunning the cultivation of the country, where population is unnaturally congested, and which Jefferson called "eye-sores on the body politic," these are everywhere seen to be the result of foreign commerce. So far as they constitute an exception or impediment to the natural tendency of things, towards the distribution of exchanges among numerous local centres, it is the consequence, not of physical laws, but of subjection to institutions which tolerate the effort to thwart men's natural inclination, to conform to those laws and make their exchanges at home rather than abroad.

It has now, we conceive, been rigidly demonstrated, that inland or domestic trade maintains at least double the number of producers that could be sustained within the country by the opposite system, and that it necessarily tends to increase the efficiency of all those labourers, while foreign commerce tends to rob the earth of the aliment, by which alone its fertility can be maintained. The proposition is especially true of that kind of commerce which the teaching of the modern English Economists, and the steady policy of the British Government, has sought to impose upon the nations—a commerce to consist in the production, by all the countries that can be coaxed or coerced into the arrangement, of raw materials for food and clothing, to be transported to the workshops of the Islanders, for conversion, and carried, in the shape of the finished wares, back to the producers for consumption. Against the enactments by which that Government deprived us, while yet in colonial subjection to her rule, of freedom of trade and of freedom of production, the indispensable basis of trade, Adam Smith remonstrated with indignant energy. Among the regulations which he denounces, the following are enumerated.

"While Great Britain encourages in America the manufacture of pig and bar iron, by exempting them from duties to which the like commodities are subject when imported from any other country, she imposes an absolute prohibition upon the erection of steel furnaces and slit-mills in any of her American plantations. She will not suffer her colonies to work in those more refined manufactures, even for their own consumption; but insists upon their purchasing, of her merchants and manufacturers, all goods of this kind which they have occasion for.

"She prohibits the exportation from one province to another by water, and even the carriage by land upon horseback, or in a cart, of hats, of wools, and woollen goods, of the produce of America; a regulation which effectually prevents the establishment of any manufacture of such commodities for distant sale, and confines the industry of her colonists in this way to such coarse and household manufactures as a private family commonly makes for its own use, or for that of some of its neighbours in the same province."

The same course pursued in regard to these States, has characterized British policy in the treatment of her colonies the world over; the uniform object being, to compel them to export their raw products, in the rudest shape, and to effect their exchanges at her mills, and forges, and shops, instead of effecting them at home, by means of the construction of the requisite machinery of conversion. It required a seven years' war for us to obtain the freedom of trade, so far as it depends upon freedom from direct legislative prohibition. When that was accomplished, the new States were sorely deficient in industrial education, which England had prohibited them from acquiring, and which she still exercised the power of impeding them in acquiring, by prohibiting the emigration of artizans and the exportation of machinery. With the advantages she possessed and maintained, by the monopoly of machinery and of the workmen skilled in its construction and use, her manufacturers were able to undersell and ruin the adventurous artizans, who in other countries made the attempt to imitate her machinery, and educate themselves in the modes of employing it.

It is obvious that a monopoly of the trade of conversion, has the same effect upon nations who submit to it, whether maintained by superiority in art, or by superiority in arms. In either case, it compels them to make their exchanges in a manner that wastes and exhausts the sources of production, and robs labour of its legitimate reward. They have to determine the question whether they will permit themselves to be forced into a course of operations, contrary to the order of Nature and to the natural inclinations of man, or will vindicate their freedom to conform to that order and to pursue those inclinations. The question is to be resolved by a comparison of advantages and disadvantages. The disadvantages of acquiescence which we have enumerated are permanent in their nature. The advantages of internal production and domestic exchange are likewise permanent, and, what is more, increasing. Increased diversification of employment, and consequent skill—increased capital, from increased productiveness in the earth and diminished waste in transportation, necessarily facilitate still further increase in skill, and in capital for the future. The people that once begins the improvement of its productive power, finds every step in its progress more easy than the last; while every moment that it permits itself to be driven on the downward path, diminishes its ability to make a stand or retrace the way. On the other hand, there is an immediate and palpable disadvantage in resistance. It involves an apparent sacrifice, that of paying a larger *price*, counted in coin, for domestic wares, than that at which they are offered by the foreign nation. Such, at least, is the temporary effect. If it be made to appear that this effect is to be permanent, and that the money-price is a true indication of the cost in labour at which the foreign wares can be procured, the propriety of substituting domestic production for purchase from abroad, must be justified by other than mere Economica. considerations.

In the State of Tennessee, cotton grows in one field and corn in the adjoining. Water-power runs to waste in a thousand streams. Timber, and stone, and iron-ore, for the construction of buildings and machinery, are abundant upon their banks. If we are told that the planter, who grows the cotton and the corn, can obtain cloth more cheaply by sending the cotton to Manchester to be spun and woven, and sending with it the corn to generate and maintain mechanical power in the spinners and weavers, than by having the cotton manufactured upon his own plantation or that of a neighbour, by men who eat the corn, we may well demand the proof. If the Price-Current of New York or New Orleans is offered as evidence, showing that Manchester cloths are imported at lower prices than similar fabrics made at Lowell or Cannelton, we cannot fail to conceive a suspicion that the true state of facts is not indicated by the money-price. The planter has, in the first place, infallibly to pay for the transportation of his cotton to the English mills — it may require, perhaps, one-tenth of the cotton to meet this charge, and nearly as much more is rejected as *waste* in the spinning. In the next place he has to pay for the transportation of the corn which feeds the spinners; and this absorbs three-fourths of its value, as is indicated by the fact that its price is four times as much when it reaches Manchester, as it bore when it left the plantation. It is bought by the spinners and weavers at the enhanced price, constituting a great part of their wages; it enters into the value of the cloth at that price. The planter sells it at twenty-five cents, and buys it back at a dollar a bushel. In the third place, a portion of the cotton is subtracted, to remunerate the mill-owner for the use of his machinery, and the operatives for the trifle of wages not paid by the corn. Finally, he must pay for the transportation of the cloth from Manchester to the plantation. The fact last mentioned deserves attention in this point of view. In estimating the advantage in price of a foreign product, the price at the various internal places of consumption must be regarded, and not merely that at the docks or warehouses upon the seaboard. The difference may be quite inconsiderable in an island like Great Britain, but in the

United States, extending from ocean to ocean, or in an empire like Russia, the difference may well be large enough to counterbalance at some points and exceed at others, the superior cheapness in money of the imported merchandise at the ports of entry.

Of the items of cost above enumerated, the only ones common to domestic and to foreign production, are wages, and the charge for the use of machinery, or profits. All the rest are an absolute waste; expenses which profit neither country. If the foreign commodity can be permanently imported at a cheaper rate than it can be produced at the source of the raw material, it must be because the foreign producer possesses advantages in the cheapness of labour and capital, more than counterbalancing the loss sustained in the other items of cost. In regard to wages, it has been sufficiently shown that a low price, instead of indicating cheap labour, betokens the reverse. It is no reason to apprehend a failure to reduce the cost of production, when the requisite skill shall have been obtained by practice, that high wages must be paid to the workmen during their education, and even higher when it is completed. Wages, moreover, are mainly expended in food; and the lower their rate, the more nearly are they exhausted in supplying this primary want. It is quite obvious that it makes no difference to the Tennessee planter, whether he pays a spinner in his immediate neighbourhood a bushel of corn, or one in Manchester a peck, expending the other three pecks in defraying the cost of carrying that one to him. If it be desired to adhere to the money-gauge for testing the comparative advantages, it makes no difference whether he pays twenty-five cents a day for the wages which are incorporated in his cloth, and obtains but twenty-five cents a bushel for his corn, because its price is regulated by a market four thousand miles distant, or pays a dollar a day for wages, selling corn for a dollar a bushel, because its market is at his own door. What is true of corn is true of all other agricultural products, which must be exported unless consumed in the country. Internal manufactures, therefore, have a necessary tendency to reduce the labour-cost of commodities, by giving increased value to the food and raw materials with which they must be purchased, and to the labour which these represent. In looking, however simply, at money-price, this consideration escapes notice. So, too, of the impoverishment of the soil resulting from the exportation of its products. Every fabric imported in return for such products, should have a certain sum added to its nominal price on this account, before that price truly corresponds with real cost.*

The rate of profit affects the price of a commodity, only to the extent of that portion of profit which is derived from a single article

* The following extracts from letters addressed to the Patent-office, in reply to the annual inquiries as to the agricultural condition of the various portions of our country, exhibit the result of the two systems. The first is from Chester District, South Carolina, where the system of exportation and foreign trade prevails.

"The breadth of land we cultivate, and the few cattle we are able proportionably to keep, seems to paralyze efforts. * * * * * Plaster, which could be had at Charleston at $5 the ton, would cost $20 more to bring it up here. *We could buy three acres of fresh land for what it would cost to lime one.*"—*Agricultural Report for* 1850–51, *page* 237.

Here land is made worthless by the exhausting system, and must be abandoned, because manures cannot be obtained so cheaply as fresh land, to exhaust in its turn. Dispersion and poverty are the necessary result.

The following are from Connecticut, where the soil is poor; but manufactures have made a market in the neighbourhood for its products, and enabled the manure to be saved:

"Twenty-five years since much of our plough-lands was exhausted, and presented as forbidding an aspect as does much of the worn-out lands of Maryland and Virginia. By judicious cultivation these lands have been most completely renovated, and their productiveness and value have increased from 100 to 500 per cent. The same land, which a few years since would hardly pay for cultivation, will now produce 60 bushels of corn per acre, and other crops in proportion."—*New Milford, Litchfield, Connecticut.—Agricultural Report for* 1851–2, *page* 178.

"This is a very prosperous part of the country, which is evidenced by the price of labour, which, for a man to work on a farm, is not less than $150 per year, with board. * * Everything the farmer has to dispose of he can get as high a price for as is obtained in any part of the United States, and gets the *cash;* and what he buys he can buy as cheap. Here, likewise, the small capital of $2000 may be obtained by any young man by the time he is thirty. * * Market gardening is carried on as extensively here, perhaps, as farming proper." — *Grt ton County, Connecticut. — Ibid, page* 186.

of the kind. The absolute quantum of profit contained in the price of a single yard of cloth, is the thing to be considered in comparing the cost of two methods of procuring it. A given rate of profit upon the capital employed, may be as well obtained by the sale of a large quantity, with a small profit upon each unit, as by a large profit upon a smaller number of units. It is indifferent whether the mill-owner receives a profit of half a cent upon each of two million yards of cloth, or of one cent upon each of one million, if the same amount of machinery which produces the smaller quantity is adequate to the production of the larger. It is for this reason, among others, that the extent and regularity of the market for any fabric, has a considerable influence upon its cost. But it is in the power of every nation to secure for its own manufacturers a market to a certain extent, that of its domestic consumption. By excluding foreign competition, and enabling them to enlarge their sales, it enables them to secure the same *rate* of profit, with a reduction of the *amount* of profit upon each sale, in other words, by a reduction of price.

But this is not all. Every bushel of grain saved from the waste of transportation to foreign markets—every bushel of increased production, due to the saving of manure, which would otherwise be sent abroad in the shape of food and raw materials, creates a new purchasing power, to the full extent of its value. These furnish a market for a domestic manufacture, which had no existence, nor could have by possibility, for its foreign counterpart. The market for the domestic produce is, therefore, necessarily a larger one than the country could afford to the foreign merchant. The exclusion of the latter gives *more* than he is deprived of to his internal rival. It is not a mere transfer from one to the other of a fixed demand for his wares, but of a more enlarged demand than was previously shared by the two. This fact implies a still greater increase in the power of the domestic producer to reduce prices, without a sacrifice of profit, than if his market were confined to that which was supplied by foreign trade. We have seen, too, that an extension of the market tends to reduce the cost of production, for another and independent reason, the increased division of labour which it induces. Whatever, therefore, may be the price at which the domestic production of a commodity commences, that price may be reduced without a reduction of wages or profits, by excluding foreign competition, and thus giving the producers in the country the possession of its entire market, in place of a part of it.

That competition among new producers will reduce price, so as only to afford the ordinary rate of profit, is admitted by Ricardo, Mill, and all the respectable Economists. None of them conceive that the excess of price, while it exists, can afford any extraordinary profit to the domestic manufacturers, except for the briefest period; for if it should it would stimulate a competition, until profits in the favoured employment should be reduced to the common level. There is no reason to fear that the entire community will not obtain the benefit of every diminution in the cost of production, or in the price remunerative to the manufacturer.

The method usually adopted by nations, to obtain the free use of their natural advantages, is the imposition of duties upon the importation of the foreign commodities which people desire to produce at home. These are known as protective duties, and the policy which sanctions their imposition as the protective system. That policy is condemned by most of the modern Economical writers, upon grounds which have been sufficiently examined—the principal one being that there is no difference in point of advantage to a nation between foreign and domestic trade. The most enlightened of them, however, admit an exception, broad enough to cover every case which can come within the range of the preceding argument. It is admitted on substantially the same grounds, by Say, Rossi, Scialoja, J. S. Mill, and others, who adhere generally to the opposing theory. The latter says:

"The superiority of one country over another in a branch of production, often arises only from having begun it sooner. There may be no inherent advantage on one part, or disadvantage on the other, but only a present superiority of acquired skill and experience. A country which has this skill and experience to acquire, may in other respects be better adapted to the production than those which were earlier in the field; and, besides, it is a just remark, that nothing has a greater tendency to promote improvements in any branch of production, than its trial under a new set of conditions. But it cannot be expected that individuals should, at their own risk, or, rather, at their certain loss, introduce a new manufacture, and bear the burden of carrying it on, until the producers have been educated up to the level of those with whom the processes are traditional. A protecting duty, continued for a reasonable time, will sometimes be the least inconvenient mode in which a nation can tax itself for the support of such an experiment."—*Political Economy, vol.* 2, *page* 495.

This concession, it will be observed, takes no account of the compensating circumstances which, from the very beginning of the experiment, diminish, if they do not wholly counterbalance the temporary excess of price which is regarded as a tax. The impoverishment of the soil, the waste in the transportation to distant markets of agricultural products, which must be exported to pay for the labour of conversion—these, and the other *sacrifices* attendant upon the system of foreign trade, go for nothing; they are ignored in the school, of which Mr. Mill is justly among the most distinguished teachers. But, irrespective of these, the one fact remains, which gives the widest application to his admission. Every country necessarily possesses advantages for the conversion of materials, drawn from its own domain, above every other country, in the saving of the cost of transporting those materials, and the articles which are given in exchange for them, after the work of conversion has been effected. The manufacture of beet-sugar furnishes a striking example of the extent to which these advantages may counterbalance those resulting from superiority in other respects. The manufacture owes its origin in France to the blockade which shut out the sugar of the tropics from the ports of the Continent. Though very expensive in the first instance, it grew up slowly, under the protection derived from the duties imposed for the sake of revenue upon the exotic product, until it was found that the production had become so large as to supersede the *cane* sugar to a large extent, and seriously to impair the revenue. In 1837 it was subjected to a duty, fixed at a rate which it was supposed would restrict its production to the amount of one-third the annual consumption of the kingdom, retaining the other two-thirds of the market for the tropical colonies. The beet-sugar, however, exceeded the proportion, and continued to displace that made from the cane. In 1847 the domestic beet-sugar was subjected to the same duties as were imposed upon colonial. Its production continued to increase, and, of course, to supplant the cane sugar, to the injury of the revenue; and, in 1851, a law was passed, the operation of which was suspended until 1852, by which for four years the sugars of the French colonies are to pay six francs per

19

100 kilogrammes (220 pounds) *less* than the indigenous product. The domestic production has increased very rapidly, rising to 76,151,128 kilogrammes in 1851, in place of 62,175,214, in 1850,* in spite of the fact that a larger weight of cane is raised to the acre than of beet-root, and that the cane yields a much larger proportion of sugar. In the States of the German *Zoll-Verein*, the culture of sugar has increased still more remarkably, being nearly four times as large in 1851 as it was in 1844.

Every country begins the work of converting its native products with an advantage in prospect that it is sure to realize, provided only its people have the capacity to educate themselves up to the degree of skill, the prior possession of which gives a temporary superiority to foreign manufacturers, and that they can obtain the use of equal machinery. Unless prepared to concede that its artizans are inherently stupid and unteachable, there is no reason why it should not make the effort. The requisite skill once obtained, there can be no difficulty in regard to capital. Food and raw materials exist everywhere; and the materials for the construction of machinery, wood and iron-ore, the remaining constituents of capital, are abundant throughout the world, only waiting for the intelligence to combine them in proper forms, and put in action the slumbering energies imprisoned in the forest and the mine. The machinery of foreign exchange, moreover, is ordinarily quite as costly as that of domestic conversion. The labour and materials expended in building a ship to carry cotton to Manchester and bring back cloth to Mobile, would suffice for the erection of a factory, which would long outlast the vessel, and convert more cotton into cloth than it could do in its life-time by fetching and carrying. No matter who furnishes the machinery of exchange, its use must be paid for, and that at a rate sufficient to provide for its renovation within the time during which ordinary employment wears it out. Although the first cost may be advanced by foreign merchants, it is necessarily replaced by the charges levied upon the producers who furnish freight. To an individual, whose powers are limited and whose lifetime is brief, it may be a matter of importance, if not of absolute necessity, to hire the

* Annuaire de l'Economie Politique, 1852, page 175.

more costly machinery of foreign exchange, instead of combining existing materials in the more durable machinery of conversion. A community, however, is immortal, and, by means of combination its powers are adequate to any object which far-sighted economy may dictate. Having continuity of succession and eternity of duration, it can never afford to sacrifice the permanent interests of the unlimited future to the convenience of the fleeting present.

It is objected to the protective policy that it is hostile to commerce, that the nations of the world, from their differences of climate, are adapted to the production of different commodities, which their mutual interest requires them to exchange. Neither figs nor cotton can be raised in Russia or England, but both are wanted. They can be obtained only by the exportation from those countries of other descriptions of merchandise, for the production of which they have peculiar advantages. Nature has indicated what has been called "the territorial division of labour," and this can be maintained only by international exchange. In this there is an undeniable truth; but it in nowise militates with the considerations we have presented. The question is not of the exchange between nations of their respective natural products, but of the form in which those products shall be exchanged. Doubtless it is the interest of every people, after its own wants are supplied, that the surplus of its productions should be exchanged at the least possible expense, for the surplus, which other communities may have for barter, of other kinds. What is really exchanged, however, is the labour embodied in commodities on either side—value resulting from labour, and representing mainly the food by which that labour was maintained. The distance between two parties who desire to trade being given, the natural obstacles to the accomplishment of their purpose are measured by the bulk of the wares they respectively possess, in proportion to the labour that produced them. Each will have more to exchange, and will receive more in exchange, in proportion as he compresses a large value into a small compass. Between the miners of Illinois and of Pennsylvania more lead will be bartered in bars, for more iron in pigs, than could possibly be exchanged if both or either were offered in the unsmelted ore. Foreign trade is facilitated, and can be extended in the same way as domestic. Adam Smith has embodied the whole philosophy of the matter in the following passage:

"An inland country, naturally fertile and easily cultivated, produces a great surplus of provisions beyond what is necessary for maintaining the cultivators; and on account of the expense of land-carriage, and inconveniency of river navigation, it may frequently be difficult to send this surplus abroad. Abundance, therefore, renders provisions cheap, and encourages a great number of workmen to settle in the neighbourhood, who find that their industry can there procure them more of the necessaries and conveniences of life than in other places. They work up the materials of manufacture which the land produces, and exchange their finished work, or, what is the same thing, the price of it, for more materials and provisions. *They give a new value to the surplus part of the raw produce, by saving the expense of carrying it to the waterside, or to some distant market;* and they furnish the cultivators with something in exchange for it, that is either useful or agreeable to them, upon easier terms than they could have obtained it before. *The cultivators get a better price for their surplus produce, and can purchase cheaper other conveniences which they have occasion for.* They are thus both encouraged and enabled to increase this surplus produce by a further improvement and better cultivation of the land: and *as the fertility of the land has given birth to the manufacture, so the progress of the manufacture reacts upon the land, and increases still further its fertility.* The manufacturers first supply the neighbourhood, and afterward, as their work improves and refines, more distant markets. *For though neither the rude produce, nor even the coarse manufacture, could, without the greatest difficulty, support the expense of a considerable land-carriage, the refined and improved manufacture easily may.* In a small bulk it frequently contains the price of a great quantity of the raw produce. A piece of fine cloth, for example, which weighs only eighty pounds, contains in it the price, not only of eighty pounds of wool, but sometimes of several thousand weight of corn, the maintenance of the different working people, and of their immediate employers. *The corn which could with difficulty have been carried abroad in its own shape, is in this manner virtually exported in that of the complete manufacture, and may easily be sent to the remotest corners of the world.*"

We are thus brought round to the proposition, that the true way to extend and increase foreign trade is to foster the domestic, which, in the order of Nature, precedes it, and from whose overflowings it must be fed. It also appears that the way to provide a vent for the surplus of raw agricultural produce — the necessity of finding a larger vent for which than our domestic consumption affords, is presented in this country as the chief argument against restrictions upon importation—is to work up that produce into the form admitting of the most distant transportation, which is therefore the most widely merchantable. It is because Great Britain has done so in so eminent a degree, that it has been truly said by a member of her Parliament, himself a strenuous advocate of that policy of foreign trade which in England filches the good name of free trade, "that Great Britain is the largest grain-exporting country in the world, as her grain, after being converted in the human laboratory into broadcloths, calico, hardware, &c., finds its way to every country of the world."

It is not within the scope of this treatise to adduce history or statistics, any farther than is necessary for the illustration of principles, otherwise we might examine at some length the results in the cheapening of production, in some of the principal countries that have sought to effect that purpose by a system protective of domestic trade. We find, however, a brief statement in a late British Review, which is unimpeachable testimony to the general success of such efforts.

"We have now many rivals, where thirty years ago we had none; we formerly supplied nations, which now partially or entirely manufacture for themselves; we formerly had the monopoly of many markets, where we are now met and undersold by younger competitors. To several quarters we now send only that portion of their whole demand, which our rivals are at present unable to supply. A far larger proportion of our production now than formerly, is exported to distant and unproducing countries. A far larger proportion now than formerly, is exported to our own colonies, and our remote possessions. More, relatively, is sent to Asia and America, and less to Europe. Countries which we formerly supplied with the finished article, now take from us only the half-finished article or the raw material. Austria meets us in Italy; Switzerland and Germany meet us in America; the United States meet us in Brazil and China. We formerly sent yarn to Russia: we now send cotton-wool. We formerly sent plain and printed calicoes to Germany: we now send mainly the yarn for making them. All these countries produce more cheaply than we do—but as yet they are not producing *enough:* we therefore *supplement* them. Partly by our old restrictive system, partly by the natural effect of an increasing population, they have been driven from the plough to the loom — or have been driven to add the loom to the plough; and henceforth our manufacturing production can increase only, not by underselling or successfully competing with our rivals, but by *the demand of the world increasing faster than our rivals can supply it.* This is more or less the case with all our principal manufactures; it is pre-eminently the case with our chief manufacture, the cotton." — *North British Review, for November,* 1852, *page* 156, *American edition.*

The Reviewer supports his statement by tables relating to the cotton manufacture, which show the consumption of the raw material has increased since 1837 more than twice as fast in the Continental States which have adhered to the protective system, as in Great Britain, and at a more rapid rate than in the United States, and declares that the comparison of 1852 will be still more against the country. "Something of the same process," he observes, "is going on in the wool trade — the Belgian manufacturers are now competing on more than equal terms with the Leeds clothiers," the result of which is seen in a greatly increased exportation of wool from England, to be spun and woven in Germany. Upon this point there is abundant evidence. Thirty years ago the States of the Zoll-Verein exported wool and imported cloth. Since 1816, as appears by the Prussian census of 1849, the production of wool in that country alone has doubled, while the population has increased but 58 per cent.; yet it now imports wool and exports cloth. Within the last year the French Government has reduced the duties upon wool brought from Australia and South America, on the express ground, that it had become necessary in consequence of the supply from Germany and Spain having ceased, owing to the increase of their manufactures.

The point, however, to which the testimony of the North British Review has been adduced, is simply that the power to manufacture at as cheap a *money*-price as Great Britain, has been attained, in the countries that have sought it, through efficient protection. In every such instance, the duties imposed for protection have obviously ceased to be a pecuniary tax, and the advantages which are not indicated in the *price* of manufactures, are a great and permanent acquisition. Russia, France, the States of the Zoll-Verein, and the other countries who adhered to the policy which promotes domestic production, and secures what alone can justly be called free trade—that which accords with human nature and human inclinations — are rapidly advancing in wealth and power. Turkey and Portugal, the nations which, possessing nominal independence, have been most submissive to the British policy, and Ireland, which has been coerced, are the most backward nations of Europe, and have now less power to resist than they had a generation ago. As against these, what are called the natural advantages of England are constantly increasing, while in respect to those who saw that the advantages were artificial, they have constantly diminished and are diminishing. The invention of Mr. Ericsson promises greatly to detract from one advantage which the British Islands have heretofore possessed over several of the Continental nations, in the possession of cheap and abundant coal to propel her machinery. If five-sixths of the quantity which has heretofore been necessary to procure a given motive force, can henceforth be dispensed with, the advantage of cheap coal must diminish in the same proportion, and those who are now most hampered by the dearness of fuel, will derive the largest benefit. As they succeed in the effort to combine their materials and food in manufactured fabrics, England will cease to find employment in *supplementing* them, will be forced to buy materials at a dearer, and sell fabrics at a cheaper price, and at the same time to seek more distant markets for them. The final result must be, to compel her to raise her own food, which she can do more cheaply than it can be procured elsewhere, whenever her rulers become willing to let the labourer have his fair share of it, and to allow him to become that most efficient of all food-growers, the tiller of his own fee-simple land. Retiring from the business of keeping "the great workshop of the world," dismissing the colonies, kept as customers, and the fleets and armies necessary to guard them, she can make a market at home worth more than all that are relinquished, and whose magnitude will measure what those do not, the wealth, prosperity, and happiness of her children. In proportion to the intensity of her struggle against this consummation, will be the misery through which it must be reached.

CHAPTER VIII.

MONEY AND PRICE.

We have thus far treated of Exchange, so far as it was possible to do so, as if it were conducted by simple barter. There are, however, many inconveniences in such a method. The man who has a quarter of beef to dispose of, may desire to procure bread, knives, calico, and shirtings, tea, books, and a variety of other articles. It would occasion him a great deal of trouble to go round to the various persons who possess the commodities he desires, and to apportion to each the share that, upon discussion, should be fixed as the equivalent of his merchandise. The man who owned calico, which he was ready to barter, might happen to be already supplied with a stock of beef. From the earliest period at which men established any considerable association with each other, they have endeavoured to obviate the inconveniences of direct barter by the adoption of some general medium, in which the values of other commodities are expressed, and which is generally accepted in exchange for products and services, in the first instance, with a view to its being subsequently bartered for other products or services. There are several properties belonging to the precious metals, gold and silver, which render them peculiarly fit for this purpose, and indicate that their general adoption is by no means accidental or arbitrary. One of these is their absolute uniformity in quality. Being simple substances they are everywhere alike; the gold of California and that of Australia are identical; the silver of Mexico and that of Russia are precisely the same substance. Another is, their capacity of minute division, and of being converted back into large masses by fusion. They are extremely durable, sustaining little injury from the action of fire, and none from rust, and enduring a great deal of handling without sensible loss from abrasion. They are very ductile, not liable to break, mix readily with the alloys of other metals, by which their hardness can be increased, and from which they can be separated again with very little loss, and they receive and retain an impression, which denotes the weight and purity of metal. The qualities which have been enumerated give them a high value for use in the arts, independent of the service that they render as coin; a very material circumstance, inasmuch as it puts and keeps them upon the same footing as other useful products.

Another circumstance, specially adapting them for use as a medium of exchange, is that they include a large value in a small bulk. This has been due, in part, to the comparative rarity of the known deposits from which the precious metals could be extracted; in part, to the inferiority of machinery which has been employed, and of the workmen who have pursued the business of mining. The employment has always presented dazzling temptations, and has always been attended with great hazards and insecurity. It has almost universally been the occupation of barbarians, or barbarized those who yielded to its allurements. It has, consequently, been a costly and unprofitable trade. Two advantages result from this circumstance, in respect to the use of precious metals as the general intermediary of exchange. The one is, that a small quantity of them suffices to facilitate the transfer of a large quantity of other useful wares. The second is, that it has tended to maintain the uniformity of their value, by limiting the additions which, in any given time, have been made to the existing stock. Considering their great durability, and that the quantity in use suffers less diminution than almost any of the things which it aids in transferring from hand to hand, it is plain that a trifling annual addition to the stock of coin—though inferior to the yearly augmentation of the general mass of commodities—would rapidly reduce its purchasing power, and deprive it of that stability of value which is the chief recommendation of a circulating medium. The circumstance is important, also, in regard to the degree of uniformity of value existing between gold and silver at different places. Like everything else, their value is limited by the quantity of labour necessary to produce them at the market where it is estimated, and this necessarily includes the labour of transportation from the place of their origin. Silver was cheaper in Mexico, in the immediate vicinity of the mines, than in New York, to which it was carried; and cheaper there than in London, which is still more remote. Gold is cheaper at San Francisco than at New Orleans, by the cost of carriage. The difference, however, is less than it would be in the case of silver, because the latter, in the same bulk, represents but about one-fourteenth as much labour, and the addition caused by the cost of transportation must constitute a larger proportion of its value. In regard to both of the metals, the expense of transportation is so light as to make but an insignificant variation in their value at places within any moderate distance from each other, as between the sea-board and the interior towns of an island like Great Britain.

It is very evident from the preceding considerations, that gold and silver are signally adapted to serve as the common measure of value in comparing commodities, and as convenient instruments for effecting their barter. It is equally clear, however, that at any given time and place, wheat is as much the measure of the value of gold, as gold is of wheat, or of any other desirable object. While gold may vary less at different places, and at different times, it nevertheless is subject to variation, not only in respect to a particular commodity like wheat, but in respect to silver and to all other commodities. A change of this kind has been going on since the discovery of the Californian and Australian diggings, which we may express at pleasure, by saying that gold has fallen and is falling in value; or, that the mass of commodities has risen in value when compared with that metal. This necessity results from the fact, that the quantity of gold now added annually to the stock in circulation in the world, is about four times as much as the annual increase previous to 1848. Gold being obtained with less labour directly devoted to that object, must be obtained with less of the labour which obtains it *indirectly*, by producing articles, which gold is only valuable as the means of purchasing.

The precious metals, when offered in the market as an article of merchandise, in the shape of dust, nuggets, or bullion, are readily perceived to conform to the general laws which regulate the traffic in other wares. It may be supposed, however, that when they have passed through the Mint, and are issued by government in the form of coins, bearing the denomination of dollars, francs, or sovereigns, they have assumed a new character, and become in some degree exempt from the incidents which attach to the ordinary products of industry. It is obvious, however, that coin differs from its material only in the circumstance that it has been refined to a certain degree of purity, mixed with a certain quantity of base metal, and issued in masses of an established form and weight, which is indicated by its name. The good faith of the government is pledged for the accuracy and honesty with which the assaying and other necessary operations have been performed; and the name which is stamped upon the coin is but a brief method of stating the facts. The service which the mint performs, is that of ascertaining and certifying, for the benefit of every individual to whom the coin may be offered, what, at some trouble and expense, he might ascertain for himself. To the extent of the cost of this important service, coin should be worth more than the value due simply to the weight of its constituents. The charge for this service of the Mint, where any is imposed, is called a seignorage. From the fact that the operation, being conducted by government upon the largest scale, is susceptible of greater economy than could be attained by individuals doing it upon a smaller scale, it may be a trifle more than is absolutely necessary to cover expenses, without leading to private coinage. If, however, the government attempts to secure anything more than the minutest profit, it creates an inducement to export bullion to the nearest country where coinage is done upon cheaper terms. The very great facility with which it may be transported and concealed, effectually defeats any regulation designed to prevent exportation; and if legislation for such a purpose could be successful, its effect would be to repel the importation of bullion, and deflect some portion of the natural current to the territory of more liberal States. Where, however, as is the case with the gold coinage of Great Britain,* the government makes no charge for its services, the difference between the value of coin and the metal of which it is composed, sinks to the amount of interest lost in waiting the few days that may be required for assay.

The extreme sensitiveness with which coin feels and obeys the

---

* This was true of the United States; but a law has just been passed, subjecting gold made into *bars* to a seignorage of one-half of one per cent., and reducing the weight of silver in the half-dollar and smaller coins nearly seven per cent. It has been generally stated that gold *coin* is subjected to a seignorage, but I do not so construe the law.

general laws of commerce has been shown, wherever the attempt has been made to maintain both gold and silver as standards. It is possible at any one day to adjust the double coinage in accordance with the value of the metals. There is no difficulty in ascertaining what weight should be given to-day to the eagle, in order that it may be currently accepted as the exact equivalent of ten silver dollars. But before the next session of Congress their relative values may change. The eagle, which is here a legal tender for but ten dollars, may purchase a quantity of silver in England or France, for which the Mint will give ten dollars and sixty-six cents. Such was the case previous to the alteration of the gold coinage in 1834. The consequence was, every eagle coined for years was sent abroad as an article of merchandise. On the other hand, the value of gold may decline, so that ten silver dollars, which the owner can tender in payment only as the equivalent of an eagle, will actually buy as much gold as will procure at the Mint an eagle and thirty cents. Such has been the case recently, and the result has been the disappearance of our silver change; an inconvenience for which Congress has, within the last few days, sought a remedy in the debasement of the silver coin. It may or may not be effectual for a short time: it is clear that there can be no warrant for believing that it will permanently adjust things, which in their nature are subject to continual fluctuation.

Whoever is honestly in possession of a portion of the precious metals, can have obtained it only in requital of labour directly expended in procuring it, as by mining, or of services rendered by his labour or by his capital, which is but the accumulation of past labour. He holds it, *ad interim*, as the means of procuring other services when he shall need them. It can neither be eaten, drunk, nor made to minister to any other want, until it shall be exchanged. If in the shape of coin, it is a token issued by public authority that the bearer has rendered a certain amount of service, for which he has not yet been remunerated. In one of those admirable pamphlets by which Bastiat sought to communicate fundamental notions of Political Economy to the people of France, after the Revolution of 1848, when so much inquiry was directed to its problems, he writes out at length what he truly remarks is the substantial import of the inscription upon a coin. Its language may be freely translated thus, "Render to the bearer in exchange herefor, services equivalent to those which he has rendered to society, the value whereof was measured by that of the ninety-six grains of pure silver contained herein. In witness whereof this piece has been stamped by agents, appointed by the public for that purpose, with the name of half-dollar, and other devices established by the general consent." Money is thus the index of a credit, which its owner has extended to the rest of mankind. Its office, as a currency, is that of a Bill of Exchange, drawn upon anybody to whom it may be presented, and which everybody is willing to hold temporarily, because its material has an inherent utility in the arts, and a value founded upon the labour requisite to produce it at any given time and place.

It is apparent that the use of such a medium does not affect the essential laws of exchange. It facilitates the process, just as a yard-stick or a quart cup does, in so far as its office is that of a measure of values. So far as it is an instrument of transfer, it promotes exchange just as do wagons, railway-cars, and canal-boats. The more that population is concentrated the fewer of these are requisite; and precisely the same economy results in the quantity of coin which a community finds it necessary to employ. It is easy to see that the smaller the quantity the better; for the expense of repairing the annual wear and tear is proportionate to its amount, and all that can be saved from use as coin may be devoted to productive purposes in the arts. The stock, great or small, must be obtained and kept up by labour; and to save any portion of that labour from being expended upon the machinery of exchange, is to put it at liberty, to aid in swelling the production of things to be exchanged. The richest nations are, accordingly, those in which the metallic currency bears the smallest proportion to the mass of wealth. In France the quantity of coin is much greater than in England; it is larger in Spain than in the United States. In England and this country, credit, without its metallic sign, has superseded the use of coin in an immense proportion of business transactions; cheaper tokens having been found equally significant and effective.

Perhaps the simplest form of credit is that upon book-account, between persons who have numerous transactions with each other which are adjusted at the end of the year by the payment of a balance, which must be less than the entire amount of values which have been transferred from one to the other, and may bear the least assignable proportion to that amount. The next is that by which A., to whom a debt is due by B., transfers it to C. in payment of his own debt. If C. happens to be indebted to B. in the same or a greater amount—which is probably the case that first suggested a bill of exchange — then their accounts are at once liquidated, and commodities to three times the value of the bill have been exchanged without the use of a single coin. If, however, C. does not happen to be indebted to A., he takes the bill in the faith that the latter will pay it at maturity, and with the additional security which the law imposes upon A., the drawer, to pay in the event of B.'s failure. If, however, before the maturity of the bill, C. desires to obtain actual payment for the services or products, in acknowledgment of which the bill was originally given to him — that is to say, desires to purchase commodities — he transfers the bill to the person with whom he deals. If the latter should have entire confidence in the solvency of A. and B., he might accept the transfer without any further security. In practice, however, it is usual for C. to endorse the bill, by which he becomes liable to pay the holder, upon being notified of non-payment by the previous parties. In this way it may pass through any number of hands, effecting a fresh transfer of commodities at each negotiation, and at each serving the same purpose as a quantity of coin equal to its value. It has been calculated, from the data furnished by the receipts of the Stamp-office, that the amount of bills of exchange outstanding in circulation, in Great Britain at one time, in the year 1847, was £113,000,000 sterling, or $500,000,000; while the average of bills in circulation at the same time, during the preceding five years, was £99,306,000. They exceed the currency of all kinds, taken together. It is stated that it is not uncommon to see bills with twenty or thirty endorsements, and occasionally with a much higher number.

There is a manifest insecurity in the private custody of money, which naturally leads to the establishment of Banks of Deposit by individuals or associations, who undertake to receive and safely keep the money of their customers, and to pay it out on demand upon their checks. A convenience resulting from the use of checks is, that they can be drawn for the precise sum required; and if the receiver keeps his account with the same banker, a debit to the drawer and credit to the holder, upon the banker's ledger, effect the transfer without the trouble of counting the coin, or carrying it from one place to another. In a large town, where there are numerous bankers, though the deposits are made with different houses, the same result is obtained, by each banker receiving on deposit the checks drawn upon others, and subsequently adjusting the accounts among themselves. The London Clearing House is an establishment maintained by the bankers of that city, at which they daily exchange the checks and bills which each holds, drawn upon other bankers. The Clearing House credits each banker with the bills and checks that he sends in, and which are accepted by the parties on whom they are drawn, and charges him with those drawn upon him; each paying or receiving at the close of the day's business the balance of his general account. By this means payments to the amount of $15,000,000 are daily effected, without using more than $1,000,000 in bank-notes. No coin whatever is employed; the residues of balances, which would require coin for their payment, being carried over to the account of the succeeding day.

It would require but a brief experience to show to the bankers, that of the entire amount deposited with them, a considerable portion remains in their hands, and that they could safely loan it, without danger of being able to meet promptly the checks drawn upon them. It is by so doing that they remunerate themselves for the trouble, risk, and expense of keeping deposits and making payments for their customers. The advantage to the public is, that a larger proportion of the money belonging to its members is kept in active circulation, than if it remained in the custody of the individual proprietors. The economy is precisely that resulting from running a number of wagons along a road, at known hours every day, and thereby enabling those who dwell upon it to dispense with keeping the much greater number that would be necessary, if each provided his own vehicle. Money, like wagons, aids production only while it is in motion; and the number of exchanges which either can effect depends upon the rapidity of circulation. It will be seen that the arrangement tends to reduce the rate at which loans can be obtained, for it brings into the market, looking for opportunities of investment at interest, a quantity of coin, which would otherwise be lying idle in the pockets or iron chests of its scattered owners. It increases the readiness, moreover, of everybody to part with his money in exchange for commodities, if he knows that, in case of an unexpected want, there are facilities for obtaining the use of money until he shall be able to procure it by the sale of property. The banks of the State of New York, on the 4th of September, 1852, with capitals amounting to $62,207,216, had on deposit $66,897,497, and their loans and discounts were $130,124,403; their notes in circulation at the same time were a trifle less than $30,000,000. It is apparent from this statement, how large a share of their power to make loans is derived from deposits.

Instead of an individual drawing a check upon his banker, which is simply an assignment of funds in the hands of the latter, it is more convenient for many purposes that he should possess the banker's acknowledgment of the possession of those funds, coupled with a promise to pay them to the bearer on demand. It is also convenient that such assignments, taking effect by mere delivery, should be of such sums as will answer for small payments as well as large. Such are bank-notes. The credit of a banker, or association of bankers, is ordinarily matter of more general notoriety, although it may rest upon no more substantial basis, than that of the drawer of a check, who, therefore, is able to employ a bank-note in exchanges with persons, who might be distrustful of the payment of his check, or, if not, be reluctant to take it because it would involve the trouble of presenting it, on account of its being indivisible. Bank-notes, moreover, possess advantages over specie in their superior portability. This recommends them to all persons whose business involves the receipt and payment of large sums. The bankers who issue them find their advantage in the fact that the notes, instead of being immediately presented for redemption, remain outstanding, in circulation, for a period varying according to circumstances. The notes of a bank in New York city which are issued one day, are returned upon the next through some other institution, to such an extent that little or no profit is derived from their emis sion, and it is kept up mainly for the convenience of their customers. The country banks, on the other hand, are able to keep out a large circulation. They exchange their notes, payable on demand and bearing no interest, for notes of individuals, payable at a future date, and bearing interest, without having parted with the use of any capital, for the period which elapses before the bank-notes come back for redemption to the issuers, except that which is necessary to repair the wear and tear of the paper on which their promises to pay are engraved. Each banker learns by experience what amount of specie it is necessary to keep on hand, in order to provide for the immediate redemption of his notes. The commercial paper which he has discounted, the drawers and endorsers of which are under the same obligation to redeem them in coin as the banker, is obviously the general and ultimate source from which the funds to cancel his notes and pay his depositors are to be drawn. The property which bank-bills serve to exchange, is that which provides for their payment. A dealer in grain at Buffalo contracts for the purchase of a cargo of corn or flour, in the hold of the vessel which has brought it from Cleveland or Milwaukie. Having transhipped it to canal-boats, he draws upon the consignee in New York for its value, and procuring the bill of exchange to be discounted by a banker, takes his bills and pays them to the person of whom he bought the grain. The consignee in New York sells the grain, and thereby puts himself in funds to meet his acceptance, and when it matures, transfers them to the Buffalo banker. They are now standing to the credit of the latter on the books of his correspondent at New York, and when a merchant at Buffalo wants money at New York to pay for goods purchased there, the banker draws in his favour upon the depositary at New York, receiving a premium to remunerate him for saving the merchant the cost and risk of conveying coin. The banker is now prepared to redeem his bills, or so many of them as remain outstanding, having been obliged to keep in his vault meantime so much coin as sufficed to pay those presented at his counter. The advantage to the banker is sufficiently obvious; that to the community consists in the substitution of a cheaper and more convenient instrument of exchange in the place of coin.

If the profits of the banker are not reduced to the general rate so that the community obtains all the services which his skill and credit can render, as cheaply as any other service is obtained, it is because impediments are thrown in the way of free competition. Such has been almost everywhere the case. The business of banking has been made the monopoly of a few, and granted as a special franchise. Even when individuals have been permitted to engage in it singly, restraints have been imposed, preventing them from freely combining their capital and credit in such numbers as to secure the greatest economy. Perhaps the nearest approach to free banking is that which has been effected under the General Banking Law of New York, enacted in 1838, and since substantially copied in several of the States, and in the Province of Canada. Its leading feature is, that it permits any number of persons to form themselves into a corporation for the purpose of banking, and permits such corporations, or an individual, to issue circulating bills upon certain uniform conditions. The principal condition, designed for the security of bill-holders, requires the banking association, or individual, to deposit with a State officer securities, consisting of stocks of this State or of the United States; or, to the extent of one-half, of mortgages upon lands in this State, at not more than two-fifths of their value independent of buildings. The banker is thereupon furnished with circulating notes, which are countersigned and registered in a department created for that purpose, to an amount equal to the value of the securities—with the exception that nothing is allowed for the premium which the stocks deposited may bear in the market. The interest upon the securities is paid to the banker so long as he continues to redeem his notes: when he fails to do so, the securities are sold by the Superintendent of the Banking Department, and the proceeds applied by him to the redemption of the notes. The amount of circulating notes thus issued was, on the 1st of December, 1852, $19,159,056, about two-thirds of the entire circulation of the State, and securities were held for their redemption to the amount of $20,230,312, of which $10,000,000 was in New York State stocks, $4,747,162 in stocks of the United States, about $1,000,000 in the stocks of States formerly, though not now, receivable, and $4,114,443 in bonds and mortgages. The Constitution of 1846 deprived the Legislature of the power of granting any special charter for banking purposes, and established it as a part of the fundamental law, that corporations or associations for such purposes shall be formed under general laws.

A question may be raised in regard to the necessity or advantage of the legislative provisions for the security of bill-holders, into which our limits do not permit us to enter. Their design is to prevent the establishment of banks by persons not possessed of actual capital, and who, under pretence of lending, would be mere borrowers from the community. By permitting the capitalist to receive the interest upon the securities which he deposits, he suffers no loss in consequence of his capital lying dead; and the knowledge that his bills are thus secured gives them a credit and circulation, from which he derives a profit. It moreover protects the community from the sudden and extreme fluctuations in the paper currency, to which they might be exposed if the bankers were enabled to extend their issues without the deposit of fresh securities. Their private interest is an ample guarantee that they will keep in circulation all the bills representing their original securities, that they esteem themselves able to do with safety. If actually possessed of capital, and therefore entitled to credit, beyond that indicated by their existing circulation, they can obtain a further supply of bills from the Banking Department; provided, only, that there are persons willing to borrow on bond and mortgage, or willing to sell State stocks, or those of the United States. If they have not the capital, there is no reason why they should obtain any factitious credit; certainly none, further than what depositors are willing to extend to them. The character of the securities to be received is a matter of detail, not affecting the principle. That they should be such as are certainly and immediately saleable at their nominal value is all which that demands. A community which accepts the promises of a banker as the equivalent of coin, does so in the confidence that he possesses sufficient property of this character for their redemption. The question between absolute freedom in the trade of banking, and such approximation to it as the New York system permits, appears to me to come simply to this: Whether it is easier and cheaper for a community to assign the labour of ascertaining whether its confidence is well founded, to agents specially employed for that purpose, or to have each person ascertain it at his individual peril and labour?

There is one portion of the securities for the issues of the New York banks, which so well exemplifies the essential character of capital as to be worth a passing remark. The ten millions of New York stocks represent labour performed in digging the canals of that State, almost entirely by emigrant Irishmen — men with stout arms and willing hearts, whom the modern Economy of England regarded as *surplus* in their native land, though one-third of it is waste and uncultivated; though there are bogs to be drained and roads to be made, sufficient to employ their energies for a generation at least. The interest upon those stocks is nothing but canal-tolls— the share which the State receives as a partner in the business of transporting the produce of the Great West, and the goods for which it is exchanged. That same labour reappears in the shape of the circulating medium, thus effecting the exchange from owner to owner, as it does from place to place, of the commodities which float through the canals, and the value of which about equals every year the entire import or export trade of the Confederacy. The fact is pregnant with a whole brood of inferences, which we leave it to the reader to deduce.

The principal forms in which credit assumes the offices of currency have now been stated. They are bank-notes, checks, and deposits subject to immediate draft, which will obviously be regarded by the proprietor in the same light as coin or bank-notes in his own strong-box. Bills of exchange are often regarded in England as forming a part of the currency, and as operating upon prices in the same way. It is plain, however, that they are nothing more than contracts for the delivery of money at a future day, clearly distinguishable from money at immediate command. The distinction is the same as that between a bill of lading, which is assigned as a symbol of goods, and a contract to deliver goods at a future date. The man who parts with property in exchange for a bill of lading, supposes himself to have perfected a transfer; he who parts with property for a promise to give other property at the expiration of a specified time, is conscious that he is lending capital. Bank-notes and checks, or certificates of deposit, answer to the first

They are capable of effecting the immediate transfer of property to a person, in exchange for his transfer of the right of property to money, understood to be in the vaults of his banker, coupled with the right to immediate possession. They act upon prices, in ordinary circumstances, precisely like the coin which they symbolize. Every person owning the symbol has the same power of purchasing, and no less disposition to purchase, than if he was actually the master of coin to the same amount. Bills of exchange or promissory notes can possess this character, only when the individual who exchanges wares for them is confident that he can procure them to be discounted immediately, or at the moment when he may need money. Such confidence may be wide-spread among the commercial class, and be justified for long periods by the fact. When it is, however, it is evident that the fact will appear in the amount of deposits in the hands of bankers, and of their notes in circulation; for, when a discount is effected, the proceeds are either paid over in coin or bank-bills, or are carried to the credit of the party procuring it, and swell the banker's account of deposits.

We may pause here to consider the relation subsisting between Prices and Values. It needs no demonstration that Value, or the amount of labour necessary to reproduce a given article in the market, is the standard by which Price, or the notation of that value in coin, must tend to adjust itself. Price may oscillate upon one side and the other of the mid-point marked by value, but it is at that point it seeks to rest. Where labour is free, it will cease to devote itself to the production of a commodity, whose price secures less of coin and of other commodities than is obtainable by labour expended in their direct production. The change, however, cannot be made instantaneously. Men who have acquired skill in a particular employment, although a reduction of price compel a reduction of wages, may for a long time do better by continuing in it, than by betaking themselves to another employment, in which they will be obliged to serve an apprenticeship before they acquire even a low degree of skill. So, of material capital. It is better to wear out machinery, which produces a profit below that which would tempt the owner to construct it, if he were free to choose the form his capital should assume, than to permit it to lie idle, or to break it up and sell the material for old iron. The question for both labourer and capitalist is, not one of securing the maximum of profit, but of escaping with the minimum of loss. A change in price, however, and the immediate decline of profit which attends it, though it may not actually withdraw a single individual from the production thus affected, will operate to deter others from engaging in it. In a natural state of things, the demand for any commodity, whose use is not superseded by a better, should be constantly increasing; for the population increases, and its ability to purchase more rapidly than its numbers, both from the general increment of wealth, and the distribution of a larger proportion of it to the class whose poverty formerly limited their power to purchase, if it did not entirely preclude them. The very diminution of price which pares down profits enlarges the circle of consumers, by bringing the commodity within the means of a greater number.

It is material to observe, that each successive reduction of price brings the commodity within reach of a larger number than the preceding, or secures it a larger market. Those who were purchasers at a given price, are the purchasers of a larger quantity when the price is reduced; and the circle of those who could not purchase at all at the higher price, but can at the lower, increases in its area at each reduction. This holds true, if the price of the article in question falls from causes which do not affect the prices of other commodities, and which do not diminish the means of payment of producers. If, in this country, the price of broad-cloth should be reduced by means operating in an equal degree to reduce the price of corn and wheat, the market for broad-cloth, instead of extending, would be narrowed. The entire value of the breadstuffs vastly exceeding that of the broad-cloth required by its consumers, they would sustain a loss much greater than the cheapness of cloth would compensate, and their general ability to purchase be diminished in a greater proportion than the facility of purchasing was increased. The proposition is therefore to be limited to the case of the fall in price of a single species of merchandise, all others remaining unchanged. In this case we can see, that while the absolute supply may not be diminished, the proportion of the supply to the demand will speedily decline.

When goods are brought to a market in excess of the wants of purchasers, or of their means of payment, it becomes evident as soon as the fact is ascertained, that the surplus must remain unsold, and be carried away at the expense of the owners, unless the demand can be stimulated to advance sufficiently to absorb it. If the goods of which there is an over-supply should all belong to a single owner, he might be able to calculate the extent of his loss; he could reckon, at all events, that it would be confined to the depreciation upon the surplus beyond what the market would take off at existing prices. This he might carry away to another market, at the cost of transportation, and the risk of finding that already filled, or store in a warehouse, with the loss of interest and charges, to wait the chances of another day. For the purpose of avoiding this necessity, he would be willing to reduce the price of the whole, by an amount equal to his estimate of the certain and the contingent losses from keeping a portion unsold. By so doing he would increase the means of purchasers, that is, would enable them to procure a larger supply with the same amount of money. His purpose, however, would not be fully answered, unless the whole of his wares were sold. If any portion remained unsold, he would be in the position of having submitted to a sacrifice, for the sake of avoiding expense and risk in keeping that portion, yet remaining under the necessity of incurring so much of that expense and risk as belonged to the residue in his hands. If, instead of one proprietor there were several, each of them would feel himself exposed to the chance of not selling, in the same proportion as the entire demand bore to the entire supply. If there were eleven sellers in the market, and a demand existed for the goods of only ten, no one could be secure of selling ten-elevenths of his stock at the existing price, and every one would be subject to the hazard of being left with his whole stock unsold, and thus bearing the whole loss without any contribution from his fellows. Suppose, and it is scarcely possible that it should be otherwise, some one of them, by superior economy of machinery, skill, &c., had produced his wares at less cost than the others, so that the existing market price paid him a higher profit. He would have a greater ability to reduce his price than the others, and would naturally be the first to do so. If the others should permit him to sell out in consequence of such reduction, the chances of each of the remaining nine foi being left in the lurch would be increased. They can prevent it, however, only by submitting to a still further reduction, which he can endure better than they, and can, if need be, exceed; for he can always keep somewhat below the others, without any greater sacrifice. In short, the sellers compete with each other until the demand and supply are equalized. The demand rises as the price falls, till the point is attained where, if the whole quantity originally offered is not taken, the remainder is driven to other markets, or withdrawn, in the hope of a future rise in the same.

We have seen how a fall in the price of a commodity, from an excess of supply, is followed in time by a reverse state of things, in which the demand is in excess. In that case, instead of the holders of goods competing with each other to get possession of the amount of money in the market, and ready to be exchanged for goods, we have the holders of the money competing with each other for the possession of the goods. Prices advance: it requires more money to obtain the same quantity of merchandise, for precisely the same reasons as in the other case it required more goods to obtain a given amount of coin, or its symbols. In the first instance money was up at auction, and the owners of goods were the bidders; in the second, the goods are at auction, and the money-holders bid against each other. This case, like the other, sets in motion a train of operations that bring about its opposite. The profits upon the commodity of which there is an insufficient supply are enhanced, its production is stimulated at the same time that the consumption decreases, until the equilibrium is restored. This fact, however, is not manifest until *after* commodities have been produced and offered in the market, in such quantities as again to effect a reduction of price.

We have thus far confined our attention to the fluctuations of price consequent upon the variations in the demand and supply of a single commodity. The principles by which they are regulated are the same, to whatever standard values may be referred. When the supply of corn is unusually large, no change having taken place in the supply of other descriptions of merchandise, a bushel will purchase less of any other commodity, as well as less of money than if the crop were short. It is obvious that the supply of money and of its symbols in any particular market is subject to ebb and flow, and that consequently there may be a general rise or depression of prices, everything except the unit of currency preserving its relative value. Currency is cheap and redundant at one time, it is scarce and dear at another: and the same diversity may exist if we compare different places, as when we contrast different times. As all the forms of currency in which credit is made the substitute for the precious metals, exert the same effect upon prices as coin, while their amount may be contracted or expanded with greater facility, the method in which such expansions and contractions take place is a subject of great importance.

Let us suppose a particular community, in a state of apparent prosperity, no cause of a political or other character being known or apprehended as likely to impede its regular industry, or interfere with the ordinary briskness of exchanges. Security in the present and confidence in the future inspire every trader with a disposition to enlarge his business, and a willingness to borrow capital, with the hope of obtaining a profit exceeding the interest he is required to pay. He desires to make the most of his credit, and either becomes indebted for goods, for which he accepts bills of exchange or gives promissory notes, or procures similar paper to be discounted, and purchases with the proceeds. If he takes the first course, the person who has given him credit is desirous of replacing his capital, that he may obtain a fresh profit upon another sale, and for this purpose he desires the paper he has taken to be discounted. There may be more or less removes, but eventually the paper, or an equivalent amount of substituted paper, comes to the banks to be exchanged for currency. The latter are desirous of keeping the largest amount out upon interest which they can possibly do with safety, and discount freely in a period of general confidence. The amount of the discounted paper, less the interest for the time it has to run, is either to the credit of their customers upon their books, thus swelling the nominal amount of deposits, or emitted in bank-notes. In either case the currency is increased, and with that increase there is a tendency to a general rise of prices. If notes are emitted by one banker, they are after a time deposited with another. The bankers adjust their balances with each other, and the notes are redeemed by the transfer of coin, equivalent to the difference, and are ready for reissue, while deposits to their entire amount stand to the credit of their customers. Checks drawn against the deposits effect, as the case may be, one or half a dozen transfers of property, and come back to the same bank, either as the deposit of a customer—in which case the amount of deposits is not varied — or are redeemed when presented by other bankers, by the payment of balances trifling in comparison with their aggregate sum. The deposits thus increase with every fresh discount; and every increase in his deposits appears to the banker a safe basis for discount, to some portion at least of its amount. The following extracts from the statements of the condition of the banks of the State of New York, made on the 20th of December, 1851, and 25th of December, 1852, will give some light on this point:—

	Dec. 20, 1851, 230 Banks and Branches had		Dec. 25, 1852, 274 Banks and Branches had
Specie	$8,306,829	......	$11,493,743
Bills of other banks on hand	2,900,187	......	2,880,784
Deposits	46,836,682	......	74,923,943
Circulation	26,228,553	......	33,416,100
Capital	58,621,422	......	65,449,703
Bonds and Mortgages	4,276,697	.....	5,282,062
Stocks, (public securities)	15,269,425	......	18,110,316
Loans and Discounts	104,039,788	......	134,876,930

From a comparison of these statements, it will be seen that the increase in circulation corresponds very closely with that in capital. There is an increase of nearly $4,000,000 in the State stocks, and bonds and mortgages, and this corresponds with the increase for the same period, in the securities deposited with the Banking Department, to guarantee the redemption of circulating notes issued. The increase in deposits is over $28,000,000, while the increase in specie and notes of other banks — the only things in which deposits could be paid—is but $3,000,000. There is indeed an increase of about $10,000,000 in what are called "Cash Items."* These consist of

* Not included in the above abstract. Nine-tenths of what was returned under the vague head of "Cash Items," in the statement of 1851, and nineteen-twentieths in that of 1852, are in the New York City Banks.

uncollected checks, which one bank may hold, drawn on another, or other evidences of indebtedness which are not in point of fact cash, though reckoned as immediately convertible. The loans and discounts have increased more than $30,000,000. If we separate the banks in New York city from those of the rest of the State, it will appear their deposits have increased over $21,000,000, and their loans and discounts over $20,000,000.

From the whole, it is apparent that the discounts and deposits have been advancing at an equal pace, to the great profit of the bankers, who have been trading very largely on credit themselves, and encouraging others, by the facility with which they extended credit to them, to enlarge their business. With a currency swelling from day to day, prices necessarily rise. Whatsoever a man buys he sells at an advance, and is of course anxious to repeat the operation as speedily and as often as possible. A speculative disposition is engendered; money is said to be plenty, and a great deal of it is thought to be lying idle, because the bank accounts show large deposits, which, in point of fact, exist in the shape of promissory notes or other commercial paper, not idle at all, for they are producing interest for the bankers—to whom they serve the purpose of money—and not money, but only contracts to produce money at their maturity. The proprietors of the deposits draw checks against them, buy, and stand ready to buy, precisely as if they were in the shape of gold, and thereby exert the same influence in pushing up prices. New enterprises, involving the expenditure of large capital, are readily undertaken in such a state of things; exchanges being brisk, railroads make large dividends, their shares advance in price, and the temptation is presented to construct new ones, the shares of which are paid for with borrowed money, so far as is necessary to get a track graded, when rails are bought with the bonds of the company, and the corporate credit substituted for that of the individual stockholders, to buy engines and equip the road. It is unnecessary to dwell upon the course of things during a period of expansion and speculation. It is unfortunately too familiar. The process through which the expansion is checked, and what is called a commercial crisis brought about, demands a brief notice.

A country in which the prices are high and rising, is a good country to sell in. It naturally attracts imports in a larger quantity than when its currency was contracted. For the same reason it is a bad country to buy in, with a view to exportation. Those products which before the expansion began, could be carried to another country, and leave a profit when sold according to the scale of prices prevailing there, admit of less and less profit as prices rise in the exporting country, and it may soon entirely disappear. In the natural course of things, the ship which brings a cargo from Liverpool to New York, should be freighted for the return voyage with products bought at New York. The inward cargo, however, is not bartered for an outward one, nor does the ship wait for sales to be effected. Though the exported wares, in the mass, and in the long run, pay for the imports, each particular transaction in the foreign, as in the domestic trade, is effected through the medium of coin or its representatives. It follows that, as the imports enlarge and the exports decline, an indebtedness grows up on the part of the country in which the currency is inflated, to that in which it is in a normal condition. The individual importer at New York who has contracted a debt at Liverpool, discharges it by the purchase of a bill of exchange, drawn by an exporter upon parties at Liverpool who are indebted to him for cotton, corn, or whatever else he sold. If bills upon England are not to be had in sufficient amount to discharge the indebtedness of American merchants, bills upon Havre, or Amsterdam, or other continental ports, may be obtained, remitted to Liverpool, and sold there to English merchants, who may have payments to make in those places. The risk and expense of shipping specie is not undertaken until the means of adjusting international balances by bills of exchange, direct and circuitous, have been exhausted. Bills bear a premium as the necessity of shipping coin increases. If there is a balance above what bills can be found to discharge, every importer being desirous of escaping the necessity of a remittance in coin, all will be disposed to offer a premium somewhat less than it would cost him to export specie, and the price of all bills rises in consequence of their competition. An increasing amount of money, however, is necessary for remittance, and the premium required to purchase bills will, after a time, exceed the expense of the transportation and insurance of the precious metals

The depositors now require payment of the bankers in actual coin. Bank-notes, checks, certificates of deposit, local credit in any form, will not answer for exportation, and are depreciated in reference to specie, with which they were before on a par. The bankers, to put themselves in funds, are under the necessity of converting their discounted bills into money as rapidly as possible. They stop discounting and call in their loans. If by such means they do not actually obtain specie, they redeem their notes, which might otherwise be presented for redemption in coin. Prices begin to fall. The merchants, deprived of their accustomed facility for borrowing, and with obligations coming round every day, upon which they are liable as principals or endorsers, are anxious to sell, while none of them want to buy. The pressure begins in the great marts of foreign trade, and extends from them to the dealers in the interior. The latter are crowded for payment by their distressed creditors, and crowd their debtors in their turn. Property of all kinds depreciates and becomes difficult to sell, when everybody wants to sell, and is anxious to restrict his purchases to the lowest practicable amount. Sales, nevertheless, are made upon credit, for the purpose of obtaining contracts to deliver money at a future day, which can be sold to usurers, who riot in their harvest. Collections are enforced by suits at law, and effected at the expense of a heavy toll to attorneys and sheriffs' officers, out of the proceeds of forced sales. Persons whose property is adequate, even at the depreciated rates, to the payment of their debts, become bankrupt from the failure of their debtors to pay promptly. When the doors of the banking-houses are closed in the afternoon, and a merchant's obligation is protested, his credit is gone, and he ceases the effort to maintain it by ruinous sacrifices. The failure of one increases the embarrassment of his creditors, and repeated failures spread general distrust. As one after another goes down, however, there is one less engaged in the scramble for money, and the survivors experience the same sort of relief as men in a crowd do when some of them faint and are carried out.

The fall of prices in a panic obviously tends to check importations, and to make it profitable to export commodities, which in the time of inflation were kept at home. The drain of specie ceases, and the current sets inward. The bankers, relieved from the demand for metal, cautiously resume the discount of commercial paper Prices begin to rise, and, as they rise, traders regain the disposition to purchase. The stagnation which had suspended the circulation of commodities is at an end, and the activity of exchanges revives. In short, all the causes which led to the reduction of prices are reversed, and the series of operations begins, which conducts in time to another revulsion. The country, meantime, has suffered in the paralysis of its productive industry, for production always slackens when exchanges are difficult and slow. It suffers immensely, too, in the demoralization which attends the sudden reduction to poverty of those who thought themselves affluent, the violent change in the distribution of property, and the general decline and uncertainty in the rewards of labour.

It is the object of this treatise only to elucidate principles, leaving their application to the reader. We may suggest for his reflection, however, the questions, Whether the course of things in this country for some time past has not been such as tends to a convulsion? Whether the unexampled influx of gold from California is not the main circumstance, which, for two or three years back, has postponed the crisis? Whether its efficacy for that purpose has not depended, for the most part, upon this country's being in an exceptional condition, as the great gold-producing country of the earth? and, whether it does not diminish as our gold is distributed by the operations of commerce, and especially, since the working of the gold-fields of Australia is putting Great Britain, with whom we have the greatest trade, in a similar position to that of the United States? While we were producing gold cheaper than it was produced anywhere else, it could be exported with a profit in exchange for merchandise; that profit, however, decreases as it comes to be produced with equal cheapness elsewhere. The gold which our people have scraped up in California has gone to Europe to pay balances, which would otherwise have exhausted the bankers: meantime we have put railroads under construction, which will require iron costing at least $70,000,000, for which we must export gold, which is going down, while iron is going up. There was nothing of which we were in less want than gold, when the sands of California first began to be washed, nor anything more needed than iron. The mines of the latter are under our feet; yet, our people have gone across the continent, to become barbarians on the coast of the Pacific, that they may obtain a metal which, after crossing the continent, is to go over the Atlantic in search of iron.

In treating of supply and demand, no reference has been made to the notion, by which some writers have been bewildered, of a general over-production of commodities. The proposition that any good thing has ever been produced in excess of the wants of humanity, will not bear a moment's examination; nor is there the slightest reason to apprehend that such an event is likely to occur. The truth of the matter may be quite as correctly rendered by the statement, that the supply of other commodities is deficient, as that any particular one is redundant. Where has it been, in any community sufficiently numerous to permit the application of the general considerations in which Political Economy deals, that any product of industry has been offered in such a quantity as to surpass what the comfort of all its members would require? The trouble is, that many of those who would gladly be consumers, have not produced enough to enable them to be. The true remedy for what is called over-production, in any article, is an increased production of other things. This is consistent with all interests; for every one is the producer of but few kinds of commodities and the consumer of many: a consumer, directly or indirectly, to the full extent of his production. He either exchanges all that he produces, for commodities actually used by himself and his dependants in contributing to their personal enjoyment, or he converts the excess into machinery for further production, which, at the next remove, must enter into the round of exchange; or, he lends it, in whole or in part, to some third person, who must employ it in one of these modes. Production and consumption are equal, and the latter can be increased no otherwise than by enlarging the former.

The surplus which any nation produces beyond the ability of its own people to consume, must evidently seek foreign markets, and in doing so must be burdened with the cost of transportation, and whatever toll may be required at the port of entry. The price at which it leaves the country of its production, must be less, by the full amount of these charges, than the price of similar wares, produced in the market which it seeks. If we suppose the case, that wheat is produced in England at the same cost at which it can be delivered upon the seaboard of the United States, then, if a surplus be brought to the Atlantic ports, which *must* go to England, the holders of that surplus must content themselves with a price, as much below that of the English markets, as the cost of shipment and of any duty which may be laid upon its importation by Great Britain. The owners will obviously be ready to sell it in New York for the same net price as they could realize, after paying charges and duties, by its exportation to Liverpool. It will stand in the domestic markets bidding for purchasers, at the price thus reduced, and, therefore, tend to reduce the price of the whole crop to the same level.

Such is the case of the Canadians with regard to wheat. They have the liberty of sending it through the New York canals, for the purpose of exportation to Europe, upon executing a bond for the duty of 20 per cent., *ad valorem*, which is cancelled upon its shipment at New York for England. For this trade they have the same advantages as American citizens. They find it necessary, however, to sell a portion of their annual crop in our markets — paying the duty. The result is, that the price of wheat at Toronto ranges at a price lower than that of the same quality on this side the Lake, by the entire amount of the duty and the cost of transportation.* They have, accordingly, for years been seeking the remission of the American duty, by the passage of an act which is facetiously called a Reciprocity Bill, because it gives our people the

* Abundant evidence of this fact might be adduced. It will suffice, however, to cite the statement of the Hon. William Hamilton Merritt, who was despatched to Washington by the Governor-General of Canada, for the purpose of urging the passage of the so-called Reciprocity Bill. That gentleman drew up a memorandum, which was transmitted by the British Minister to the Secretary of State, in which he says, in regard to Canadian wheat:

"The imports from Canada since 1847 have in no instance affected the market in New York. The consumer does not obtain a reduction of prices; *the duty is paid by the grower, as shown by the comparative prices on each side of the boundary*, which have averaged in proportion to the amount of the duty exacted."

liberty of exporting wheat to Canada — that is, of carrying coals to Newcastle — and other privileges of equal value.

What is true of a nation is true of an individual farmer. He may sell a part of his wheat to feed weavers and miners in his immediate vicinity, at sixty cents a bushel, and send the surplus to New York, where he sells it at a dollar, which, after deducting the cost of transportation, nets the same price as that sold at his door. The New York merchant pays more than the neighbours of the farmer, by the cost of transportation, and may thereby be led to think that its burthen falls on him and not on the producer. But the reason why the farmer sells grain to his neighbour at sixty cents is, that unless he did so he would be obliged to send it to New York. However small the surplus that *must* be sent to a distant market, its *net* price regulates the gross price of all that remains. It is for this reason, among others, that the producer can afford to tempt consumers to his side, and thus make a home market, by paying them higher prices for their labour, embodied in commodities, than would suffice to obtain the same from abroad.

If, on the contrary, a nation is compelled by the insufficiency of internal production to import a portion of its supply from abroad, it is plain that the demand for this supplementary quantity pushes up the price of all that is made in the country; and the price at which it is sold must determine the price at which the native product is also sold. We are under a present necessity of procuring railroad bars from Wales, and must therefore pay for rails made in Pennsylvania, a price which is enhanced by the duty on those imported. As the internal production approximates to the wants of the country, the price must fall; and when the supply from our mines is adequate, those who import rails from abroad must do so at the expense of paying the duty themselves, without enhancing the price to the purchaser. Lead is now imported under an *ad valorem* duty of twenty per cent. When the duty was three cents a pound, the price upon the Mississippi was generally less than the duty, and lower than it now is; it being then exported at as low a price as it is now imported. The effect of a duty in respect to price depends upon the question, whether it increases or diminishes competition. The reduction of a duty may so diminish domestic competition as to increase price; the imposition of a duty not sufficiently high to stimulate domestic production, must infallibly tend to enhance price, for it puts the duty upon the purchaser, while a higher rate might extort it from the foreign producer. In support of the general doctrine of this and the preceding paragraph, Mr. M'Culloch, commenting on the modifications of our Tariff, proposed by Mr. Meredith in his first Treasury Report, gives his opinion as follows:

"Freedom of importation is, speaking generally, the best rule to follow; but there are no absolute rules in politics, or, indeed, in most other things. The Americans formerly compelled us, by their retaliatory proceedings, to make, greatly against our will, though greatly for our advantage, important changes in our navigation laws. And are they quite sure, since they will not follow our example, that we may not diverge a little from the course on which we have entered, to profit by their example? Suppose we laid a discriminating duty of 3*s*. or 4*s*. a quarter on corn and flour from America, to continue as long as the proposed new duties (if passed) on cotton goods, iron, &c., imported into the Union are to continue, what could the Americans say against such a duty? To be consistent, Mr. Meredith should write a report in its favour. And yet it would be far more severely felt in the States, than the duties they propose to lay on imports will be felt here. *The Americans must come to us for iron and cottons, and must, therefore, themselves pay the duties imposed on them. But we may supply ourselves with corn in fifty other places besides the Union; and hence the duty on it would fall entirely on the United States' grower and exporter, and not on the English consumer.*"*

Mr. M'Culloch fails to remark, that when our necessity for importing iron and cottons disappears, it will relieve us from the necessity of exporting corn and flour. It will then be a matter of supreme indifference to us, what duty England may impose upon breadstuffs which we do *not* send her. Her power to fix the prices at which we shall sell, and at which we shall buy, will then have gone. The producers of American corn and flour will exchange with the producers of iron and cotton, at prices fixed by themselves, and will thus have won freedom of trade.

---

* Supplement to Commercial Dictionary for 1850.

CHAPTER IX.

GOVERNMENT.

The widest form of association known among men, is the political. Families grow into tribes, the tribes combine into nations; sometimes, as in the case of the United States, nations are confederated for so many purposes, that they are spoken of collectively as one nation, instead of thirty-one. In all the forms, a body of agents, denominated in the aggregate the government, is charged by the society with certain duties, and necessarily entrusted with powers adequate to their performance. The general limitations of those powers are established in some instances by written constitutions, in others by prescription; while there are still others, in which, while scarcely any limit is recognized in theory, to the powers of the government, their practical exercise is restricted within narrow bounds, and the individual members of society, though nominally the subjects of a despot, enjoy as much freedom, and exercise self-government in a greater degree, than the citizens of what have been called Republics. The Danes are in this situation, compared with the people of France under the Republican administration.

It is only the Economical functions of government with which we are concerned. In considering them, we have a great advantage over the writers of the Old World. They cannot help regarding the government as something distinct from the people, upon whom and among whom it operates — as imposing regulations upon the latter without consulting its will — as controlling affairs by an inherent force. Even where representative institutions exist, as in Great Britain, the elective franchise is restricted to a portion of the population, and its members are denominated "the governing classes." We, however, have before our eyes the working of things under a system, in which the *whole* people appoint the administrators of government, portioning out to them such powers as they deem expedient; restricting their exercise, or resuming them at will; holding the public servants to strict responsibility for their conduct, and changing them whenever they exercise their acknowledged powers wrongfully, or fail to exercise them in such a manner as to promote what the entire community regards as its interests — at all events, what a majority regard as the general interest. Something of this kind has been imagined by European writers, for the purpose of deducing from the theory of a social contract, the functions and powers which men would be likely to assign to government. But what is theory with them is with us a dry fact. We need not conjecture what men, acting freely, would seek to accomplish by State agency—we have only to inquire what duties they have, in point of fact, assigned to the general agents of the State associations they have formed. As we are constantly seeing constitutions amended, and new constitutions formed by communities passing from the Territorial condition to the full assumption of sovereignty in State organizations, we can also study the tendency of humanity in respect to the reservation of power, or the grant of it to common agents.

A writer* who has most thoroughly investigated the antiquities of England, informs us that the primitive germ or unit of an Anglo-Saxon kingdom, was the Mark or March. It was a district comprising arable lands held in severalty, and pasture lands occupied in common, fenced in by an exterior boundary of forest, heath, or marsh. "It was a miniature State; the principles of whose being, as regarded other similar communities, was separation—as regarded itself, was an intimate union of all its individual members." The process of association between adjoining Marks is thus traced by Mr. Kemble:

> "Take two villages, placed on such clearings in the bosom of the forest, each having an ill-defined boundary in the wood that separates them; each extending its circuit woodward as population increases and presses upon the land; and each attempting to drive its Mark (the word is used as indidating the boundary, as well as the territorial district itself,) farther into the waste, as the arable land gradually encroaches upon this. On the first meeting of the herdsmen, one of three courses appears unavoidable; the communities must enter into a federal union; one must attack and subjugate the other; or the two must coalesce into one, on friendly and equal terms."

The reader cannot fail to be struck with the exact correspondence between the course of things here described, and that in the forma-

* J. M. Kemble: "The Saxons in England."

tion of our New England States. Plymouth, Boston, Salem, &c., were entirely independent towns, settled by the emigration of distinct colonies, each exercising all the powers of self-government within its own limits, and subsequently coalescing into the Province of Massachusetts Bay, now the Commonwealth of Massachusetts. In like manner, Hartford, Windsor, and New Haven combined by voluntary compact to form the Province of Connecticut. In these unions, each of the former petty sovereignties retains the management of its internal affairs, and the large power of local self-government, with which De Tocqueville was so much impressed. The instinct of "separation as regarded other similar communities, of intimate union of all its individual members, as regarded itself," controlled after the union as before; the union affording fresh security for its indulgence, against the interference of the surrounding savages, or of the British Crown. When the Revolution occurred, the Provinces became independent nations — each as distinct from the other as India and Canada will be, when their connection with Great Britain shall have been severed. The citizens of any one were aliens in all the others, and each formed its own institutions according to its own wants and enlightenment. When the Constitution was formed, the States confederated for certain determinate purposes, and each retaining to itself the general attributes of sovereignty, created a body of common agents in the Federal Government, to which they granted special and limited powers, carefully enumerated, with a jealous reservation, in terms, of all powers not delegated by the Constitution, nor prohibited by it to the States. The result is, that while the Federal Government possesses no power for which there is not an express grant, the State governments possess all power which is not expressly prohibited to them by the people.

This course of things in the organization of government, and the distribution of its functions among different orders of agents, seems to us to correspond with what might be anticipated in the natural development of society. In point of fact it has been a natural development. Constitutions, it has been said, are not made, they grow. The proposition contains most truth, when men have had most freedom to adapt their systems of government to their wants;

and this has been confessedly enjoyed by the citizens of the United States more than any other people. We have better warrant, therefore, for inferring what are the natural and appropriate functions of the public agents, from their example, than from any other, or from abstract speculations.

Our practice gives the negative to the very restricted view which many writers are disposed to take, of the proper limits of governmental action. What is it that we call the State? asks Mr. Herbert Spencer.* He answers, "Men voluntarily associated for mutual protection:" and argues that the State cannot exceed its office of protector—cannot attempt a single supplementary service—without producing dissent; and, in proportion to the amount of dissent, losing protective power, and defeating the end for which it was established. Government, says Bastiat, acts only by force; its action, he argues, is therefore legitimate only when the employment of force is legitimate. By force, he evidently intends bayonets and the like—constables, staves, imprisonment of the person. His conclusion is, that it can have no other rational duties than the defence of individual rights. The same doctrine is expressed by others, in the declaration that the true office of government is simply to repress force and fraud.

Perhaps the most general expression of the purpose of government is, that it is an agency to promote and facilitate the association of the individuals by whom it is instituted. Defence against foreign aggression; the repression of force and fraud in the intercourse of its constituents; the establishment of uniform systems of weights and measures; the construction of roads, bridges, and canals; the defining of the rights of property, and the remedies for an injury to them; the coinage of money; the postage of letters—all these, and the other offices, in which most governments agree, are plainly subsidiary to the general purpose of promoting association. It would, we think, be impossible to find in the powers of the Federal Government, enumerated in the Constitution, or in the prohibitions to which the States subject themselves by that compact, a single one which is not clearly referrible to that object. There are many which tran-

* Social Statics, page 275.

scend the purpose of defence: and the administration of private justice between the citizens of the same State; the relations of its citizens to each other; the defining of what is the subject of property and what is not, and of the modes of its transmission — of crimes and their punishment; almost everything that could grow out of domestic force or fraud, is left to the regulation of the States.

We have here the example of a government — the only government by which we are represented in foreign intercourse, and, consequently, the only branch of our governments of which foreigners take much note — which has scarcely any duty or power within the sphere to which the writers in question would confine government; and all whose functions of any consequence whatever, are outside of that sphere.

A particular examination of the Federal Constitution would, we think, show that the dominant idea in its formation was the same as that which characterized the Anglo-Saxon Mark. Its object was, to preserve the complete separation between the States, and their respective citizens in certain relations, and thus to promote that intimate union between the members of each individual State, which the similarity of their local character, circumstances, and wants naturally produces, and which a connection for the general purposes of legislation with peoples in many respects dissimilar, would disturb. At the same time it facilitates the association of the members of the different States, in all those relations in which there is a common interest, and guarantees to the citizens of each an equality of privilege in all. It secures unqualified freedom of trade between the States, by prohibiting any State from laying imposts or duties on imports or exports, or any tonnage duty, without the consent of Congress, and by prohibiting Congress from laying any tax or duty on articles exported from any State, and from giving a preference, by any regulation of commerce or revenue, to the ports of one State over those of another. It gives Congress the power to regulate commerce with foreign nations — the restrictions above-mentioned preventing any discrimination between the States in the exercise of that power—and thus secures the ability to counteract any foreign interference with domestic freedom of production and trade, through temptations held out to the immediate selfish interest of individuals

Against any embarrassments which the States might interpose, from a supposed local interest, it has guarded by interdicting them from entering into any treaty, alliance, or confederation. The Confederacy thus acts as a unit in its dealings with the rest of the world. The States preserve the equality of power in internal legislation by equality of representation in one branch of Congress; and in regard to arrangements with foreign powers, they have a *double* negative strength. Treaties can only be made with the concurrence of two-thirds of the Senators present. The two Senators from Rhode Island, representing less than 150,000 people, by their votes against a treaty, counterbalance the four from New York and Pennsylvania, representing about 5,500,000; Delaware, with 92,000 inhabitants, counterbalances Ohio and Virginia, with near 3,500,000. It is a possible thing that, in a full Senate, a treaty may be rejected by the votes of Senators from States containing but one-twelfth of the inhabitants of the United States. Thus jealously have the States guarded their isolation from all nations not combined with them in the Union.

Our system, by combining the energy of local patriotism, and the freedom of local self-government, with the strength derived from extended territory and population, seems to have solved the problem of expansion without weakness. "Variety in unity," it has been said, "is perfection." It certainly is the law of all natural organic development; and it is manifested in our system, not only in the whole but in all the fractions, from the Union down to the school districts, of which there are more than ten thousand in the single State of New York, each a little Republic, working out its purposes by universal suffrage. What speculation on the natural offices of government can enlighten us like our own history?

The object proposed by those writers who are desirous of restricting the functions of government within the narrowest limits, is to secure the largest freedom in production and trade for the individual members of society. Confining ourselves solely to Economical considerations, this object is desirable, not as an end, but as the instrument and means of the largest aggregate production. It is because freedom is a necessary condition of the greatest efficiency in industry, that Economists are solicitous that it should be everywhere established and maintained. It is obvious, however, that the thing to be sought is the greatest *aggregate* of freedom. This may well be consistent with some degree of restraint upon individuals. Every organization implies this. Every combination involves the subordination of the separate powers of its members to a common purpose, for the sake of attaining greater power. The savage rights his own wrongs by the strong hand. As he becomes civilized, he resigns his freedom to do this, for the sake of obtaining redress more cheaply and effectually through the combined action of his tribe or nation; and it then becomes necessary to establish general regulations, according to which the whole force of the community is brought to bear upon the aggressor. Every man who enters into a commercial partnership subordinates his individual will, in regard to the mode of conducting its business, to that of the majority of his associates. The rule sometimes restricts one, sometimes another; but it manifestly secures a greater aggregate of free action to the partners, than if the majority were liable at any time to be thwarted by the arbitrary volition of a single one. What is a State but a great partnership for such purposes, subordinate to the general purpose of promoting association among themselves, as its people choose to define? What principle of rational freedom forbids restrictions that are *self-imposed?* forbids a people voluntarily agreeing upon a mode in which future agreements may be made, through legislative agents freely chosen, that shall be binding upon all? What else are laws than the popular will, ascertained and recorded in the mode which the people have themselves agreed upon and designated?

It is quite apparent, we think, that the hostility which prevails so much among European Economists, not simply against particular governmental regulations relating to trade, but to regulation in the abstract, arises from their inability to make the answer to the foregoing questions which the American makes. It is the consciousness that the powers of the State are wielded, not by the many but by the few, that is at the root of the aversion. We have no occasion for such a feeling. We may regard a regulation as unwise and injurious, but it is the agreement of the people who are to suffer by it if it is so, who have, therefore, every motive for enlightening themselves in respect to its operations, and who have the power to repeal it when they choose. Education is not the monopoly of a class or a party. The laws of Nature tend to its diffusion, and our institutions co-operate with them. We have no reason, therefore, to fear that if we are right the people will not find it out; and great reason to distrust our judgment, if the people do not concur in it.

The progress of society in population and wealth naturally tends to diminish the *proportion* of its members who are occupied in the duties of government; or, what comes to the same thing, the labour that it is necessary to devote. A people, thinly scattered over a large territory, requires a large portion of the time of its males to be spent under arms. Its feebleness invites aggression, and aggression provokes reprisals as well as defence. A vast deal of military service is therefore imposed in the first stages of society upon its members. "War," said Napoleon, "is the science of barbarians." Every man is a soldier, and alternates between the camp and the farm. He is an enormously expensive soldier, as all experience with militia troops has shown; and the intermitting service which makes a poor soldier, spoils the man who might have been a good agriculturist or mechanic. Robberies, and other similar causes of internal insecurity, abound in inverse proportion to the density of population. To guard against their commission, and to detect and punish the offenders, requires a greater *share* of the labour which a sparse community has at command, than when it has become dense. Labour is most unproductive at that stage of social progress when the burden of defence is greatest; and governments are relatively most strong, employ proportionately most men as soldiers, constables, judges, &c., when their constituents are least numerous, when their accumulated capital is smallest, and the labour devoted to its increase is least effective. Taxes paid in money or personal service are then more onerous, than when, at an advanced stage of progress, the absolute amount collected is vastly greater. The occasions for governmental interference, and the need of governmental agencies, diminish as the power of private association grows with the increase of numbers, and the curtailing of the distances which separate men from each other. It is the same with the purely industrial operations of the State. It is only thirty-five years since the construction of the Erie Canal was deemed an enterprise of such magnitude as to strain the powers of the State of New York. The idea of its being made by a private corporation would then have been regarded as visionary to the last degree. Since that time a single corporation has constructed a railroad within the State, of more than double the cost of the Erie Canal. Nobody doubts the wisdom of the construction of the canal *by the State* at that time; while no one would now regard it as a sufficient reason for the State's undertaking an industrial enterprise, that its cost would be ten times as great.

There are palpable objections to States assuming any industrial employment, when individuals can be found with adequate means. The vigilance of individual supervision, and the keenness of private interest, secure an economy, which is never obtained where the loss caused by neglect is not borne in its entire weight by the guilty party, but is divided among a multitude. This is so well known as to dispense with the necessity of enlarging upon it. If the State could secure the same profit as one of its citizens, or an association of them, it is difficult to perceive any reason why the community should forego an advantage, in which all its members would share. But unless it can render a specified service at the same or a less cost than individuals, it is plain that it imposes a tax upon those with whom it deals, which is unjust because it is partial, or must make up the loss by a tax on the whole for their exemption, which is equally unjust.

When it is said that no objection can be perceived to operations by government for pecuniary profit, except the general inability of government to work with the same economy as individuals, it is on the supposition of the free consent of the people, who can determine the questions of expediency relating to a particular case, or inhibit the government by permanent restrictions from undertaking such classes of industrial enterprises, as they deem it wise to reserve for private action. If government, in pursuance of what we deem its most general purpose, facilitates and encourages association among individuals, it thereby extends the power of private competition with the State, and diminishes the temptations for it to attempt any operation for pecuniary profit. When the people of the State of New York revised the Constitution in 1846, they deprived the government of the power to retire from the only business relations which the State sustains towards the public, by providing that "the Legislature shall not sell, lease, or otherwise dispose of any of the canals of the State, but they shall remain the property of the State, and under its management for ever"; and that "the Legislature shall never sell or dispose of the salt springs belonging to this State." They, at the same time, made the enlargement of the Erie Canal, and the completion of certain others, obligatory. The security which they took against future industrial enterprises on the part of the State, consists in provisions prohibiting the credit of the State being loaned to, or in aid of any individual, association or corporation; and prohibiting the State's contracting debts to exceed $1,000,000, except to repel invasion, suppress insurrection, or defend the State in war, "unless such debt shall be authorized by a law for some single work or object, to be specified therein; and such law shall provide for the collection of a direct annual tax, sufficient to pay the interest of the debt as it falls due, and redeem the principal within eighteen years"; which law is inoperative until it shall have been submitted to the people, and ratified by a majority of those voting upon it. These provisions have been substantially copied by several States which have revised their fundamental law since the year 1846.

The same constitution deprived the government of a power, which it had formerly possessed, of impeding private association. In order that numerous persons should be willing to unite and contribute their capital to be employed for a common purpose, it is necessary that they should be at liberty to contract with each other, and those with whom they may have dealings, upon such conditions as they deem proper. If a thousand persons combine to build a railway or a factory, they must entrust the management of their property to a few agents. The stake which each has in the skill and fidelity of those agents is proportionate to the amount he contributes. It would be the most natural arrangement in the world, that the partners should agree that their power, in regard to the selection of those agents, should be proportioned to their several risks, and that they should divide the profits resulting from their operations, or contribute to the loss in the same proportions. To such an arrangement, as between themselves, the law has presented no obstacle. Suppose, however, that one of them has embarked in the undertaking, not only the whole of his own property, but capital which he has borrowed for the purpose from a third person, who chooses not to invest his means for the sake of a contingent profit, but is willing to entrust them to the probity and judgment of his friend for a stipulated interest. Others may contribute but a small portion of their capital, preferring to buy State stocks with the remainder, or to employ it under their personal supervision in agriculture or commerce. Upon the arrangement above stated being proposed, the exceptional individual might well say to his associates, "Gentlemen, I embark in this business with the hope and expectation of profit—so do you all. You have, nevertheless, very properly made a provision in the case of loss, which is undoubtedly equitable. I think it fair, however, to inform you that the provision, so far as I am concerned, will prove entirely nugatory in case we sustain a loss of capital. You have the whole of my property already, and more, too. I shall have no means of contributing to make up a loss. If I should obtain the means by my future earnings, I should feel bound to repay the borrowed capital entrusted to me, the owner of which gains no profit by our success, as you will, and, therefore, in justice, should suffer less by our failure. I propose to promise only what I can perform. When the capital I contribute is gone, I intend to be under no liability to make it good." If the others accede to his views, still the law makes no objection to the contract between themselves. They were prevented, however, by the common law of partnership, from making the same arrangement with the public. The law held each partner liable for the entire debts which the copartnership might contract. After the entire capital had been exhausted, any creditor might resort to the individual property of any one of the partners for satisfaction, leaving him to obtain from the others what he could. Another difficulty in regard to partnership was, that a member desirous of withdrawing his capital, or selling it to another person, who might be willing to take his place and continue the business, could not do so without the consent of all the partners; and if he obtained it, he still remained liable to creditors for all debts previously contracted.

The only mode of association in which the difficulties above enumerated, and some others of minor importance, could be avoided was that of a corporation. This is a species of partnership in which the shares are assignable, and in which the liability of the members extends only to the loss of the capital they invest. It was for these reasons, among others, much the most secure and convenient method in which a large number of small capitals could be combined. Those who traded with it, did so with a full knowledge of the terms on which they contracted, and ordinarily with more ability to ascertain its means and debts, than in the case of an individual or an ordinary partnership. Unfortunately, however, the creation of corporations was originally a royal prerogative, and descended to the legislative department of government. To be a corporation was a franchise obtained by special grant, which the Legislature gave or withheld according to its notion of expediency. The power of the government, and the opportunities for favouritism and corruption, were very unnecessarily enhanced, and the capacity of association among the people injuriously trammelled. The Constitution of 1846 redressed the evil, by depriving the Legislature of the power to create corporations by special act, "except for municipal purposes, and in cases where, in the judgment of the Legislature, the objects of the corporation cannot be attained under general laws;" and, provided, that all corporations, and all "associations or joint stock companies, having any of the powers or privileges of corporations not possessed by individuals or partnerships," should be formed under general laws, to be enacted by the Legislature.

In accordance with the Constitution, general laws have been enacted, prescribing very simple and inexpensive proceedings, by which any persons who desire may form themselves into corporations, for the purpose of building railways or plank-roads, or for prosecuting any manufacturing, mining, chemical, or mechanical business. The members are held personally responsible that the nominal capital shall be actually furnished, and for the payment of wages due to labourers in the employ of the company.

General acts, for the formation of corporations to establish public libraries, and for the formation of religious corporations, have long been in force in New York. A general act, authorizing the formation of corporations for certain prescribed manufacturing purposes, is also of old date. The recent extension of the principle, however, is mainly due to the success of the experiment in divesting the trade of banking of the character of a special privilege, a few years before. There was some opposition to both measures on the part of men troubled with apprehensions, that those who dealt with corporations would not be able to judge which of them were worthy of credit, and to what extent, and that individuals would be tempted to combine, upon wild expectations of profit, that would have failed to deceive them, but for a certain charm connected with the name and attributes of a corporation. These fears have proved visionary. Now that corporations have ceased to possess the recommendation of a special legislative sanction, people are neither as anxious to take stock in them, nor as ready to trust them, as when they partook of the character of a monopoly, and bore the stamp of State approbation.

The Constitution of 1846 abolished "all offices for the weighing, gauging, measuring, culling, or inspecting any merchandise, produce, manufacture, or commodity, whatever," and prohibited the future creation of any such office, with the exception of offices created for the purpose of protecting the public health, and of supplying the people with correct standards of weights and measures, and protecting the interests of the State in its property and revenue, tolls and purchases. The object of this provision was mainly to restrict the patronage of the government, and to leave inspections to be made, and the agents for that purpose to be selected, by the voluntary arrangements of individuals.

We have confined ourselves to the course of things in the single Republic of New York, as well because it is the most populous in the Confederacy, and exerts a great influence by its example, as because the recent revision of its fundamental law exhibits the intervention of the people in their highest act of sovereignty, to impose such restrictions upon their governmental agents as they deemed expedient. Enough has been shown to prove the natural tendency to confine government to its necessary functions, or to those which could not be discharged with the same efficacy by minor associations. When the natural laws are permitted to operate, which increase the numbers, the wealth, and the equality in condition of the community, all classes will obtain political power, and will not employ State officials to do what they can do better themselves. Where rulers resist those laws, it requires something more convincing than lectures on Political Economy, to induce them to abdicate any power they have exercised.

In one thing all governments agree. All require taxes in some shape or another. Although no tax-gatherer should go his rounds, and the remuneration of the government agents should be paid by revenue derived from a public domain, or from the profits of a business carried on by the State, yet, as it can hold property and get gains only in trust for the community, withholding, is equivalent to paying over with one hand and taking back with the other. In regard to the methods in which the necessary means for the support of government should be collected, there are two principles, in respect to which there would seem to be no room for dispute. The only difficulty arises in the details of their practical application.

As government renders services to each and every one of its constituents—at all events, does so in proportion as its actual administration corresponds with its objects and profession—every one ought to contribute to the expense of its maintenance in the ratio that he receives advantage. It gives him security for his person and his property. So far as his property is concerned, it is apparent that his contribution should be estimated as it would be by a private insurance company, by the amount at stake. If he purchases insurance at any less rate, it can only be because some one else is made to pay more than his fair proportion, and to take from his property for the purpose of adding to that of another. This is manifest robbery, and the government which fails to prevent it fails in the chief purpose of its institution. Every poll-tax is liable to this objection, whether paid in money or by personal service. That a labourer, whose exertions are required for the support of his family, should be compelled to expend a day in militia duty, or pay the same commutation as the man with a large revenue, is palpably unequal and unjust.

The value of protection to the person is incapable of estimation. If left to different individuals to declare at what price they would purchase indemnity from injury to life or limb, the rich would be more apt to pay in a proportion exceeding their property, as compared with the poor, than below it. The greatest number of the offences attended with violence to the person, have their origin in designs upon property, or arise from controversies relating to property. These reasons excuse any attempt to regard the value of personal security as the basis for taxation. If it be a consequence, that those who are destitute escape contributing to expenses of which they share the benefit, there is the countervailing advantage, that it tends to facilitate the acquisition of property by them, and to diminish that inequality of condition which impedes the association of producers.

The principle of equality demands that all taxes for the sake of revenue should be imposed directly, because such is the only mode in which the contribution of each individual can be adjusted in proportion to his means. Every tax upon consumption involves the difficulty, that men's personal wants and indulgences vary greatly less than their capital or income. The labourer, if he does not consume quite as much bread and meat, tea, coffee, sugar, cotton and wool, &c., as the millionaire, devotes to their purchase a large portion of his income; while the capitalist furnishes himself with the somewhat larger quantity of such commodities that he may consume, by the expenditure of a small portion of his income. Whatever articles may be selected, and however the per centage of taxation may be graduated, it is a problem of insuperable difficulty to equalize the contributions of different classes of consumers, or even to make any tolerable approach to equality.

From the preceding considerations, it is apparent that all indirect taxes imposed by way of duty or excise, require justification from their contributing to some other object than that of fairly distributing the expenses of government among its constituents. Upon that ground they are wholly indefensible. The necessity for revenue is no apology for an unjust mode of assessing it. There is another principle which may save them from condemnation. It is that taxes should be levied in such a form as to promote the general purposes for which government is instituted, to diminish the evils it is designed to avert, and thus decrease the necessity for future taxation. If, for example, an indulgence in reading should be ascertained to have a tendency to produce crime, and thus increase the expenses necessary for its detection and punishment, it can hardly be doubted that it would be just and expedient to impose such taxes upon books and newspapers as should be adequate to discourage their use, and produce sufficient revenue to defray the expenditure resulting from the crime caused by those which continue to be read in spite of the tax. A supposition is here purposely made that is the direct reverse of the fact, because it illustrates the principle without involving any question as to its application in the particular case. Government is an association for all the purposes that its constituents may from time to time agree upon and specify. The repression of crime is, indeed, among the most permanent and universal. But, if it be proper to impose taxes by way of fine and penalty, to promote one purpose, it must be for every other. It comes but to this, that the members of the association have agreed to contribute equally for common objects, and, also, that any one of them who pursues a course of action calculated to defeat any of those objects, shall thereby become liable to make a special additional contribution.

The true defence of protective duties must be put on the ground here indicated. A community judging that it is cheaper to combine its food and raw materials at home, than to procure the labour of conversion to be done abroad, and desirous of increasing its aggregate production by the change, determines to invest a portion of its means in educating its labourers in the process. This it does by submitting to a temporary sacrifice, real or apparent, in the payment of a higher price for the domestic fabric than for an imported one of the same kind and quality, a sacrifice which, becoming less and less as the education of the labourers advances, finally disappears. In other words, it agrees to give a preference to the domestic over the foreign manufacture, notwithstanding the difference of price. If all the members of the association would adhere to the agreement, there would be no necessity for a duty. The individual interest of any one, however, tempts him to save his pennies and continue to buy at a cheap price from the importer, while his fellows pay for educating the labourers, in the gain from whose skill and efficiency he will share when it is attained. To prevent this there are two methods. One is to levy contributions equally upon the whole community, for the purpose of paying a bounty to the domestic producers. One objection to this is, that it is taxing the entire community for the benefit of the consumers of that commodity, upon which the bounty is paid. Another is, that the foreign producers, by submitting to a reduction of price, can defeat the purpose of the bounty, while its burden to the community which pays it is unalleviated; the consumers alone benefiting by the reduction. On the other hand, the imposition of a fixed duty, enhancing the price of the foreign commodity, throws the tax upon the consumers who are to be benefited by any future reduction. As the cost of domestic production decreases, the foreign producer is made to pay a part of the duty, and thus contribute to the revenue of the country, and the relief of its tax-payers. Upon him it operates as a penalty, increasing as the price of the protected commodity falls with the increase of skill in the domestic producers, the improvement of machinery, and the extension of the market, until it ceases to be a tax upon the consumers.

Mr. J. S. Mill enters into an argument, in which our limits will not permit us to follow him, to show that "duties on the importation of any commodity, which could not by any possibility be produced at home, and duties not sufficiently high to counterbalance the difference of expense between the production of the article at home and its importation," are paid in part by foreigners. "A country," he observes,

> "Cannot be expected to renounce the power of taxing foreigners, unless foreigners will, in return, practise towards itself the same forbearance. The only mode in which a country can save itself from being a loser by the revenue duties imposed by other countries on its commodities, is to impose corresponding revenue duties on theirs. Only it must take care that those be not so high as to exceed all that remains of the advantage of the trade, and put an end to importation altogether, causing the article to be either produced at home, or imported from another and a dearer market." — *Political Economy, vol.* 2, *page* 413.

It is sufficiently plain, that if the citizens of a country are driven to the domestic production of an article, which could be permanently obtained in return for less labour by importation from abroad, and the revenue ceases in consequence, there is a double loss; first, of the difference in cost of the domestic and the imported articles; second, of the revenue—or, rather, that portion, if any, which would have been drawn from foreigners — which, as we must suppose it necessary, must be obtained by some other mode of taxation. An argument may be drawn, from this consideration, against duties for revenue, with a side-view to "incidental protection." If protection is an object at all, it should be the main one, and revenue the temporary incident, as being obtained in a mode which is justifiable only as a means to reach another end. If there is any valid reason for giving *any* degree of protection, it must be for the purpose of cheapening production, not for the purpose of enabling a favoured class of producers to continue a business which would otherwise be unprofitable, by making up their losses out of the pockets of consumers — the contributions of the latter, if the duty is only sufficient to substitute the consumption of a domestic commodity for an imported one, without increasing consumption by cheapening its actual cost, being just so much *withheld* from the treasury of their government. If the effect of the duty be to cheapen production, that is sufficient justification, and it needs no bolstering by a plea of the necessity for revenue. In that case it tends to defeat the purpose of revenue, except so far as it is derived from the foreign producers. There is no good reason why they should participate in the advantages of association with a community — as they do by every act of trade — without contributing towards defraying the expenses by which that community obtains the advantages of association and trade between its own members. That they find some advantage from it they testify by seeking our market; and, in every case where the duty is a protective one, they, by so doing, interpose to substitute exchange with themselves for that exchange and association between its own citizens, which it is the leading purpose of governments to promote.

Under our system, the imposition of duties upon exports from any of the States is prohibited to the Federal Government; and the States have resigned the power to lay "any imposts or duties on imports or exports, except what may be absolutely necessary for executing their inspection laws," without the consent of Congress. We need not, therefore, consider the operation of export duties, which are practically abrogated in our confederacy. The nations which resort to this method of raising a revenue, artificially enhance the cost of their products to foreign nations, and, by limiting the market for them, increase the cost of their production at home; or, what comes to the same thing, prevent the economy which might be obtained by an extension of the market. In regard to internal, or excise duties, the principle upon which they may in some cases be defended, and the general objection to them, in common with all modes of indirect taxation, have been indicated, without any discussion of the details in regard to the objects to be selected for taxation, or the manner and time of levying, with a view to economy in collection on the part of the government, and consequent diminution of burthen on the part of the tax-payers. Regarding direct taxation as the only legitimate source of revenue for the sake of revenue, we are indisposed to detain the reader by any further examination of exceptional methods of obtaining it, which are to be tolerated in proportion to their tendency to diminish the cases in which they can be applied, and the revenue which they will produce. In this, as in all the other forms of its action, government is successful in the degree to which it becomes unnecessary—in which men acquire the knowledge and the power which render them a law unto themselves, substituting self-government, the cheerful conformity to the higher law, for subjection to earthly control and direction. Obeying that law, the promise to all the children of men is,

YE SHALL KNOW THE TRUTH, AND THE TRUTH SHALL MAKE YOU FREE.

THE END.

www.ingramcontent.com/pod-product-compliance
Lightning Source LLC
LaVergne TN
LVHW010234110826
845151LV00004B/1285